Letters
Auguste and Louis Lumière

LETTERS
Auguste and Louis Lumière

———

edited and annotated by Jacques Rittaud-Hutinet
with the collaboration of Yvelise Dentzer
preface by Maurice Trarieux-Lumière

translation by Pierre Hodgson

faber and faber
LONDON · BOSTON

Originally published in French by *Cahiers du Cinéma* in 1994 under the title *Auguste et Louis Lumière: Correspondances 1890–1953*
First published in 1995
by Faber and Faber Limited
3 Queen Square London WC1N 3AU

Photoset by Parker Typesetting Service, Leicester
Printed in England by Clays Ltd, St Ives plc

Lumière letters © Cahiers du Cinéma, 1994
Translation © Pierre Hodgson, 1995
Photographs and drawings courtesy of Association Frères Lumière; Association Musée du cinéma de Lyon; Lumière family collection; Dr Beaulaton; Mrs Couteaux; P. Vigne

Pierre Hodgson is hereby identified as translator of this work in accordance with Section 77 of the Copyright, Designs and Patents Act 1988

A CIP record for this book
is available from the British Library
ISBN 0–571–17545–7

2 4 6 8 10 9 7 5 3 1

Contents

Acknowledgements

We are particularly grateful to the following people and organizations who made letters available for publication in this book:
Mesdames Cuteaux, Yvette Lumière, Yvonne Meyer; Messieurs Auboin-Vermorel, Henri Borges, Paul Génard, Jean Seyewetz, Max Lefrancq-Lumière, Jacques Trarieux-Lumière, Maurice Trarieux-Lumière, Max Vernet; Madame Marie and Monsieur Jacques André; the Académie des Sciences, the Bibliothèque de l'Image-Filmothèque, the Cinémathèque Française, the Conservatoire National des Arts et Métiers and the Musée Ciotaden 'Les amis du vieux La Ciotat'.

We also thank François Ede for his information about integral photography; André Barret, Alain Bideau and Emmanuelle Toulet for their general encouragement; and the following institutions: CERTC-Université Lumière, the Université Lumière, the Association Frères Lumière, the Institut Lumière and the Musée du Cinéma de Lyon.

The translator wishes to acknowledge the help of Francis Hodgson, whose expert pen and knowledge of nineteenth-century photography proved invaluable.

Preface

'A day spent without learning something new
is a day wasted . . .'
'Driven by a thirst and a need for knowledge,
I have madly enjoyed working all my life'

The first of these statements is by Auguste Lumière, the second by his younger brother, Louis. They are plain statements of belief, made towards the end of their lives, which seem appropriate here, introducing this.volume of letters which I am privileged to preface.

Either sentence might have been spoken by either one of the brothers. Both reflect an outlook and an ethic which they held in common. By temperament – I remember them both fondly – they were indefatigable workers. When they were young, fourteen-, even sixteen-hour days in their laboratories were not unusual. They were driven by curiosity. They were eager to study physical, chemical and biological phenomena, and discover rational and practical solutions to all sorts of problems they faced in their various disciplines.

Much of their work they did together. They signed nearly three hundred and fifty patents jointly, as well as, in photo-chemistry alone, nearly two hundred and fifty memoirs and other communications, whether at the Académie des Sciences or at other learned societies like the Société Française de Photographie or the Société Française de Chimie.

Later in life Auguste abandoned photo-chemistry. From an early age he had been strongly drawn to the natural sciences. In the fields of biology, physiology, pathology he published nearly sixty books and hundreds of articles, becoming, as his studies evolved, a true humanist. Louis, the younger, carried on with his research into photography, and successfully tackled related problems arising in the fields of mechanics, optics and acoustics.

As children, they had sworn to share and publish the fruits of their research jointly under both Christian names, regardless of which of the two had initiated any particular discovery. For forty years, they kept this agreement, until their fields of inquiry diverged completely, as I have just mentioned.

There are not many examples of such practice anywhere. It can only be explained by deep, mutual fondness. We, their descendants, are much attached to the memory of this sentiment, which the warmth of the phrase 'the Lumière brothers' evokes.

Remember that, for decades, the two brothers and their families shared the same house in Lyon, and until Louis left for Paris when my grandmother died in 1925, they took every meal together – though they sometimes hurried to get back to work – eating in each other's rooms on alternate weeks. They worked in the same factory, which they had established with their father to make constantly updated photographic plates and papers, and they shared laboratories.

I am sure that the unusual extent of their shared sympathy contributed to their astonishing creativity.

Innumerable historians and biographers having produced descriptions and investigations of their scientific research; I should like to consider, instead, their respective personalities, such as I recall them and such as they emerge in the letters.

Louis died at the age of eighty-two in Bandol, where he had gone into retirement. He maintained a two-storey, custom-built laboratory there. I was twenty-five years old at the time. That is to say, I had been old enough for several years to enjoy listening to him and to appreciate what he had to say. He liked talking about his life as an inventor, which was a mine of stories of every kind. University vacations were sufficiently long that I could spend two or three weeks with him every September. We shared our meals on the beautiful terrace of the house, and in between meals, he would settle down to work and I would go . . . to the beach.

I have all sorts of memories. But one has to choose. The picture which comes back to me, as I write, belongs to that world in which a grandfather and his grandson live quiet days of family harmony, flitting from past memories to the events of the day.

Sometimes, I would tell him things I remembered from my childhood in Paris. He used to come to see us often, and we used to go to see him. It was better when he came to us, because my brother and I – and later our cousins – knew that he had a particular talent: he repaired our toys – all our toys. Every one of his jackets was filled with an arsenal of weird and wonderful tools, hidden in special inner pockets designed by a cunning tailor. The incredible weight of his jackets still makes me shudder. But that wasn't the point. He wanted to be ready, at the drop of a hat, to mend whatever needed mending, whatever the cause of the break. I never remember him being stumped.

The usual picture of a scientist is a man lost in thought, sullen or grumpy . . . It could hardly be less appropriate. The Lumière brothers were a delight. They were naturally jolly, even-tempered, warm, never talking shop when they were with family or friends, always in the thick of a conversation which was never without humour.

My great-uncle Auguste died six years after his brother, in Lyon, a town he loved. He was just as extraordinary. Unlike Louis, he was very shy. He was also very gentle and deeply kind. But he was also resolute in the defence of the ideas he believed in; he knew how to find the right arguments and express them in a language he handled most adeptly. He would challenge anyone he considered a danger to the humaneness he advocated, namely out and out conformists and the rootedly pompous. One of his books, from before the war, was called *Les Fossoyeurs du Progrès: les mandarins contre les pionniers de la science* [The Gravediggers of Progress: the Medical Establishment against the Pioneers of Science]. He was profoundly mischievous and there was always a twinkle in his eye. He was a member of the French Association of Conjurers and we were delighted when he would do a trick for us, although, in the time-honoured tradition, he would never tell us how it was done.

As to the letters that are gathered here, most of them were unknown to me. To choose only the most significant, two subjects of correspondence seem to me to stand out. Curiously, and this is coincidence, they each concern a different brother, and they are quite unlike each other.

One is the exchange of letters between Louis Lumière and Jules Carpentier. Carpentier was a highly qualified engineer, a graduate of the Ecole Polytechnique, who met Louis at the first performance of a film projected on to a screen, at the Society for the Advancement of National Industry, in the rue de Rennes in Paris, on 22 March 1895. The film had been shot on a prototype Cinematograph, built in the Lumière factories and Carpentier offered to manufacture this prototype industrially in his workshops in Paris, guided by Louis.

Their correspondence shows how well these two brilliant mechanics got on with each other; it also shows the problems caused by the distance between the towns in which they lived, so that they were unable to have the daily chats which they needed. But – and I was surprised to see this – the postal system at the end of the nineteenth century was incredibly fast. Every letter sent from Paris to Lyon or vice-versa arrived the next day without fail.

Which was just as well, because they were in a hurry. It was crucial to the Lumières that everything should be ready for 28 December 1895, the date booked for the first public performance in the Salon Indien of the Grand Café. Firm commitments had been made. There was not a day to lose and every letter, all handwritten, from the one or the other reflects that concern.

There was no point being ready on time if the machine was not perfect. Consequently, every detail is carefully analysed; every adjustment made described with extreme precision, with a sketch to help. On the evening of 28 December everything was ready for the first performance, and the Lumière Cinematograph set out on the royal road that we now know it to have followed.

For me, the Carpentier–Lumière letters bring us realistically close to the birth pangs that accompanied a masterpiece of precision engineering.

The other main body of letters which has captured my attention, is, on the contrary, extremely dramatic, particularly when one knows the context in which it was written.

The letters to which I refer concern the death, at the age of twenty-four, of Auguste's daughter Andrée Lumière, a few days after the armistice, on 26 November 1918. The world was in the grip of the terrible epidemic known as Spanish 'flu (because it was supposed to have come from that country), which caused untold damage. Auguste's letters to his son Henri, who had joined the Army Aviation Service at the age of 17, are particularly moving.

The first is a letter dated 18 November in which Andrée, who is about to get engaged, accompanies her parents to a fête. Everything seems peaceful after the terrible storms of the last four years.

Then, on 20 and 22 November, there is a scare: the epidemic is worsening. Mention is made of a relapse, which suggests that Andrée must have been ill before 18 November, but without causing undue anxiety, since everything had gone back to normal. This time, he is not so sure, but he thinks it is going to be all right: 'Andrée is a little better, but her temperature was 38.5 last night,' he writes to his son. Then suddenly, nothing. The irreparable tragedy has occurred. His beloved daughter has died. After the funeral, the letters to his son, who has had to rejoin his regiment, are heart-rending. 'You must come back. Life is not liveable apart like this, after that other terrible eternal separation.'

These letters of Auguste Lumière's, both before and after the terrible event, before he can conceive of it and after it has hit him, seem to me, in their inexorability, unusually powerful and touching . . .

I should like to close by thanking those people who have enabled me to evoke the Lumière family – the *Cahiers du Cinéma*, Jacques Rittaud-Hutinet and Yvelise Dentzer – by allowing me to preface this collection of letters. It is a cliché to say that, unlike friends and acquaintances, one does not choose one's relations. This allows me to say that Providence has truly smiled upon me. I have been lucky enough to have been on intimate terms with two remarkable men, to appreciate their kindness, their extreme decency and their admirable intelligence . . .

I am very pleased to have been able to pay my respects to them here. I have no doubt that my feelings are shared by every member of my family and all those who knew them, for to know them was to admire and to love them.

Maurice Trarieux-Lumière

Introduction

A century ago, to communicate meant to write, just as today it means to telephone. It took longer, but more was preserved from oblivion, as long as one took the trouble to fill a drawer or or an attic cupboard for a future historian.

The strictly chronological order in which we have chosen to present these letters shows the wide variety of subject matter, but it also shows the story moving forward at a pace dictated by what was then known or unknown, told by the chance survival of these letters. These letters represent the outcropping of certain hard truths on a true background, in a life forever over and gone. These letters tell a story that had no way of knowing it would in time become history. They make no mention of their own value or the value of the things they describe. They make no claim to be anything more than an exchange of words, with no other reader in view than the correspondent. As a collection of facts, they tell something that history all too often leaves unsaid about its own incompleteness. At the same time, they bear strong witness to history's reality. In presenting events cheek by jowl with oddments of opinion and anecdotes the letters force us to read between the lines, a bit like an archaeologist reconstituting an Etruscan vase from a few shards of earthenware, or a palaeontologist a whole creature from a fragment of bone. Where biographies invariably draw on the research of a previous one, collections of letters function as a re-injection of life into history, which gives it a new vitality, and may from time to time change it a little.

These letters graft on to the relatively homogeneous structure of history like branches on a tree. They are made of the same stuff, but their shapes are utterly distinct; they are a part of the same thing, yet separate from it. They link memory to its origin in a very untrammelled way. Reading them in order, a historian tries to correct their minor variations, to seize a little of the independent information they supply, to bring them back into the broad general lines of understanding, and to anchor them, when possible, to the knowledge we already have. The historian attempts to ease explanation, and maybe suggest it, without forcing it. Lively enough to be quite sufficient in themselves, these letters also summon the imagination to fill the gaps, and invite guesswork to reconstruct meanings which may survive only as fragments. Luckily enough, in some cases the answers have survived, giving us a chance to enter into dialogue. The best example of this is the correspondence between Louis Lumière and the engineer Jules Carpentier, who was in charge of finishing the design of the Cinematograph and getting its mass production under way. But more often, we have to make do with a few lines sent to a correspondent who defeats all the historian's efforts to discover who he was. Many of the Christian names of workers, such as Moussy and Perrigot, projectionist and assistant to the Lumière brothers, remain unknown. Some of the letters refer to incidents not known from any other source, coming, for example, from institutions whose archives have not survived. So the staccato commentary of the footnotes is not offered as selective analysis, by an all-seeing critic looking down on the correspondence and picking a few choice examples to reinforce some position of his own, but, on the contrary, as elucidation put at the disposal of the story telling itself. Publishing the letters, furthermore, will give them a sort of collective presence.

These letters cover three broad themes: relations between scholars and specialists (particularly on the subjects of colour photography, on the Cinematograph, and on Auguste Lumière's medical work), the commercialization of the Cinematograph and, lastly, family letters.

The early years draw attention to one of Louis Lumière's main interests: the invention of colour photography, set in motion by the work of Professor Gabriel Lippmann, future Nobel prize-winner in physics, whose early results were presented to the Académie des Sciences on 2 February 1891. The Lumière brothers eagerly formed an association with Lippmann and set about manufacturing plates. These letters confirm the long partnership that resulted. Of particular interest are two particularly important letters from Louis Ducos du Hauron. A brilliant pioneer, he lacked technical and financial resources at precisely the time when the development of research made an industrial-scale base more and more necessary: craftsmanship and artisanal work by even the most inspired minds were no longer enough to guarantee results. The shortcomings of Ducos du Hauron's own results are clearly depicted in the letters of 4 June 1892 and 17 June 1895. Reading these letters, everything makes sense: the Lumière brothers, for their part, were indeed industrialists. They were able to carry out their research with a solid financial background which allowed them to commission ever more complex, substantial and expensive pieces of machinery. Consider, for example, the machine designed and made by

Louis Lumière in connection with the coloured emulsions of autochrome plates, which was able to exert a pressure on grains of potato starch of five tonnes per square millimetre by applying tangential force. Louis Ducos du Hauron talks about his 'scientific and technical isolation'. The Lumières worked in a community, they linked up with scientists and skills across many borders. What the one discovered, another not only commented upon, but may even have got excited about: 'I love your paramidophenol!' exclaimed the Count d'Assche (26 July 1892), with the same kind of enthusiasm as that shown a little later by Demenÿ, Marey's not yet dissident follower.

The early letters show the close connection with research that rapid industrial expansion nourishes and promotes: the famous Blue Label photographic plates, sold all over the world, allow the initiation and financing of other projects, among them the Cinematograph, even while results are presented and explained to the scientific community.

The first mention of the Cinematograph comes almost as a surprise. On 12 July 1895 140 enthusiastic people witness a 'demonstration' of the astonishing apparatus on the premises of the *Revue Générale des Sciences*. This sitting quickly draws requests for information from a multitude of scientific and general journals who wish to write further about it. All good public relations for a success which looked likely to be a triumph. After this first show an order for twenty-five machines – soon to be increased to 200 – is placed with the Ruhmkorff works, headed by the engineer/instrument-maker Jules Carpentier (12 October 1895). After a first estimate of costs – which we will later see to have been substantially too low – we find a succession of letters disclosing the fruitful partnership between the inventor and the highly talented engineer, somewhat under the spell of Louis Lumière's character and standing.

The chronology of the letters then becomes very revealing. On the one hand, the Lumière company hesitates 'on the matter of marketing the Cinematograph', whose reputation is growing in Lyon and in Paris, which prompts an offer to buy it (Louis Lumière to Antoine Lumière, 14 October 1895). On the other hand, Louis Lumière and Jules Carpentier want to release a reliable, durable and perfectly designed machine. They feel obliged to wait, and to make others wait for them to be ready. And they use the enforced delay both to think about the best possible marketing strategy, and to make sure the Cinematograph machine is perfect in every detail. From then on, Louis answers with stolid patience the impatient demands of people trying to place orders. This does not seem to be the reaction of the inventors' father, Antoine, who suggests a way of marketing which is met with some slight reluctance, as we see in the letter of 14 October 1895. Antoine, having offered himself as the 'fairground barker' for the Cinematograph, draws this gently ironic answer from Louis Lumière: 'We do not like the prospect of you playing Barnum showing off his magic lantern.' The important point in this letter lies elsewhere; as early as 14 October, several months before the launch, the Lumière brothers seem to have broadly decided upon the commercial strategy they would adopt in the coming year, and which was designed to guarantee them independence and risk-free management. They would find an employee to promote the machine and hire him out in the various places concerned, and they would train 'experimental-assistants' (not yet projectionists, let alone film-makers) to work the machines. This arrangement would depend on installations already in place (more than likely the worldwide network of professional photographers selling Blue Label plates). And they would set their prices according to supply and demand, after what can only be described as market research based on the demonstrations planned for Paris and Lyon.

After 14 October, enquiries for possible purchase and information grow more numerous, including one from The Edison-Bell Phonograph Co. (19 October 1895). Auguste Lumière politely refuses: the machine is still under construction in Paris and the company cannot yet know the release date or the price. But on 2 November, Louis Lumière mentions a rival who could become a serious threat if Carpentier doesn't make all haste to complete his machine. A quick-fire exchange of letters between Louis Lumière and Jules Carpentier begins. Most of the parts for the machine known as No.1 are tested, improved, modified: here they talk about a variable shutter, there about improvements to accessories, or about problems of light intensity controlled only by the speed of hand-cranking the film.

There is another problem: the search for somebody to supply film and, above all, for a way of coating film without the buckling and loss of shape that occurs when it is hot-coated. Victor Planchon, owner of the first factory to make flexible film, known as 'autotensile' film, had already had dealings with the Lumière Company. He starts experiments on the strength of film and on coating techniques.

Technical problem succeeds technical problem, from 'the little mirror which presses on the film' to the 'receiving container' or even 'mass production' (9 November 1895). In the same letter, Carpentier reveals a first hint of his character. He announces that he has abandoned his own machine, the Cinegraph, in favour of the Cinematograph, knowing that his might have become a serious rival. He will even go so far as to use for the advantage of the Lumière Cinematograph the film-perforating machine he had designed for his own. None the less, Louis Lumière's letters reveal a certain discouragement which he occasionally confides to Carpentier (25 November 1895). His trials show Planchon's film to be too supple, the emulsion too thin, re-winding awkward . . . and always the terrible rush! (25 November 1895).

On 28 November 1895, the first machine finished by Carpentier according to Louis Lumière's designs and instructions is sent to Monplaisir. Carpentier sends it under the reservation that he could not complete the order for two hundred if more modifications were to be incorporated (27 November 1895). Carpentier's troubles are not over. Louis Lumière, while apologizing for being 'a bore'(30 November 1895) continues a highly precise technical conversation. His worry about detail looks like perfectionism, and Carpentier tells him never to 'say that he is a bore' when 'pointing out mistakes to be put right or improvements to be made'.

Meanwhile, with Planchon, it seems that nothing is going right, for Louis threatens that he will look for another supplier (6 December 1895). First estimates of film stocks needed suggest that they will need a hundred rolls a day, a huge number if one takes into account how very few films had then been made. Louis Lumière was certainly thinking of the future. Everything is smoothed out, and the products are deemed of high enough quality.

At last, on 14 December, Louis can write that 'the mechanism of the machine we have just received [No.2] is now perfect'! Apart from a little fine tuning which only regular use of the machine will be able to point up (15 December 1895 and 20 December 1895), everything seems ready for the first show on 28 December.

On 30 December, Carpentier offers his congratulations to Louis Lumière for the success of the first projection, on 28 December 1895, in the Salon Indien of the Grand Café on the boulevard des Capucines, in Paris. But he complains at having received no invitation other than an anonymous circular. An oversight by Antoine Lumière, who had insisted on organizing the show himself. Louis Lumière apologizes by return of post. That misunderstanding sorted out, Carpentier manages the feat of finishing and sending three machines to Louis Lumière on 31 December.

As the machines begin to be delivered at the end of January 1896, 'perfection' seems just around the corner for Louis Lumière, in spite of a few last-minute hitches. The commercial operation continues to be planned, with a proposal for a screening-room in Lyon put forward on 11 January 1896. The Lumières are going ahead with their centralizing policy, bringing to Lyon Planchon's firm and buying a share in their suppliers: glass-makers, paper-mills, chemical firms and so on. This creation of satellite companies will turn out to be a very efficient way of supporting the planned commercial onslaught. The first commercial contract for operation of the Cinematograph is agreed on 16 January 1896 with the Marquis d'Osmond for Belgium. The second letter to the Marquis (23 January 1896) shows that the commercial arrangement is already set in the form it will take throughout that year of expansion: each team consists of two Lumière employees, one to operate the machines and one to take charge of the box office. They are to be paid by the contracting party, but picked by and from the staff of the Lumière company.

The Cinematograph now spreads sometimes in direct rivalry with X-rays, which have only recently been discovered by Professor Roentgen. Auguste Lumière talks about his enthusiasm for a technique in which he was to become pre-eminent as one of the pioneers of medical radiology. He was, a few years later, to become the first person to X-ray a fracture, set by Professor Ollier of the Lyon medical faculty. This letter (1 February 1896) marks the very beginning of a major interest.

The preparation for the worldwide spread of the Cinematograph involved not only the registration of an American patent and various operating plans (8 February 1896), but also the precise working out of the accounts for the teams of projectionists. The machine-handler was to receive ten francs per day, plus a small commission (one per cent of profits, as we learn from the travel book of Marius Chapuis, projectionist in Russia). The Lumière brothers insisted on the use of a book with stubs and tear-out forms to be sent daily to Monplaisir. This would establish the takings and provide the data for the project's commerciality. Charles Rossel, in Paris, seems in no hurry to send his in, and a sharp letter (12 February 1896) reminds him. It is true that many abuses were to occur later, when false accounting by concession holders made it difficult to establish the true financial position. Improvements continued to be made from a distance, and the refinement of the Cinematograph and its effect stayed under close scrutiny. The Lumière brothers were not so much selling a machine as a whole spectacle, which is why they insisted on being regularly informed.

Spring and summer 1896 see the Cinematograph making its way in the world, and the autumn of that year is rich in honours: King Umberto I of Italy and his Queen, Margareta, go to a special screening on 20 November (18 November 1896) and a demonstration at the Imperial Polytechnic Society in St Petersburg on 29 December (6 December 1896). The following autumn the President of France demands a private view at Rambouillet on 7 October (30 September 1897).

The success of the Cinematograph does no harm at all to their work on colour photography. Constant Girel, a projectionist who also seems to have been made responsible for sales and marketing of colour photography, writes (14 March 1897 and in an undated letter of 1898) of the enchantment in Paris of the members of the Institut and the press.

Prosperity encourages the family to philanthropic gestures. A pension fund is set up for their workers, for which the staff warmly thank Antoine Lumière (2 October 1896). So we see the industry developing in all its facets: technical, financial, social and marketing.

The universal Exhibition of 1900, planned for Paris from as early as 1897, pushes the Cinematograph towards gigantism. For the exhibition, a giant screen twenty-one metres wide and eighteen high will be put up in the old Machine gallery.

At the very beginning of the new century, we see two types of letter: those referring to the generosity of Auguste Lumière, and those on technical subjects like colour photography or medicine and, of course, business. They allow us to see clearly the variety of tasks the Lumières engaged in: from technical advice on the manufacture of photographic plates sent to the Burlington plant (set up in Vermont in the United States) to congratulations to Auguste on his work, to gifts made to the Lyon bacteriological institute, we see a burgeoning of activity, underlined by Auguste's increasing interest in biology. Not that the partnership between the brothers is on the wane. They continue to live, as we have seen, in that same house (now vanished) where the two families occupy matching wings, connected by a corridor where the two brothers meet each evening to exchange news and views. And they continue to manage their huge business together. If their activities gradually begin to diverge, they can be seen as complementary. Auguste has a lab built, then a clinic where much of the care will be administered free of charge. His reputation was a double one, as a scientist and as a philanthropist, which is why he receives so many letters asking for help. Auguste takes a more prominent place in these letters, to match his generosity. There are innumerable letters, of which we publish only a small fraction, from people he has treated or helped: a veterinary surgeon he has helped to get started, a gift to a medical school of a Cinematograph machine for use in parasitological research, or more gifts to the Ducos du Hauron family.

Suddenly, in 1917, Léon Gaumont bursts on the scene (8 May 1897). There is a a rumour abroad that Demenÿ, who had recently died, had invented the cinema. A lengthy debate, still running now, begins about the origins of the invention. The Lumière brothers print a 'right of reply' to their detractors (here published after Gaumont's letter). To re-establish the facts, they draw on Marey's account of 18 August 1899 (they were in friendly correspondence with Marey from 1896 on), which is corroborated by the German inventor Max Skladanowsky's letter of 1 July 1935. Marey had said to the congress of learned societies at the Sorbonne in 1897 that 'Auguste and Louis Lumière had first made this kind of projection with their Cinematograph'.

Auguste's work and activity seem from these letters to have been at their height in this period, and Louis is hardly less active. He invents a system whose principle is still in use today, the catalytic heater which allows aeroplanes to take off in freezing conditions. That, too, is done for no gain. No less generous than his brother, Louis pays for a hospital with a hundred beds throughout the war of 1914–18, and Auguste underwrites all the radiological expenses of the patients for the then astronomical sum of 200,000 gold francs. Auguste Lumière writes to his son, and we see something of what a father feels when his son exposes himself to dangerous acrobatics in the air. Henri is what we would today call a test pilot. In the war, he has the job of making sure that planes which have been shot down and repaired are fit to fly. At his own risk. He is such a good pilot that he invents a manoeuvre to pull a plane out of a corkscrew dive, an occurrence which had been fatal until then. After the death of his daughter Andrée, from which Auguste was never wholly to recover, the letters to Henri suggest the pain of affection transferred to his son, sometimes with desperation: 'You must come back. Life is not liveable apart like this, after that other terrible eternal separation.' (7 December 1918). But Auguste also writes, often very agreeably, about his daily round as a scientist. He talks about the idiosyncrasies of 'Rolland', the car he had built specially so that ladies could use it without removing their hats, which became a well-known sight on the streets of Lyon. He goes fishing at La Ciotat, with differing degrees of success, suffers from the heat, and trains his dog to acquire sea-legs. Auguste is a simple and clever man who seems to take pleasure from everything.

Then the letters take a surprising turn. The paternal worries begin to alternate with vigorous technical research. Rodolphe Berthon (12 January 1919) writes to say that he has made a machine which makes it possible to look again at Lippmann's integral photography, which Auguste and Louis Lumière had abandoned twenty-five years before. So Louis and Gabriel Lippmann start once again a friendly and technical correspondence about emulsions, bases, hydraulic presses for colour photography and so on. Theories and analyses about bakelite or celluloid are punctuated by the terrible letter in which Auguste announces that the whole family has the Spanish 'flu (which killed several million people in Europe). Photo-chemical experiments, cameras, filters, lenses: twenty-five years later, Louis Lumière shows the same perfectionist sense of attack as he did while building the Cinematograph.

From 1920, Henri heads the factories, allowing his father and his uncle to devote themselves entirely to their scientific work. He defends the inventors of the Cinematograph, correcting an error in the *Illustrated London News* (8 September 1922). At one and the same time family letters, and business and scientific ones, the letters between the wars break up into fragments of often unclear information.

Auguste continues to be very successful in medicine, and writes (11 August 1928) that he has too many patients to have time for research. Both a field-worker, as we would now put it, and a scholar and inventor, he lets us hear his 'immense satisfaction at treating so many patients whom conventional therapy had been unable to help'. He continues to try to alleviate distress wherever he finds it and gives without counting the cost. From time to time old friends ask him favours. The photographer Nadar, who resumes his career aged 79 (6 November 1934), recalls his old friendship with Antoine Lumière, who had died in 1911. Perhaps this letter offers us a key to the real meaning of a calling which is more than simply a way of earning one's crust, more than a speciality, but more of a vocation, a way of filling oneself with 'sincerity' that puts financial interest to one side.

Auguste's fame grows and grows (he is elected a correspondent member to the surgical and medical sections of the Académie des Sciences on 26 November 1928).

The brothers continue to collect honours, although even there they do not forget the pioneers. Louis agrees to sponsor Georges Méliès to the rank of Chevalier de la Légion d'Honneur (4 September 1931). They seem to share honours fairly and efficiently. A letter from Albert Trarieux (23 October 1931) gives a good example: the two scholars seem to be obstructing each other for a double promotion to the rank of Grand Officier de la Légion d'Honneur. Auguste offers to step down in favour of his brother, particularly since a double promotion, although extremely rare, might still happen. Auguste will himself be promoted to that rank on 30 July 1935. But behind this glory are a few shadows: Auguste seems to feel a black-out by the press on the subject of his research, orthodox medicine having decreed that he should be 'neutralized' by silence (21 September 1931). His ideas are taken up without acknowledgement, he is often challenged. But nobody can call into question his extraordinary productivity: either alone, or with others, including his brother Louis, he wrote nearly a thousand articles and books, a body of work of almost encyclopedic proportions.

The fortieth anniversary of cinema brings a new honour to Louis Lumière, who accepts the idea of a solemn evening at the Opera to celebrate the day (6 May 1935), and a suggestion that a stamp might be printed bearing the portrait of . . . Louis Lumière alone. It starts as a misunderstanding, a letter from Auguste in which he says the idea for the Cinematograph came to his brother one evening. But the origin of the invention was certainly due to both brothers equally. Auguste, having built a prototype with Charles Moisson, had passed the torch to Louis, and they had proceeded to work together from then on. The business is sorted out: the stamp would bear Auguste's portrait behind that of Louis (3 July 1935). More serious is Georges Méker's suggestion to Alphonse Seyewetz (25 June 1935) that the jubilee celebrate Louis alone, with Auguste having one of his own some months later. Auguste is delighted on behalf of his brother, and shows no bitterness, but refuses to have a jubilee himself as long as his work is not fully accepted by the medical establishment. Louis' jubilee takes place, and Auguste is very visible by his absence. He chooses to write the introduction to a book on magic tricks that day. A rumour circulates that Auguste has died, which would explained his absence (18 December 1935).

A tireless writer, Auguste publishes (see his letter of 4 October 1937) his *Horizons of Medicine*, a work which draws more new patients to his clinic. An ex-Minister of Health and an ambassador are among those who congratulate him, but the medical press remains silent. 'The big chiefs will not allow that one can come up with original work outside their domain, and my work hits them in their pride and in their wallet,' he writes bitterly. The establishment may give him the cold shoulder, but the patients do not. His timetable is crushing: he is consulted from all over the world. This great workload helps him to forget the alarm raised by the German offensive (4 September 1939). He loathes Hitler – he calls him a 'barbarian' and 'the greatest criminal the world has seen'. For his part, Louis puts himself at the service of the Ministry of Defence: he makes parabolic mirrors for naval spotlights.

A letter of 20 June 1940 makes us relive the fear brought on by the débâcle, the dark days of the Occupation, the hostage-takings and the news black-out. None of which stops Auguste from publishing *The Gravediggers of Progress: the Establishment against the Pioneers of Science*, and in pamphleteering mood, his doggerel of the 24 March 1941 which insults the Germans while pretending to flatter them.

The end of the war and the years that follow see the cinema come back into Louis Lumière's life. Louis' corrections of a mistake by the historian Coissac, of an incorrect identification of an actor in *L'Arroseur Arrosé* (22 July 1945), his objection to and refusal to allow a plaque in honour of Méliès and Marey (7 January 1946) on the wall of the Grand Café show his will to preserve his standing as the inventor of cinema, however willing he might be elsewhere to see the other pioneers justly acknowledged. Although quite seriously ill in the summer of 1946, Louis sharply criticizes Georges Sadoul, who seemed to have had access only to doubtful or pejorative sources while preparing the first edition of *The History of Cinema* (published in 1947). But everything is sorted out, and the following letters show a friendly collaboration taking shape between the two of them. Louis even furnishes historical data of great importance. Then a fruitful relationship develops between the Lumière family and the Cinémathèque Française, which leads to negatives being printed. While preparing his exhibition on the birth of cinema, Henri Langlois takes over from Georges Sadoul, and proposes to screen all the Lumière films in a permanent exhibition, to re-build the Photorama, and to put all available machines on show: Cinematograph, Kinora, and so on.

Louis Lumière's health worsens by the month, without diminishing his enthusiasm for research: 'I hope to find a bit more energy to continue my studies into diverse problems,' (16 December 1946). After a last letter to Henri Langlois (20 December 1947), Louis Lumière dies at Bandol, aged 86, on 6 June 1948.

A handful of letters from Auguste Lumière finishes this volume of letters. One particularly eloquent phrase sticks out from them, which seems to echo what his brother had written: 'I seem to be bearing up reasonably well despite my ninety years of age, since I continue to work and spend every morning at the clinic.' (29 May 1952). He died on 10 April 1954.

In modern times, specialists have been divided in their approach to the work of the Lumière bothers: 'Lumièrists' come close to hagiography, while the opposition want to diminish the importance of their invention by writing it into a long process of development. These letters, without wishing to add fuel to the flames of controversy, show the excellent relations the Lumière brothers maintained with at least some of the pioneers: Marey, Ducos du Hauron, Méliès. They help us also to find certain less well-known aspects in the life of humanist scientists of the nineteenth century and in the life of worthy industrialists who financed not only their own research but that of others. And they help us, finally, to learn something of men of a stamp which is sadly too little found, men of great ethical probity, whose scientific objectivity was in no way diminished by philanthropic and moral subjectivity. None of which takes anything away from other pioneers in their field. Far from it. Louis Lumière wrote modestly of his invention of the Cinematograph: 'I was just lucky enough to be the first to get there.'

I would like to thank warmly André Fayot, Chantal Leclerc-Chalvet, Antoine Morin and Laureent Loriot for help and support in some very dark hours.

Jacques Rittaud-Hutinet

Lumière Letters

Auguste Lumière to an unknown correspondent

Lyon, 30 September 1890

Dear Sir,

You were kind enough to appreciate our research into haloes[1] and I now have the pleasure of submitting the results of a process of microphotography invented by my brother and myself.

Please expect a post office parcel under separate cover containing photographic prints of microbes coloured according to the original preparations.

In addition, we include a written description of our process. Please do with it as you wish.

If by any chance you should have any similar preparations which you would like photographed, we are entirely at your disposal.

Yours sincerely,

A. Lumière

1 The Lumière brothers were the first to study and analyse photographic haloes. They identified a phenomenon by which the crown of white dots around the image is broader in diameter in proportion to the thickness of the photographic plate. They suggested that this phenomenon was caused by light reflected on the reverse of the plate, and then produced mathematical proof of their theory. In February 1890 a note was addressed by them to a Paris correspondent, Monsieur Vidal, for him to present to a forthcoming session of the French Society of Photography, and he duly arranged for this to be done. A Monsieur Cornu, fellow member of the Society, asked to be given an advance copy of the written text, as he was 'personally' interested in it. On 7 March, despite not being listed to speak, and before the Lumière brothers' note could be received, Cornu proceeded to make a personal communication on his own account, in which he gave an explanation for the phenomenon identical to theirs. He even managed to get this communication published in the March edition of the Society's Bulletin under his own name. The Lumière's brothers' note was not published until June. Worse, Cornu presented his research to the Académie des Sciences* without referring to the Lumière brothers' research. Years later, as is evidenced in this volume of correspondence, Auguste – who went on to run a medical research establishment and clinic – was to suffer similar malpractice at the hands of the medical profession. Louis and Auguste Lumière's study into haloes was eventually published as 'Analyse expérimentale des phénomènes connus en photographie sous le nom de halos' in *Société Française de Photographie*, vol. VI, 2nd series, 1890, p. 182.

*Translator's note: Académie des Sciences: one of the five Académies which together make up the Institut de France. The others are the Académie des Beaux-Arts (Fine Art), Académie des Belles-Lettres et Inscriptions (Literature), Académie de la Musique (Music) and the most famous of all, the Académie Française which is pre-eminent and cross-boundary. All these Académies are housed within the same golden-domed Institut building on the Quai de Conti in Paris, which Louis Lumière was to frequent with pleasure until the very end of his life.

Gabriel Lippmann[1] to Monsieur Lumière

Paris, 2 August 1891

4 Carrefour de l'Odéon

Dear Sir,

I have seen Monsieur André here in Paris and he tells me that you have made some attempt at producing colour plates[2] with disappointing results. I am sorry if this is so, for I have discovered that one can produce decent gelatine bromide plates.[3] Perhaps the best thing would be for me to tell you how I did this.

I spread gelatine bromide on glass. One gram of potassium bromide for 20 grams of dry gelatine. Once dry, the plate is dipped in silver nitrate, to which a small quantity of acid has been added so that the plates don't mist. Then a bath of cyanide solution, and drying.

Plates thus prepared have all produced some colour, even the very first ones, though these were heavily fogged.

No doubt for the purposes of industrial manufacture, and in order to achieve a smooth process, ready-mixed emulsion should be used.

I have made too few experiments to call them conclusive, but I have to say that so far I have only managed to produce residual traces of colour in that manner. Now it's the holidays and I have had to interrupt my work.

If, in the autumn, you have produced colour plates, I could certainly try them out.

In any case, could you perhaps send me a supply of gelatine bromide plates in October, even if I have to prepare the baths myself?

It is true that the silver bath is not particularly easy to handle. It is unstable. On the other hand, it is most convenient to be able to dip the plates in the bath and dry them without worrying about exposure to light.

Yours faithfully,

G. Lippmann

1 1845–1921, eminent French physicist, professor at the Sorbonne. He devised a system of colour photography called interferential. This provided spectacular confirmation of Fresnel's theory of light waves. On 2 February 1891 – a landmark date in the history of science –

Lippmann exhibited the first photograph of a solar spectrum. 'I was so astonished and delighted by the vividness of colours in the photograph of a spectrum,' he wrote, 'that I dared not move lest the experiment was the consequence of an accidental play of light and I was unable to reproduce it.'

The Lumière brothers took an early interest in Lippmann's work and soon embarked on a programme of joint research with brilliant results. We are able to present here, with some unfortunate gaps, the small number of letters which the two parties exchanged. It has the merit of showing the day-to-day progress of their work.

The first result came in May 1892. Lippmann's use of special photographic plates made up by the Lumière brothers enabled him to show the Académie des Sciences a series of colour photographs which caused a sensation: a stained glass window, a plate of oranges with a red poppy, a parrot, a group of flags. Unfortunately, the exposure time was, in each case, several hours. Louis Lumière rapidly reduced this to half an hour, and then to four minutes. He devised and put on the market a set of special plates complete with screen and filters, development fluids and colours.

Success came in 1893 when the Lumière brothers exhibited a series of portraits at the International Congress in Geneva in which they were to be seen with one of their sisters, sleeping on a table laden with fruit. These prints were displayed at the Congress of the Photographic Society in London and then sent to the United States where they were universally admired. On 28 March 1894, Louis and Auguste Lumière received prizes from the Académie for their work on colour. Despite this, they abandoned the Lippmann route, because it demanded an exposure time that could not be reduced below one minute. Other disadvantages of this process were that each image remained unique: prints could not be made on paper; and that, under identical conditions, with the same batch of plates acted on in the same way it was impossible to make two identical photographs. The brothers started again from scratch and evolved a system of indirect photography, which led eventually – in 1903 – to the discovery of autochromes. The Lumière brothers nevertheless remained on excellent terms with Lippmann. In 1919, Louis Lumière resumed the collaboration – as we shall see later – with the joint study of what they called *photographie intégrale*. Lippmann entered the Académie des Sciences in 1896, received the Nobel Prize for Physics in 1908 and died in 1921.

2 This letter is significant. It proves the Lumière brothers' strong interest in manufacturing plates for colour photography, according to the Lippmann process, before their association with Lippmann himself. It is worth noting, however, that at this stage the work is still in an experimental phase.

3 In 1881, aged seventeen, Louis Lumière perfected a faster and more regular emulsion formula than Monkhoven's, needing no washing and capable of industrial production. They were to become known as dry plates. But the small scale of production presented intractable problems. Despite the family's back-breaking work, from five in the morning to eleven at night, they could produce only one hundred and forty dozen plates a day, not enough to cover their costs. A deficit of 200,000 francs forced Antoine Lumière to announce imminent bankruptcy to his boys. Auguste and Louis took over the business, obtained a delay, and a further loan (thanks to fellow old boys of a Martinière school), which enabled them to devise and put into effect machines to industrialize the process. They saw to their marketing, built a worldwide distribution network, and hired staff – the end result being the famous extra-fast Blue Label plates which made their fortune and led the market for sixty years until 1944.

Aimé Laussédat[1] to Messieurs Lumière Sons

Paris, 9 March 1892

Dear Sirs,

Monsieur Léon Vidal has passed on to me your most kind offer of a donation to the Conservatoire National des Art et Métiers of a print of the solar spectrum which one of you has obtained by Monsieur G. Lippmann's process.

I am most grateful to you for the gift of this remarkable object which we are currently having framed in order that it may be placed, together with the appropriate description of its nature and origin, in the gallery which we have specially arranged for the display of objects pertaining to the history and applications of photography.

Yours faithfully,
Laussédat
The Director
Conservatoire National des Arts et Métiers

---

1 Aimé Laussédat, 1819–1907, Professor of Geodesy. From 1871, he was Director of Studies at the Ecole Polytechnique, one of the elite university level schools set up under the Napoleonic system, called *grandes écoles*. The Ecole Polytechnique is attached to the army and produces top-flight engineers, civil servants and managers. In 1881, he became director of the Conservatoire National des Arts et Métiers, another state engineering institute. A keen astronomer, he was responsible for a law of 14 March 1881 establishing the concept of legal time. He also encouraged the use of photography in cartography.

Société Française de Photographie to Monsieur Lumière

Paris, 29 March 1892

76 rue des Petits-Champs

Dear Sir,

I have been privileged to see two very fine specimens of colour spectra which you have obtained according to the Lippmann process.

The Society has no specimen of this sort and we should be most grateful if you would be good enough to honour it with one of your excellent spectra. Our next session is Friday, 17 April and if you were able to supply us by then, I know the members of the Society would be most interested.

Yours faithfully,
Comany

Société Française de Photographie to Messieurs Lumière

Paris, 7 April 1892

76 rue des Petits-Champs

Dear Sirs,

The Society received, at its session on 1 April 1892, the magnificent image of a spectrum which you obtained according to Monsieur Lippmann's process and which you were kind enough to donate. I have been asked to pass on to you the Society's thanks.

Yours faithfully,
Baulle
President

Louis Ducos du Hauron[1] to Monsieur Lumière

Algiers, 4 June 1892

Dear Sir,

I have the honour of enclosing a print of a colour photograph, taken in the neighbourhood of Algiers according to a process which I have devised. I made the print myself on a small photocollographic press which I possess.

There is nothing particularly remarkable about this piece of work, other than the extraordinary optical principle which it illustrates. I am scarcely more than an amateur photographer, both as regards the use of gelatine plates and the making of phototypes. My equipment, in other words, is not up to my invention[2] and I am constantly having to improvise techniques which I know to be perfectly adequate elsewhere but which Algiers, with its limited resources, outside the strict bounds of conventional photography, cannot provide.

Whatever its lesser imperfections, I send you this colour print (another copy of which is currently on display at the International Exhibition of Photography at the Champ de Mars) as a feeble token of my ancient and undying gratitude; for, though I may have been out of touch for some time, I shall never forget that, nearly a quarter of a century ago, you were good enough to sponsor my invention at the Société Française de Photographie on 7 May 1869.

My invention has had a difficult childhood, and a troublesome adolescence. Two terrible obstacles stood in its path. On the one hand, the poverty of means at my disposal and, on the other, widespread prejudice. What I mean is that my system of colour photography did not fit in with received opinion as to how the grand puzzle of colour photography would be solved. The general public, and the world of photographers in particular, expected to be presented with a photographic plate chemically and physically capable of capturing, at each point, the particular colour of the ray that strikes it. Monsieur Lippmann has showed us that such an expectation could be met. But what was not realized was that, remarkable as it is in scientific terms, direct chromophotography[3] is no more suitable for the multiplication of solar creation than the daguerreotype. By its very nature, direct chromophotography cannot partake of the essential scheme to which we all, consciously or unconsciously, aspire, namely the idea that we must multiply, *crescite et multiplicamini*, for that is the ideal of any industrial process and indeed of the expansion of the human race itself. From the very beginning, I looked to the print-process for a solution to the question of colour photography. Inking three times, whatever the subject matter, inking, not according to the dictates of light but according to invariable rules which provide us with a very realistic imitation of nature. Thus did I sever the Gordian knot. I am sure that taking this approach would have earned me, from the start, as it did Charles Cros,[4] the plaudits of both the general public and of photographic experts, if a diversion had not been created in people's minds by the existence of another school of thought. The choice of three colours, adopted by us, is not in any way arbitrary, whatever people say. They relate to three types of radiation, engraved, from an early age, in the brains of all men. In other words, our solution to the problem was both scientific and compatible with the demands of industry. I believe our invention deserved to be treated not as some passing guest but as a host, for it was the natural corollary of an eternal truth, a law of optics of the first importance. It is absolutely certain that the twentieth century, as well as the nineteenth, will use a system of inking and only inking for its printing, whether black and white or in colour. The printer's press will never use the sun's own rays as part of its equipment.

Such were the real principles of my invention but they were so easily misunderstood! I cannot pretend that, even today, they command the unanimous support of the representatives of official Science.

No matter. Truth will out. Numerous, unmistakable signs indicate that my notions are making rapid headway. Certain recent events make that quite plain. Today, printers have triumphed with their new rapid presses. Will they not soon be able to produce immense quantities of my three-colour photographs? I am certain they will. Then shall all controversy end and the late lamented Charles Cros and I shall be fully acknowledged. One thing I shall never forget, sir, and that is that from the very beginning, you were clear-sighted enough to come to our defence and, your energy undaunted by the incredulous smiles of many people about you, you foresaw, at least implicitly, the eventual triumph of our ideas. Once more, I thank you for your masterful support which, together with Monsieur Blanquart-Evrard's favourable comments and those of several other princes among scientists, forestalled my discouragement. Your friend, Monsieur Armand Malaval, a superior man, brought me last year your message of comfort and this had a profound effect upon me. Please accept this expression of my gratitude and please also pass my thanks on to him for his kind visit.

Yours ever,
Louis Ducos du Hauron

P.S. I intend to travel to Paris at the beginning of July: if I do, I shall not fail to call you and tell you, *viva voce*, how very grateful I am. I enclose a few copies of a memorandum which I have given the Institut.

1 Despite the ill-fortune which dogged him for most of his life, Arthur Louis Ducos, known as Ducos du Hauron, (1837–1920) was a genuine visionary. He took out nearly thirty patents for various inventions, between 1864 and 1907. On 1 March 1864, he patented 'a device intended to reproduce photographically any scene, and its transformations over a given period of time'. This description foreshadows the Lumière Cinematograph by some thirty years. It probably never got beyond the conceptual stage. But Ducos du Hauron was best known for his work on colour photography. In 1862, in a memorandum to the Académie des Sciences entitled 'Solutions to colour problems', he defined a method known as 'indirect' photography. From 1869 onwards, he tried to market polychrome photographs. They were not a great success, though they appeared in several exhibitions. In 1885, just when he had found backers to establish his process on an industrial scale, his workshops burnt down. In the end, Lumière bought out his patents, at which point he emigrated to Algeria where his brother was living. They both returned in 1896. Ducos du Hauron remained a somewhat isolated figure, and financial difficulties prevented him making the most of his inventions. He was given a stipend of 1800 francs by the Lumière family firm, and a state pension of 1200 francs. The average civil service salary, before the First World War, was 250 francs per month. Ducos du Hauron died in Algiers in 1920. He published *Les couleurs en photographie, solution du problème* (1869); *Les couleurs en photographie et en particulier l'héliochromie du charbon* (1870); *L'Héliochromie* (1874); *Traité pratique de photographie en couleurs* (1878); *La photographie indirecte des couleurs* (1901).
2 An indication of the extent to which absence of technical means could render powerless the most ingenious and innovative theories. In the matter of colour photography, as we shall see, the fact that the Lumière brothers had at their disposal considerable industrial capacity was of paramount importance.
3 The term chromophotography refers to a theoretical archetype of colour photography. The vocabulary of technical innovation draws on a series of speculative inventions, some of which were brilliant, like Daguerre's daguerreotype, the grandfather of photography. Ducos's invention is one of those.

4 Charles Cros (1842–1888), a poet much loved by the surrealists, for whom Manet illustrated a volume entitled Le Fleuve; he was also a keen student of oriental languages, of physics and mechanics. In 1869, he published a description of a trichromatic photographic process, similar to that which Louis Ducos du Hauron was perfecting at the same time. There followed a controversy between the two men and an exchange of letters to determine who had thought of the process first. In the end, it was decided that the discovery had been simultaneous. These letters were published in a periodical called *Cosmos*. They are available in *Oeuvres complètes de Charles Cros* (Gallimard, 1970, La Pléiade).

Dr de Pegoud[1] to Monsieur Lumière

Grenoble, 21 July 1892

Dear Monsieur Lumière,

We received a few days ago your microphotographs[2] and you may be sure that we have done our best to display them well.

May I remind you that we are still counting on your spectrum which is so much more successful and more exemplary than Monsieur Lippmann's.[3]

I now write about a different matter. I should like to invite you, on behalf of the Society, to be one of the prize judges at the Exhibition. We are particularly anxious to see your firm represented. I am however ashamed to say that though I have had excellent relations with both the Lumière brothers, I am not sufficiently acquainted to be able to tell one from the other, and that is why I cannot address this request to one or another. In truth, I now write to whichever of the two can most easily manage the dates. We are thinking of assembling the jury in Grenoble towards the end, the middle or the beginning of August.

I should say that you would be in very good company, with members of the Societies of Chambéry, Lyon, Grenoble and so on. I hope that you are able to grant our request.

Yours sincerely,
de Pegoud

1 Albert de Pegoud, graduated 1881, taught that year at the School of Medicine and Pharmacy, then Professor of Pathology. In 1890, president of the Society of Medicine, Surgery and Pharmacy of the Isère, which is in the region of Grenoble.
2 Small photographs that collectors and exhibition organizers would pass on to each other. The author refers to an exhibition which took place in Grenoble towards the end of July, one of the many exhibitions organized by photographic societies in order to publicize their research and its results.
3 At this time, Lippmann and the Lumière brothers were making colour photographs according to the same process, but the Lumière brothers soon achieved better results.

Count d'Assche to Monsieur Lumière

26 July 1892

Dear Monsieur Lumière,

I am absolutely enthusiastic about your paramidophenol;[1] I have been able to develop prints very quickly, with no ensuing harshness. I rather think I use less concentrate than you do. I think you recommend 10 grams of param. and 6 of lithin for 1000 cubic centimetres of 25% sulphite solution, whereas I use 7 grams of paramidophenol, 3 grams of lithin, 5 grams of ferrous cyanide, 100 grams of sulphite in 1000 of water. I've had never had such an excellent developer. The silver is more finely reduced and, providing one does not go too far, the resulting negative is well-detailed, without excess opacity in the whites: a marvel. And no fogging, because of the yellow prussic acid.

Since receiving the sample you sent, I have called on Monsieur Demeny[2] of Dr Marey's[3] physiological research laboratory and given him a ready-mixed sample of the developer. He is delighted with it and is giving up the crystals[4] he has been using until now. From now on, his one thousandth of a second negatives will be developed using paramidophenol, but he would like to mix it up himself and he does not know where to obtain supplies of your product in powder form. Does Monsieur Thibaut keep it?

I must congratulate you for giving us such excellent results. I am abandoning my pyrogallic acid[5] for all my snapshots and perhaps for the landscapes too.

Is there any point in using bromide, even though the developer is diluted? I reckon it has very little effect on the paramidophenol. What do you think?

Yours sincerely,
Count d'Assche

P.S. Perhaps you saw the note in *Photogazette*. Is it satisfactory?

1 The Lumière brothers published frequent articles in learned journals, notably in the *Bulletin de la Société Française de Photographie*. Their eminence in the field of photo-chemistry was unquestioned. They discovered the use of photographic developers composed of paramidophenol and communicated this discovery to Professor Chauvau of Lyon in order that he could present it to the Académie des Sciences. For what it is worth, this professor replied that, as their discovery was of practical interest, and would have industrial and commercial applications, it could not be listed in the proceedings of the Académie des Sciences. In 1893, Auguste Lumière observed that diamidophenol, used to develop photographic plates, was dangerous. It clotted the blood in guinea pigs' capillary veins. Consequently, users were advised to take special care in the handling. Furthermore, he found that his hair and moustache changed colour if he spent too long poring over test tubes of

diamidophenol. Indeed, he soon took out a patent for a cosmetic dye, though this had no commercial results. Among the more important articles on this subject, signed jointly by Auguste and Louis Lumière, the following may be of interest: 'Paramidophenol developers' in *Société Française de Photographie* t. VII, 1891, p195; 'A comparison of the properties of paramidophenol, hydrophenol and iconogen', ibid, 2nd series, p. 232.

2 After protracted studies, Georges Demenÿ (1850–1917) became Etienne-Jules Marey's (see below) assistant at the Collège de France, the most prestigious of the Parisian post-graduate research institutes where Marey taught natural history. Marey and Demenÿ came to take an interest in the study of movement and Demenÿ, following on from this, in the study of images. On 27 July 1891, he finally presented the phonoscope, a device which coupled about thirty photographs of a person speaking, made according to the process devised by Marey, with the words recorded on to a cylinder. The system provided an effective way of reproducing sound and images together, but the tapes were very short. On one, the person says 'Je vous aime' and on the other, 'Vive la France'. Demenÿ's system left several problems unsolved: how to ensure the film passed at an even speed through the camera, and to preserve the even spacing of the photographic images. In 1893, Demenÿ added an eccentric gear to Marey's chronophotograph, which Marey had just patented, and called it the biograph. Demenÿ then left Marey and tried unsuccessfully to interest the Lumière brothers in a joint venture. His system formed the eventual basis for Léon Gaumont's camera. In a letter dated 30 May 1920, Louis Lumière describes for the record the nature of his relations with Demenÿ.

3 Etienne-Jules Marey, physiologist and Professor at the Collège de France. Conducted research into cardiac and muscular motion. Also, birdflight, human and animal gait. In order to pursue these studies, Marey developed various recording devices. He was interested in the analysis of movement and its component parts, not in synthesizing it to provide an illusion, which is what cinema does. In 1882, he constructed a device based on the photographic gun which Janssen had developed to photograph the passage of Venus in front of the sun (9 December 1874), the purpose of which is to take a series of photographs at a regular interval. The result was unsatisfactory. He then tried fixed-plate chronography in which motion is broken down into a series of poses recorded on a single plate. This was deemed useful, but still not satisfactory. In 1893, Marey took out a patent for a film-based chronograph capable of recording a succession of images of an animated subject. But this system too had a defect: the film was immobilized by a series of pincers which cannot maintain a regular interval between each shot, so that the illusion of movement remains imperfect. What Marey was missing was the idea of perforating the film. But as these letters show, his research progressed no further, though he maintained an active position in the little world of animated photography.

4 salt crystals produced in solution.

5 Phenolic acid, derived from benzene, also used as a developer.

Count d'Assche to Auguste Lumière

Paris, 8 August [1892]

Dear Monsieur Lumière,

I am writing to remind you of your kind offer of a note for *Photogazette* on cobalt salts. Perhaps you would be kind enough to send it to me in the next few days in time for publication on the 25th of this month?

I have been told that a solution of paramidophenol and lithin should be clear and colourless. I cannot get it like that. It is invariably a light Madeira colour. I attribute this to the colour of the powder which you have sent me, as this is a greyish lilac and not white. Should the solution be colourless or not?

Please let me know. When will we have supplies of pure paramidephenol powder at your Paris outlet?

Many thanks.

Yours sincerely,

Count d'Assche

Association Belge de Photographie to Messieurs Lumière Bros.

Brussels, 21 November 1893

Messieurs Lumière Bros, Lyon

It is my privilege to inform you that the session arranged specially in order to make your fine work on colour photography available to members took place on the 19th of this month and was a great success. The chemistry lecture theatre of the School of Industry, which is enormous, was full. Monsieur Maillon's lecture on Monsieur Lippmann's discovery and the considerable advance on his work which you have achieved was heard with the greatest of interest.

The photographs which you were good enough to supply were projected and the marvels you have produced provoked loud applause. A vote of congratulation was taken and I have been asked to pass on the Association's heartfelt thanks for your kindness in making these photographs available to us. I am delighted to pass this message on and to inform you of our vote.

I had had an opportunity to see your photographs in Geneva and it was with great pleasure that I saw them, once again, in Brussels, where I performed the perilous task of projecting the images.

As you requested, I returned the eight photographs which you had sent Monsieur Maes to you by post; indeed, they had gone before your letter reached us. Monsieur Maes was indisposed and very sorry that he was unable to attend this memorable session in the history of our Association.

Finally, at the risk of seeming presumptuous, I wonder whether I might ask for a photograph for the Ecole Industrielle de Bruxelles where I give an annual lecture on photography. I only ask because it would be such a pleasure to show my students the results you have obtained in the attempt to fix colours and I very much hope you will feel able to repy favourably.

    Yours sincerely,
Secretary-General
Puttemann

Antoine Lumière[1] to the Grand Chancellor of the Légion d'Honneur[2]

April 1894

Monsieur le Grand Chancelier de la Légion d'Honneur à Paris

Sir,

I attach various documents. Please also find the information you have requested, as follows:

    1) My birth certificate

    2) A summary of service: After terminating my career as a photographer, during which I obtained the following awards: gold medal, Lyon 1872; medal for progress, Vienna 1873; medal with special distinction, Paris 1874; gold medal, Paris 1878; I founded, with my sons, Auguste and Louis, our photographic plate business. Previously, there had been almost no manufacture of this product in France and it was entirely by our efforts that it was established here. We have obtained the following prizes: diploma, Le Havre, 1887; gold medal, microscopic exhibition, Antwerp, 1891; first prize, Universal Exhibition, Paris 1889. In addition, we have founded a business manufacturing and selling photographic paper and we are pleased to be able to say that more than 200 employees depend on this enterprise. Finally, I am a member of the 35 Committee and inspector at the Universal Exhibition in Chicago.

    3) A receipt for 37 francs.

    4) Among my many friends in the Légion d'Honneur, I hope that Monsieur A. Davanne, 82 rue des Petits-Champs, President, Société Française de Photographie, Officer of the Légion d'Honneur, will agree to stand as my sponsor.

    Yours sincerely,
A. Lumière

Note – There is a mistake in the decree which describes me as a manufacturer of photographic machines. We manufacture photographic plates and paper.

1 Antoine Lumière (1840–1911), father of Auguste and Louis, inventors of the Cinematograph. Born at Ormoy, Haute-Saône, in the east of France, in 1840, after a short interlude in Paris he set up as a photographer in Besançon, and then in Lyon. He encouraged his sons to help him in his work from a very young age. He soon acquired a reputation as an excellent portraitist and, in his studio in the rue de la Barre, grew relatively prosperous. This enabled him to give his sons the very best technical and theoretical training, at a school named La Martinière. Ever curious and eager to catch up with the latest technical developments, Antoine became interested in the manufacture of a more convenient, superior, 'dry' photographic plate under the name 'Etiquette bleue' or Blue Label. These were manufactured in a factory he built at Monplaisir in the suburbs of Lyon. After a few difficult years, a considerable fortune was built up. In 1894, it was he who encouraged his sons to take an interest in 'animated photography' and see if they could not improve on existing appliances.

As the number of his workers increased, he set up a pension and social security scheme for his employees, which was, at the time, comparatively innovative.

Perhaps the considerable success of his firm went to his head. He spent enormous sums, building a succession of small châteaux, to such an extent that the firm's future was compromised. It was saved at the last minute by his sons, supported by a family friend, a businessman named Vermorel.

Antoine Lumière was a man of artistic temperament – an accomplished painter, as well – which contrasts with his sons' more rigorously scientific minds, but it was he who provided them with exceptionally favourable circumstances in which to allow their talent to flower: he gave them a good education, surrounded them with artists and scientists, and played a vital part in the decision to launch the 'dry' photographic plates and the Cinematograph. It is unfortunate that his correspondence has almost entirely vanished. Antoine Lumière died of a brain haemorrhage in 1911.

2 Principal French Honours Order, set up under Napoleon. All three Lumières, father and two sons, held rank in the Légion d'Honneur.

Auguste Lumière to Marius Pradel[1]

11 April 1894

My dear Pradel,

If the letter I wrote you[2] unusually displeased you, you will hardly be astonished to learn that we too, on our side, are furious:

1) With Stéphane Girard[3] who is building up the firm thanks largely to the use of our name, and who is handing out founder members' shares in vast quantities without even bothering to keep us informed.

2) At you too, since you have accepted these shares without any consideration for your collaborators. If your collaborators do not count, then perhaps they should withdraw (along with those subscribers whom they have introduced).

No amount of explaining, no amount of excuses will convince us that there is not something most underhand in this whole business. Our intention was that founder shareholders' shares should remain largely in the hands of Girard and Leser. If we had known things were to be different, we would not have acted as we did. I am sorry I misunderstood what Leser had to say on Saturday. I regret it in every way and especially because it removes any illusion we might have had about Monsieur Girard. None of this is very frank, straight and clear. We are a little disappointed. We do not know whether to stay or withdraw.

Thomas[4] has just arrived. We will have a talk about all this.

What do you suggest?

Apart from anything, if our subscribers find out that yours have received shares, they will think we have kept the ones meant for them, and we shall look like scoundrels. Which is not funny, since we are straight.

I look forward to hearing from you, my dear Pradel. Here is a handshake.

Yours ever,

Auguste

1 Friend of Antoine Lumière and teacher at La Martinière where he taught Auguste and Louis Lumière.
2 Translator's note: He uses the familiar *tu* form, which shows particular intimacy, since this form would not normally be used to a former schoolteacher.
3 Messieurs Girard and Thomas, two businessmen of Lyon who sat on the board of the Lumière family firm from 1892 onwards.
4 See above.

Davanne to Louis Lumière

Cannes, 26 March 1895

Dear Monsieur Lumière,

I have received a letter from Monsieur Victor in which he tells me about your success at the Société d'Encouragement, first with an excellent and lucid lecture which went down very well and then with your projection of moving images which I found so interesting when you showed it at Lyon[1] and which your audience in Paris found equally fascinating.

Monsieur Victor has asked me to press you to renew your presentation of moving film at the next sitting of the Société Française de Photographie, 76 rue des Petits-Champs, and this I willingly do. The date is 5 April. But perhaps it is too much to ask you to be in Paris then, when either you or your brother will attend the Congress of Scientific Societies on the 16th?

I should be most grateful if you would let me know, when you reply, whether you will be asking for electric light for your lecture on 16 April. I am sure that, at the Sorbonne, it must be possible to obtain this.

Perhaps you could let me know what is necessary so I can arrange it as soon as I return to Paris on 8 or 9 April.

Yours sincerely,

Davanne

Note in Louis Lumière's handwriting: Autumn 1894.

1 Davanne refers here to the first projection of the Cinematograph at the Société d'Encouragement pour l'Industrie Nationale (Society for the Advancement of National Industry) which took place on 22 March 1895, in Paris, 44 rue de Rennes, nine months before the first public screening, on 28 December of the same year. Curiously, on the occasion of his lecture of 22 March, Louis Lumière showed his film, *Workers Leaving the Lumière Factory*, almost by accident, as just one of many examples of the progress being made in photography. He also showed several colour photographs in projection. The success of the moving picture was unexpected and instantaneous. Léon Gaumont, then director of Le Comptoir de la Photographie, a firm specializing in still photography, was in the audience. At the end of the session, Jules Carpentier, an engineer and manufacturer, approached the Lumière brothers and was commissioned by them to construct 25 cameras according to their design.

This letter is of great historical significance. It suggests that another session was envisaged at the Congress of Scientific Societies on 16 April 1895. We know that the screening to be arranged at the Sorbonne, which is referred to here, took place at the start of the academic year, on 16 November.

Gabriel Lippmann to Auguste Lumière

Paris, 21 April 1895

Dear Sir,

At tomorrow's session of the Académie I shall present your note together with its pretty photographs. I am sure you will be most successful. I should be grateful if you would let me have the pictures by Tuesday. They will be returned to you after the sitting, but as you may need the new ones to show at the Société de Photographie or elsewhere, I shall wait to hear from you before returning the lot.

Please send my best regards to your brother Louis.

Yours ever,

G. Lippmann

P.S. I have this minute received a note from your father who wishes to attend the sitting at the Académie. We have arranged to meet. His arrival is perfectly timed.

Henri Becquerel[1] to Monsieur Lumière

Paris, 14 May 1895

Sir,

This morning I showed my students at the Ecole Polytechnique the photographic plates you were kind enough to send me. They were much appreciated. I was careful to avoid overheating and the plates are in mint condition. The General[2] in charge of the School attended the lesson and he has suggested that it would be appropriate to show the President of the Republic your plates when he visits the School at the beginning of next week, in which case the class would be taken not by me but by the senior Professor of Physics who is Monsieur Cornu.[3] The General therefore requests that you allow your plates to remain in Paris for a few more days and that you allow me to pass on to Monsieur Cornu, if he asks for them, both your very fine photographs and the burden of looking after them.

If you would rather show the photographs to the President of the Republic yourself in other, more personal, circumstances, I would of course understand and I am quite ready to return the plates to you immediately if you so wish. Perhaps you could let me know as soon as possible.

Once again, thank you for letting me have the pictures and for allowing me to show my students what excellent use you have made of Monsieur Lippmann's discovery.

Yours sincerely,
Henri Becquerel

1 Professor at the Ecole Polytechnique, Henri Becquerel (1852–1908) in 1896 discovered radioactivity while studying fluorescence in uranium salts. Entered the Académie des Sciences in 1889 and received the Nobel Prize for Physics in 1903.
2 see note to letter of 9 March 1892.
3 see note to letter of 30 September 1890.

Louis Ducos du Hauron to Messieurs Lumière

Algiers, 17 June 1895

Dear Sirs,

I gather from newspaper accounts that you have recently sent a most interesting note to the Académie des Sciences and that it was presented by Monsieur Lippmann. Apparently, you have succeeded in producing remarkable colour pictures by triple printing, using three phototypes[1] obtained by the use of coloured filters. With your usual gentlemanliness, I also note that you have specifically stated that this photochromatic process is based on the principles of indirect colour photography as published by the late Charles Cros and myself more than twenty-five years ago.

I am absolutely delighted to hear of your success. I am sure that it is due to the ingenuity and science with which you have succeeded in applying chemical and mechanical means to make use of the various principles involved in as practical and attractive a way as possible. For I also know from the same accounts that the specimens you have obtained are of considerable charm and great beauty.

You know that, although I am not skilled in practical photographic printing, I repeatedly attempted to combine by photocollography the three phototypes of the System; unfortunately, the almost complete solitude, speaking scientifically and technically, in which I have had to live for many years, in a town which is most unscientific, and, even more significantly, that absence of capital which might, in my hands, have blossomed into invention, has meant that our theoretical work is much worthier of attention than the meagre works of art which have emerged from my tiny workshop.

The numerous and detailed data which I have assembled over more than twenty years of silent research into the subject of three-colour photography are now largely gathered together in a major work which my elder brother,[2] now judge at the Appeals Court in Algiers, proposes to publish in a few months. My brother is daily in my confidence and I have initiated him into all the secrets of my research. The mysteries of my Heliochromy[3] (I apologize for still, as is my habit, using this out-dated term, though it is no longer classical and has been replaced by the word 'photochromography') will soon be revealed and I know that this publication will rapidly popularize every means of making three-colour photographs, over and above the methods I have investigated myself. In particular, I go into the subject of producing the three special negatives in the most complete detail. I must also tell you that I refer repeatedly to gelatine bromide plates, and various other kinds, either ordinary or orthochromatic[4] plates particularly sensitive to one kind of ray or another, that are manufactured by your firm. Detailed experimentation has convinced me that your plates are of a superior quality and this is reflected in the book. My brother and I are convinced that publication will increase your sales. The work is conceived in such a way that all recent improvements to your photographic plates are relevant to the various descriptions it contains. If you like, I can enclose in every copy a short printed notice detailing the most recent changes and improvements.

As far as commercializing my colour photography is concerned, I have not so far had much success: a great deal of praise and platonic success in exhibitions is what I've got to show (notably at the International Photography Show, Paris, 1892, where, as a judge, I was disqualified, and the International Book Show, Paris, 1894). I have also achieved some notoriety, particularly of late. Still, what a father or an uncle cannot achieve for himself, a son or a nephew sometimes can. A life's work can continue in the same family, from one generation to the next. That is why my nephew, Gaston Ducos du Hauron,[5] has decided to capitalize on the honourable renown my photographic research has generated (this work is extemely varied and, most of it, unpublished) to go into partnership with some friends who are abundantly provided with capital to set up, in Algiers, an Office Algérien et Tunisien de Photographie the purpose of which will be to popularize some of my inventions and which, hopefully, will possess all that is needed to cultivate Photography in general.

Allow me to raise a particular matter with you, while we are on this subject. My nephew and his associates, Messieurs Mayeur and Baudin, would like to have exclusive distribution rights for Lumière plates throughout Algeria. Is such a thing possible?

I should explain that the establishment in question will be on a grand scale. We have chosen a spot in a magnificent location, in the most brilliant neighbourhood which is, as you know, for six or seven months of the year, rendezvous for a considerable number of distinguished tourists and travellers from the world over.

Finally, I must add that one of the photographic novelties that these gentlemen intend to launch is a kind of panoramic darkroom, for which I have taken out a patent just a few days ago and which I am sure will rapidly become fashionable. An entire landscape, within a circular circumference, is depicted, anamorphically, in the lower hemisphere of a mirror similar to a Desjardin globe: this globe[6] is placed above a photographic device which prints the image on a strip of gelatine film arranged cylindrically around a dark chamber; the image, which is deformed as it appears from the globe, is 'corrected' as it travels downwards through the lens and is printed on the emulsion. This system has the advantage of producing an instant panorama, without rotation. It will not be expensive.

It will be a privilege to hear from you.

Yours sincerely,

Louis Ducos du Hauron

Inventor

1 Old word for direct positive photographs.
2 Jean Marie Casimir Ducos, known as Ducos du Hauron, born at Courtras, 29 June 1830. In 1866, judge at Lectoure, then at Agen in 1869. On 25 January 1881, appointed to the appeals court at Algiers. In 1896, he retired to Paris where he died in 1909. Under the pseudonym of Alcide, he published several poetical works. He also collaborated with his brother and published *La Photographie des couleurs* (n.d.), *Traité pratique photographique de photographie des couleurs* (1878), *La Triplice photographique des couleurs et de l'imprimerie* (1896).
3 Heliochromy: photographic reproduction of colour. Apparently, not the favoured term.
4 Photographic plates that react to all colours except red.
5 Gaston Ducos du Hauron, nephew of Louis, would appear to have been a businessman keen to promote his uncle's interest. Together with Messieurs Mayeur and Baudin, he established as company specifically to sell his uncle's inventions. He would have liked this company to have become a subsidiary of the Etablissements Lumière, the Lumière family firm.
6 The principle is the same as a fish-eye lens, although here a panoramic and not a spherical projection is intended.

Dean Raulin to Messieurs Lumière

Lyon, 22 June 1895

Dear Sirs,

The Governing Body of the Faculty of Science has asked me to thank you for your generous contribution to the zoology department with a view to assisting the maritime expedition which Monsieur Koehler[1] is preparing.

Your encouragement of scientific research is most impressive and I am delighted to join my colleagues on the Governing Body in thanking you.

Yours sincerely,
Dean Raulin

1 René Koehler (1860–1931) submitted two theses in 1883, one in medicine and one in science. He was lecturer, then professor (1894) of zoology at Lyon. He married Jeanne Lumière on 25 September 1890.

Louis Olivier to Louis Lumière

Paris, 13 July 1895

Dear Sir,

I am writing to thank you once more for the enchanting evening you gave me and my friend last night. Wherever I was, yesterday and again this morning, people said what a brilliant session[1] it was, and how enthusiastic the audience was, as you know from the extent of the applause. We were delighted to discover these marvels, never before seen in Paris. I am sure that they will spread throughout the country.

I am most gratful to you for having given my guests a preview of this fine show which is an important landmark in the story of the photographic sciences. Allow me to compliment you, you and your brother, on the magnificent results you have obtained and to express the pleasure which I exerienced on viewing them.

Further, I enclose all the letters I received in response to my invitations, filed according to whether they are acceptances or not. Several people who said they would come did not and others who did not reply, did come. The entire Bouvier dinner came as a gang. All in all, about one hundred and fifty people probably passed through the rooms where the projection was held on Thursday night. A pleasure for everyone.

Yours etc.,

Louis Olivier

1 The session referred to is Auguste and Louis Lumière's presentation of the Cinematograph on 11 July 1895 in the reception rooms of the *Revue Générale des Sciences*. Brilliant, it must have been, if this detailed commentary by André Gay is anything to go by: 'The Cinematograph was illuminated electrically, by means of a Molteni bulb. The images were projected on to a screen five metres distant from the lens, made of fine, transparent cloth and stretched in the doorway between two of the rooms. On one side, spectators saw the image reflected and, on the other, equally sharp, but through the cloth. The first film showed trick-riding by cavalrymen with all the skill of their kind; then a military joke; then a house on fire, flames engulfing the building, smoke in the sky, firemen arriving, drenching the house with water and putting the fire out. The next film showed life-like blacksmiths exercising their trade: the iron reddened in the fire, was beaten into shape, dipped into water to let off a jet of steam. A view of the place des Cordeliers in Lyon was much admired: pedestrians coming and going, entering elegant shops, phaetons and commercial wagons dashing about in every direction. A little girl, life-size [sic] was particularly popular. She was eating out of doors, in between her parents who were feeding her. Nothing prettier than the delightful expressions of a happy child enjoying the morsels her father was giving her and holding down her bib against the wind with her tiny hands. The same child delighted the audience in another film by trying unsuccessfuly to catch goldfish in a bowl with the help of a spoon. *Revue Générale des Sciences*, 30 July 1895, pp. 633–6. This letter contains the important information that one hundred and fifty people attended this session, which may, therefore, be considered semi-public. It is worth remembering that only thirty-three people attended the first public screening on 28 December 1895 at the Salon Indien of the Grand Café, boulevard des Capucines in Paris.

Louis Lumière to Cousin

4 October [189]5

Monsieur Cousin,
Paris

We have received your letter of the 3rd of this month and noted its contents. We are most grateful to you for your suggestion that a note on our 'Cinematograph'[1] should be inserted in the *Bulletin de la Société Française de Photographie*. We are producing typographic prints[2] and we will have our Paris representative forward one to you as soon as possible.

Monsieur Louis Lumière is aware of your request concerning the Brasserie Lyonnaise. He sends his apologies for not replying in person, as he is extremely busy just at present. As Monsieur Winckler,[3] his father-in-law, a brewer in Lyon, is currently absent, he cannot give you the information you require. He will do so as soon as he can and forward it to you immediately.

Yours sincerely,
On behalf of Louis Lumière
Paris[4]

1 The Lumière Brothers' Cinematograph combined elements from the pioneering work done by such precursors as Muybridge, Janssen, Marey, Demenÿ, Edison and Reynaud and improved upon them. It was principally Louis Lumière who was responsible for perfecting the device. Towards the end of 1894, the brothers invented a claw mechanism similar to the presser foot on a sewing-machine. Auguste Lumière was to declare this the decisive revelation. Charles Moisson, chief mechanic in the Lumière factories and a close associate of Louis Lumière's, then transposed the idea to a camera. Soon, the circular eccentric ratchet system was replaced by a device known as 'Hornblower's eccentric' which had operated in sewing machines since 1877. Such was the principal innovation in the Lumière camera, described in the patent as 'a triangular ratchet which maintains the ribbon (or film) in place for two thirds of the total time.' At a pace of approximately 16 frames per second, the claw mechanism dug into the perforations, alternately stopping and starting the film at the appropriate speed to give the illusion of continuous movement, under the physiological laws of retinal persistence. The relevant research culminating in the invention was undertaken in 1894; 1895 was a year of tests and minor improvements; and 1896 the year the product was put on the market. The brand name Cinématograph Lumière first appears on 10 March 1895, in a supplementary note to the original patent which was taken out on 15 February 1895. One important detail was that the Lumière camera doubled up as a printer and projector too. See Appendix I.
2 The first photogravures made according to the Lumière process. In 1885, Louis Lumière developed a system of zinc offset, for use in printing. The first published work of photogravure was issued in Paris by Ernest Leroux and printed by Storck in Lyon. The book in question was a thirteenth-century New Testament in Provençal, together with a book of prayer according to the Cathar rite. It was a great success. A department of photographic printing was set up in the Lumière factory at Monplaisir. The pictures referred to here are probably part of a press campaign to launch the Cinematograph. See 'Le Cinématographe' in

Revue Générale des Sciences pures et appliquées, 1895, p. 633.

Louis Lumière to Diradour

7 October 1895

Monsieur Diradour
Constantinople

Thank you for your letter of 30 September. We have received the photographs you sent us and had an opportunity of examining them. As far as we can tell from the fragment, the spots appear to have been caused by the negative coming into contact with silver nitrate paper, as used in printing, before the negative was fixed. As far as the 13x18cm print is concerned, we believe that it was insufficiently rinsed and that consequently hyposulphite of soda crystals have formed beneath the varnish. We know of no remedy for either of these problems.

We will comply with your request for a print illustration to the article which you have given a Turkish scientific journal on the subject of our new device, the Cinematograph. We are most grateful to you for arranging this publication.

Yours sincerely,
L. Lumière

Jules Carpentier[1] to Louis Lumière

Paris, 12 October 1895

Monsieur Louis Lumière
Monplaisir, Lyon

Dear Louis,

I was just about to write to you this very day, since we Parisians have had three days of sun above our heads, to ask what kind of weather you are having in Lyon and how our machine is proving. Your reply has arrived in advance of my questions.

The various points which we had discussed previously were already being looked into; the new points you raise will now join them in the lab.

It is absolutely essential, as I told you,[2] that the camera is returned to us for a few days in order that we can check the various changes which have been been made during the course of construction and compare your original drawings with the current prototype. These changes are of the first importance since they are the result of successive practical experiments.

Please show your brother Auguste the prototype as soon as he returns and send it back to us straight away. We shall keep it here as short a time as possible, though we may as well use the time to make any changes which are already decided upon. Perhaps you could enclose a few sensitive strips in the parcel so we can conduct our own photographic experiments and determine the efficiency of any improvements we have introduced.

As soon as the matter is settled, we can let you have the twenty-five cameras you asked me to construct. We will have completed this first series by the end of the year; but if you so wish we can so arrange things that you have the use of a few cameras in advance of the rest, indeed as soon as possible.

As far as price[3] is concerned, I told you I expected to be able to manufacture the first series at a cost of 250 francs per unit. This figure must be treated with caution, however, since we have no firm ground for it and the construction of the first camera really gives us no relevant data. As you know, in the building of a prototype, measurement and design, trial and error and above all the process of gradual improvement all multiply costs by a factor of up to five. The first Cinematograph has thus cost us something like 950 francs not including Monsieur Cartier's time[4] or the cost of the Zeiss lens which I lent you.

We are agreed, are we not, on the notion discussed when I first came to Lyon, namely that you should preserve all rights as to the marketing of your system, my function being restricted to that of constructing the machines until further notice. I shall bill you for the cameras at a price agreed between us and you will be responsible for deciding on a retail price and the wholesale discount. It goes without saying that I count on being your principal wholesaler and representative in Paris. I would furthermore like your assurance, even if this may seem superfluous to you, that I shall continue to have exclusive rights of manufacture of your instrument, the improvement of which is an end towards which I intend to work with all my heart. Indeed, I should add that the aspect of this business which has brought us together which is most attractive to me is that it will undoubtedly make us firm friends. I was particularly struck by the kindness with which you received me the other day in Lyon and I hope you will pass my thanks on to Madame Lumière[5] as well.

Please give your brother my kind regards, as to all the other members of your family whom I have met.

Your devoted,

J. Carpentier

As far as I can tell from your notes, you have used only the small Zeiss lens. Does not the small box which you wish to eliminate prevent daylight from leaking into the grooves around the sprockets? And if we were to come to use a diaphragm, would it not provide the simplest and the best frame for it?

1 Jules Carpentier (1851–1921), a student at the prestigious Paris Lycée, Louis-le-Grand, and, from 1871, at the Ecole Polytechnique. Fascinated, from an early age, by the museum of mechanics in the Conservatoire National des Arts et Métiers, he went to work in the workshops of the Compagnie des PLM (a private railway company: Paris–Lyon–Marseille). He then took over a small engineering firm, situated in the rue Delambre in Montparnasse. He soon acquired a reputation for excellence in the field of electrical precision measurement devices and this put him in touch with the great physicists of the era. He rationalized his workshops by making each worker responsible for manufacturing one particular part, rather than a whole device. On 22 March 1895, he attended the presentation of the Lumière Cinematograph at the Société d'Encouragement pour l'Industrie Nationale and subsequently suggested to Louis Lumière that he be responsible for manufacturing the device, and for selling it in Paris. Louis Lumière accepted this proposal.

The correspondence between the two men is an example of the active exchange of views between two scientists, as first mutual trust, then friendship, springs up between them. In addition, it reveals, by a series of anecdotal incidents, the existence of stiff, albeit not yet threatening, competition to the partners' plans. The complementarity between the two men is typical of the way in which the Lumière brothers always managed to attach themselves to colleagues of particular worth. Carpentier's attempted construction of a 'Cinegraph' was useful to the making of the Cinematograph. He took out a patent on this Cinegraph some eight days after discovering the 'Cinematograph' on 22 March.

After the first public screening on 28 December 1895, Carpentier embarks on assembly line production of some 200 Lumière cameras. But Carpentier is an inventor in his own right and not just a clever manufacturer. Thus, on 18 March, he took out a patent for a mechanism based on a five-branched Maltese cross, forty days before V. Continsouza (28 April). Similarly, on 30 March 1896, he took out a patent for 'a device intended to photograph animated scenes by means of a film strip known as a "phototrope".' He also built a camera which he called a 'photo-jumelle' designed to be used at eye-level, by means of a separate viewfinder beside the lens. This camera sold fairly well and was copied, as is often the case. Finally, Carpentier invented a device called a 'Défileur Carpentier-Lumière' which adapted the basic Lumière camera to show much longer films. He also expanded on his 'phototrope' to make a 75mm camera and matching twin-blade reverse shutter projector, a system which only reappeared forty years later in America. Sadly, Carpentier's projector never worked and it was Louis Lumière's 35mm camera and films which had to be used for giant-screen projections at the Universal Exhibition of 1900. Shortly before Carpentier's death in a car accident, Louis Lumière took a three-dimensional portrait of him.

2 Translator's note: Louis Lumière and Jules Carpentier became close friends but they continued to use the formal *vous* form.

26

3 Carpentier's estimate is wrong, and he found himself obliged to revise it at a later stage.
4 Monsieur Cartier was one of Carpentier's technicians.
5 Daughter of Léocadie and Alphonse Winckler, Rose Winckler married Louis Lumière on 2 February 1893.

Louis Lumière to Antoine Lumière

14 October 1895

My beloved Dad,

Auguste and I have been discussing the matter of marketing the Cinematograph. You know that, as it is, we have received a large number of offers of different kinds. Here in Lyon, for instance, two newspapers, *Le Lyonnais* and *Le Progrès*, both suggest they take charge of the operation, including all advertising. In exchange we would receive 60% of the takings, after poor tax.[1]

The Casino de Paris in Paris has let us know of a similar offer and, as you know, this establishment has advertising agreements with all the major newspapers, as well as having a large audience capacity. We have not accepted this offer as you wish us to bring something off in the capital. But it seems fair that you ensure that we obtain a 40% share of takings, after tax. That hardly seems excessive in view of the offers we have been given. We feel that no more decisions should be taken until we have decided on locations in these two cities and I have to say that we are not in agreement with you as to the best way of arranging matters.[2] It would appear to have the following disadvantages:

1) Sizeable capital outlay.

2) High running costs.

3) Constant supervision, throughout the country, of the shows so that we can modify at short notice the costs of each operation, the advertising programme or cut the whole thing short if it looks as if the attraction has diminshed in that particular location.

4) Finally, we do not like the prospect of you playing Barnum showing off his magic lantern.

We see things differently:

Since so many people are making us offers, all we need is one intelligent employee to answer correspondence and rent out the devices at a fixed sum per evening: 100 francs, 200 francs according to the importance of the location.

We could also train operators whose expenses would be paid by people who rented the devices and who would be in charge of running the show.

This method presents several advantages:

1) Almost no capital outlay, no advertising costs, no organization of premises to establish.

2) We would benefit from existing locations, some of which are well-equipped.

3) We would be able to measure progress and advance cautiously. If our devices are much in demand, at the highest price, then our experience in Paris and Lyon will help us fix prices elsewhere. When popularity wears thin, we will be in a position to lower our prices according to supply and demand.

4) We would be beholden to nobody, free and the fact is we do not know how things are going to work out.

Even if we were to establish a company, we believe this is the best way of commercializing our invention.

So, dear Father, that is what we feel. Is it not more logical?

Our travellers arrived safely yesterday and we all ate at home. Everyone is in good health today except for Suzanne,[3] who has a cold.

It is cold and we have lit fires all over the house.

When are you coming to Lyon?

We all hug you a thousand times. We love you, dear Father, from the bottom of our hearts.

L. Lumière

1 This implies the Cinematograph would come under the same law as the theatre where a *droits des pauvres* or 'duty for the poor' was levied on box office takings. This money was spent on hospitals, on asylums and so on. Some film screenings were of course entirely for the benefit of charity, as for instance – among others – a charity gala for the Hospital of the Blind at the Prium Theatre, Melbourne, on 19 November 1896 (*Melbourne Age*, 18 November 1896, p. 8).
2 Antoine Lumière was an artisan, a photographer, whereas his sons were industrialists and much more alert to the business of making a profit. Antoine Lumière had got himself into trouble in the early years of bromide plate production. It would appear from this letter that Antoine envisaged a highly centralized, and thus costly and unmanageable, method of commercializing the Cinematograph, with him in charge of operations – 'the Barnum' as his son Louis puts it, not without irony.
3 Suzanne Lumière, Louis and Rose's daughter, born in 1894, then one year old.

Louis Lumière to Jules Carpentier

[Lyon, Monplaisir] 14 October [189]5

My dear Monsieur Carpentier,

We are today sending you the instrument which I showed my brother as soon as he returned, which was yesterday, and he was as appreciative as I was of your fine workmanship. We enclose two strips of sensitive film[1] (these strips must be 16 metres long). At present, this is our entire stock. We are currently looking into the business of preparing the film and soon we shall be ready to go into production.

In response to your request, I am happy to say that we would be glad to accept your suggestion that we give you exclusive rights of manufacture, on condition you agree to do everything you can to carry out our orders as rapidly as is reasonable. We will restrict our dealings to sales and we are delighted that you should be our principal representative and stockist in Paris. Needless to say, these arrangements only apply to sales in France, for we may license our patents abroad.

Please bear in mind that delivery of the first twenty-five cameras is urgent and we are relying on your kind vigilance in this respect.

Please be assured that we are delighted at the friendly sentiments which you express and we very much hope that they will grow over the years, as they are reciprocated.

Yours ever,

L. Lumière

I obtained the picture by means of the small, ordinary lens, which is perfectly adequate – and not with the Zeiss. The small round box I asked you to suppress will be a hindrance rather than a help, unless it is lined with velvet. But even then, it would scarcely be of any use. This box will not suppress the slight misting produced by light seeping into the sprocket grooves, unless we reverse it and fix it in front of the shutter, on the lens frame for instance. It is easy to see where the light comes in.

Please return the camera as soon as you can. Thank you in advance.

1 In 1930, Charles Moisson, chief mechanic at the Lumière works, related how such film lay at the origins of their research into the Cinematograph. 'In the summer of 1894,' he explained, 'the father came into my office; Louis was there; he took a strip of kinetoscope film out of his pocket and said, verbatim, to Louis: "This is what you should be doing. Edison is making a fortune selling this and his appointed concessionaire is looking to encourage production here in France so he can get the price down." I can still see the strip of film. It was about 30 centimetres long and exactly the same as film is today: 4 perforations

per frame, same breadth, same frame size.' The need to develop adequate support for animated photographs ran parallel with the development of the Cinematograph. At first, Louis Lumière used strips of perforated paper in his various early devices; the images were printed in negative and illuminated by arc-light. Paper was too opaque; it would have been hard to project these images even if they had been positives; but, as a manufacturer of photographic equipment, Louis Lumière was in a privileged position. He soon understood that the obstacle could be overcome by using a material that was transparent and supple and yet strong, that would hold stable images and that could be cut to a sufficient length. Transparent celluloid answered these requirements but it was a recent invention, and not yet manufactured in France. One of the Lumières' employees was despatched to America to buy supplies at the New York Celluloid Company. 'One of the first points that retained my attention,' Louis Lumière was to tell Georges Sadoul (G. Sadoul, *Louis Lumière*, p. 15), 'was the question of the resistance of the films. Celluloid was new to us and we did not know what its properties were. I elaborated a series of methodical experiments which involved piercing strips of film with needles of variable diameters and attaching increasingly heavy weights to these needles.' Covered in emulsion, cut into strips, then perforated by a machine which Moisson invented for this purpose, celluloid film turned out to be the right stuff. A succession of 900 photographic images are printed on a strip of film 17 metres long – the prototypes, as we shall see in this letter, were only 16 metres long – and 35mm wide. Once the process was defined, a separate firm, run by Monsieur Planchon, was given the task of producing the strips of film, rather like Edison and Eastman. There were, however, significant differences. For example, Lumière films had two round perforations per frame, as opposed to Edison's four square perforations, and it was Edison's standard that was later adopted worldwide.

Auguste Lumière to Ed. Liesegang[1]

19 October 1895

Ed. Liesegang
Düsseldorf

It is with pleasure that we inform you that we are today mailing you a fragment of one of our 'Cinematograph' film strips. We also enclose a copy of *Nature* and a copy of the *Revue Générale des Sciences* which both contain information about this device. We hope that this information is of use to you with regard to the articles which you intend to publish locally.

We are most grateful to you for undertaking this publication. Please do not hesitate to call on us for any further information you may require.

Yours sincerely,
A. Lumière

1 Liesegang manufactured and sold magic lantern slides in Düsseldorf.

Auguste Lumière to the Director of the Edison-Bell Phonograph Corporation

19 October 1895

The Director
The Edison-Bell Phonograph Corporation
Bradford

Thank you for your letter of 15.[1] Our new invention, the 'Cinematograph', is currently under construction in Paris and we are not yet in a position to say when it will be on sale. Nor are we able yet to determine what the sale price will be. As soon as this information is in our possession we shall forward it to you.

Yours faithfully,

A. Lumière

1 Thomas Edison (1847–1931) was aware of the success of the Cinematograph, after its early screenings. He needed to know whether it would provide serious competition for his kinetoscope and thus was attempting to find out how it was put together. The Cinematograph mechanism was not patented in the United States until 1897, and then under the name A. and L. Lumière Kinetographic Camera. Relations between Edison and the Lumières were always very competitive. In 1896, the kinetoscope's popularity faltered because of the arrival of the Cinematograph. As a result, Edison contracted Thomas Armat to establish the phantascope, a device developed with Charles Francis Jenkins including Demenÿ's ratchet which would enable kinetoscope images to be projected on to a large screen. America welcomed the Lumière Cinematograph with open arms, but this was soon replaced by an all-out trade war, the champion of which was, on the American side, Edison's Biograph. Hassle, blackmail, threats, legal proceedings were all employed to hound Mesguich and the Lumière teams out of America. It should be remembered that the brother of the President of the United States, McKinley, was one of the directors of the Edison Biograph company. It is naturally tempting to establish a connection between this fact and the administrative obstacles which were placed in the Cinematograph's path.

Perrigot, an employee of the Etablissements Lumière, was responsible for defending the company's interests at the Swiss National Show in Geneva in 1896. The organizers had suggested that the Cinematograph was installed on Edison's stand. Perrigot reports that Louis Lumière had this to say: 'Without in any way wishing to diminish the American inventor's well-deserved reputation, you will understand that nothing will induce us to place the Cinematograph on the Edison stand. If there was a Marey stand, we would certainly be happy to take refuge beneath its French flag.' (in G. Sadoul, *Histoire du cinéma*, t. 1, p. 426).

Auguste Lumière to Captain des Francs

21 October 1895

Captain des Francs
Chambéry

Thank you for your letter of the 19th.

It is true to say that citrate, gelatine-based paper does not necessarily conserve well. It is not possible to predict how long it will keep because this depends on the packaging, how long it must be transported, the various climates to be traversed and so on.

We enclose a formula for the preparation of combined toning-fixative baths.[1] The products involved are easy to transport in powder form.

Our new device, the 'Cinematograph' is currently under construction in Paris and we do not yet know when it will be ready. As soon as we do, we shall let you know.

Please do not hesitate to get in touch if there is any further information you require.

Yours sincerely,
A. Lumière

1 Colour fixatives. Toner provides a measure of the chemical transformation undergone by the image, such that it may be fixed at the appropriate moment.

Louis Lumière to H. Mesnier

22 October 1895

Monsieur H. Mesnier
Bordeaux

Thank you for your letter of the 20th. We had not overlooked your previous request regarding the Cinematograph but we have not yet settled the price, nor the moment at which we shall put it on sale. As soon as we can, we shall let you know.

The machine is not complicated; it will be easy to handle and is unlikely to go wrong provided it is in the right hands. No special knowledge will be required for its use; at least, not over and above a knowledge of photographic techniques. Its advantage over Edison's machine[1] from the point of view of performance, is that the projected images may be viewed by a large number of spectators at once, which is not the case with the kinetoscope.[2]

Yours sincerely,

L. Lumière

1 Before inventing the phonograph in 1878, Edison had improved the telegraph printer, then invented the automatic ticker tape telegraph. Considered in the United States as the father of animated photography, his interest in this field had arisen as a result of a lecture given by Muybridge. His aim was to reproduce not just movement but the sound that went with it. Edison's genius was not just as an inventor but as a leader of men. He surrounded himself with the finest teams. In order to ensure that the printed images were equidistant, they first had recourse to indented celluloid film (1888), then perforated celluloid film (1889), provided by George Eastman. In 1890–1, they devised the kinetograph, the first true movie camera, but curiously Edison believed that there was no future in projection: it was by means of individual viewing apparatus that spectators were to discover the reproduction of movement. Edison's kinetoscope arrived in France in 1894. The *Bulletin de la Société Française de Photographie* wrote: 'It is nothing more than a remarkable toy.' It goes without saying that the kinetoscope was one of many devices which inspired Louis Lumière in the construction of the Cinematograph.

2 The Cinematograph weighed less than 5kg. It was easy to handle compared to the kinetograph, whose larger weight and volume made it clumsy, particularly for reportage. Kinetoscope images could be viewed by only one spectator at a time looking into the back of a box through an eye-piece. Cinematograph pictures, in contrast, were projected in public, in darkened rooms, on to a large screen. It was an experience much closer to what we now term cinema.

Auguste Lumière to Henri Coupin

23 October 1895

Monsieur Henri Coupin
Paris

Thank you for your letter of the 21st. The pictures you require for your forthcoming article in *Chronique scientifique* about our new device, the 'Cinematograph', are at present unavailable. We expect this situation to change shortly and we will have our Paris representative send you the illustration; we are writing to him about this.

We are most grateful to you for the article in question. Please do not hesitate to contact us if there is any further information you require.

Yours sincerely,

A. Lumière

Auguste Lumière to E. Demole

28 October 1895

Monsieur E. Demole
Geneva

Thank you for your letter of 26 October. Our new device, the 'Cinematograph' is currently under construction in Paris and we are as yet unable to say when it will come on the market. Nor do we know how it will be priced. We note your interest and we shall most certainly give you this information as soon as we are able.

We enclose two press cuttings about the device. If you feel that it would make copy for your journal, we could supply you with an illustration, being a fragment of one of our film strips[1], together with some line drawings.

Yours sincerely,
A. Lumière

1 Three or four frames taken from a print. Later on, Lumière films will come with a sample of each film stuck on to the outside of the cardboard package, together with a catalogue number for identification. This use of sets of single frames was helpful both in identifying the films and for advertising purposes. (See Jacques Rittaud-Hutinet, *A. et L. Lumière, les 1000 premiers films*, Sers-Vilo, 1990, in which these single frames are published.) The line drawings are probably explanatory sketches to show how the Cinematograph worked.

Auguste Lumière to J. Casier

29 October 1895

Monsieur J. Casier
Ghent

Thank you for your letter of the 27th and for letting us have the requisite information as to where to send our device, and where your Meeting is due to take place.

We will make our chief electrician[1] available to you. He is able to demonstrate and operate the 'Cinematograph' as well as answer any questions which may arise. He will not, however, be able to perform in public and we should be grateful if you would nominate someone from your Association to discharge this duty.

We enclose two descriptions of the device which the person in question can read up before the demonstration.

Yours sincerely,
A. Lumière

1 Charles Moisson, head technician, and his assistant, Jacques Ducom, acted as projectionists for two demonstrations of the Cinematograph in Belgium: at the Palais du Midi in Brussels on 10 November 1895 for the Association Belge de Photographie; and on 12 November, at the Cercle Artistique et Littéraire, now Cercle Gaulois, also in Brussels. The 'chief electrician' referred to may be Ducom. The demonstration in question is probably a projection for some scientific society in Ghent. In any case, the information is useful because it would seem to confirm the hypothesis according to which there were a larger number of private or semi-public displays of the Cinematograph before 28 December 1895 than is usually thought.

Auguste Lumière to Carl Neweczerzal

31 October 1895

Monsieur Carl Neweczerzal
Davos-Platz

Thank you for your letter of the 29th. Our new device, the 'Cinematograph', is currently under construction in Paris and we are as yet unable to say when it will come on to the market. Nor do we know how it will be priced. We note your interest and we shall most certainly give you this information as soon as we are able.

Our super-fast, super-thin 45 x 101 millimetre glass plates are 1.90 a dozen. Red label slow plates, the same format, are the same price.

Yours sincerely,
A. Lumière

Louis Lumière to Jules Carpentier

[Lyon, Monplaisir] 2 November [189]5

Dear Monsieur Carpentier,

I am writing to ask for the return of the first machine which you have built as I assume the improvements discussed have now been implemented. We are committed to a number of demonstrations and your machine is much missed because it is so accurate.

We are also anxious for news of the first series of twenty-five. The competition is snapping at our heels and my father is particularly keen that eveything should be ready as he intends to take charge of this business.

Furthermore, De Bedts[1] (the Anglo-American import officer[2]) continues to attract as much attention as he can with his chronos[3] and it would be most unfortunate if he started before we did.

We are relying on your friendship. Construction must come along as quickly as possible. We look forward to hearing from you.

   Yours ever,
   L. Lumière

I shall have the pleasure of calling on you in Paris in a few days' time.

1 The European Blair Camera Company's representative in France for film. He also ran a shop in Paris, 338 rue St Honoré, called The Anglo-American Photo Import Office. Together with his supplies of Blair film, he stocked Edison kinetoscope 35mm film. This gave him a serious edge over other inventors, such as Lumière, who were still searching for the right film stock. De Bedts also sold Demenÿ's phonoscope and supplied Demenÿ and Gaumont with film stock for their first experiments. It seems probable that he took over sales of the kinetoscope from the Werner brothers. In 1896, he started to take out patents: on 10 January, for a 'punching machine for perforating film' and on 14 January for an 'intermittent mechanical system for chronophotography and for animated projection'.

De Bedts' kinetograph was serious competition for the 'Cinematogaph', weighing 5kg, and using 35mm perforated film in 30m strips. Unlike the Cinematograph, the kinetograph was on sale to the general public, which Laurent Mannoni (in *Le grand art de la lumière et de l'ombre*, Nathan 1994) considers an advantage over Lumière, who sold a complete show, but not the machine on its own. This view is questionable. Lumière's network induced impressive experiment with film as a medium and also established the foundations for a production-distribution system.

De Bedts was also the founder of the French photographic society, and was an innovator in the field of film as an advertising medium. In April 1896, he set up his kinetograph-projector in the Isola brothers' establishment across the street from the Salon Indien where the Lumière Cinematograph operated, but his business foundered and was liquidated on 15 July 1898.

2 Translator's note: in English in the original.

3 Perhaps an abbreviation for Marey's chronophotograph.

Jules Carpentier to Louis Lumière

4 November 1895

My dear friend,

   I shall be sending you machine no. 1 tomorrow or, at the latest, the day after tomorrow. We have had to keep it longer than anticipated because we have had to review our entire specification, starting with what works and is proven.

   Machine no. 1 has had the largest number of improvements. You will discover that it now contains a shutter consisting of two thin blades (metal) which permit variations in aperture and, consequently, in exposure. Neither of these blades will be fixed, in order that you may place them as you wish. The mechanism is not very convenient for the man in the street and if we decide to provide all the machines with variable aperture, we should have to do better; at least, fix one of the blades, so that the variation concerns only one side – front or back – of the opening. We could also supply a set of spare discs with graded aperture, but is it necessary? One element is bound to remain unpredictable and that is the speed at which the camera is cranked. Let me know what you think as soon as you can. Our manufacturing process is under way and if we leave any changes too late they will slow things down.

We have introduced several other improvements. I hope you will approve. I know, for a start, that you will be pleased to know that the actual manufacture is proceeding apace. It began even before we had produced a complete set of specifications. We have got a lot of work under our belt and I hope to be able to improve on the delivery schedule which I gave you.

I am aware of Monsieur De Bedts' efforts: his prototype is complete; he has made his films and projected them; their specifications are identical to Edison's kinetoscope films. I do not think, however, that he is anywhere near supplying machines for sale. As for us, we are not wasting a minute of our time.

I am delighted to know we shall be seeing you soon.

Yours,

J. Carpentier

I have drawn up specifications for a single spool magazine, to be used while filming. The other magazine is for making positive prints. The single magazine goes with a metal bin into which the film reels; each machine will obviously need several such pairs of these accessories, so that a cameraman can make several films without rushing to a laboratory in between. At least, that is what I have gathered. I am manufacturing more accessories than machines.

What about the film strips? Are you managing to make them now? If you let me know where the raw material comes from, I shall try to find out how it is made.

The weather is foul and I have a feeling I shall be returning the two rolls of film you sent me without having exposed them.

Louis Lumière to Jules Carpentier

[Lyon, Monplaisir] 5 November [189]5

My dear Monsieur Carpentier,

I received your kind letter this morning and am writing to thank you by return for agreeing to hurry the manufacture as much as you can. As far as the shutter disc is concerned, I believe it will be neceesary to make it up in two pieces, one fixed to the shaft and the other free to move, so that the aperture is not enlarged by use of the time the film is in motion. This is as you suggest.

I don't think we can rely on variations in cranking to provide variations in exposure because that would mean filming shorter scenes in fine weather and longer ones on cloudy days. When the film is projected, either the characters will move too slowly or there will be a waste of film because successive frames will appear on the screen with an unnecessary speed of more than fifteen frames per second. As in most cases, an exposure of 1/50 second is sufficient, if, during the making of the negative the disc had been opened as wide as possible, then the projectionist would have to double his cranking (in order to achieve 30 frames per second) to get the same 1/50 exposure.[1]

Coating American film with emulsion[2] is very difficult and, unfortunately, we have not so far succeeded. This, in spite of the fact that Blair products are manufactured in this way.[3]

If we are not successful (we are at present envisaging another solution), then we shall reach agreement with Blair Co. I think they will agree to supply us, though I would rather avoid this route if possible.

We do not know where to find the manufacturer of raw film stock. We are trying to find out. The most useful thing to know, though, would be how to coat film with emulsion. We have made various attempts and we are regularly confronted by the same problem: the film warps, it dilates with the inevitable temperature changes that are involved in the process – however much these changes are minimized.

We can discuss all this in London next week and perhaps you will be able to help us, since you are kind enough to offer.

Can you send us machine no. 1 tomorrow without fail and as fast as possible? We have promised to show some prints in Lyon on Saturday and our prototype is on its way to Brussels where Moisson,[4] our technician, is going to give a demonstration of the machine to the Belgian photographic association. We could not turn them down. Furthermore, Monsieur Lippmann has asked us to project a few prints at the Sorbonne next week and I shall make use of my trip to Paris to give him satisfaction.

Please accept my apologies for scribbling at such length.

Yours ever,

L. Lumière

Did you by any chance carry on with your plans for a machine to make the perforations? It would be most useful.

It would be handy to have, for every machine, several spool containers and several bins but will this not put a burden on cost? In any case, you can certainly manufacture some extra.

1 This really raises the matter of the diaphragm. In this device, it is fixed. Consequently, the speed at which the crank is turned should take light conditions into account. But in practice this is problematic. If the film runs at less than 15 frames per second, the threshold of illusion is crossed and the images will judder on the screen; if the film runs too fast, then its overall duration, only one minute long, will be still further reduced.
2 Having been supplied with strips of celluloid, the Lumière brothers turned their attention to the matter of laying down emulsion on to film. Edison benefited from American advance in his field. The Lumière brothers ran into trouble. Celluloid warped and expanded under a heat-based treatment. Yet they insisted on discovering the theory and practice of each stage of the process of making moving pictures, both out of intellectual curiosity and because, as businessmen, they wanted always to maximize productivity.
3 Supple, transparent film made out of cellulose nitrate – celluloid – invented by Hannibal Goodwin and manufactured by George W. Eastman had been available in the United States since 1889. The Lumière brothers did not succeed in applying photo-sensitive emulsion to celluloid film and had to apply to the Blair Company, through Fuerst Brothers, London, for supplies of ready-made stock.
4 Charles Moisson, head technician in the Lumière factor; worked with Auguste, then with Louis, to design and manufacture a prototype Cinematograph. With Francis Doublier and Jacques Ducom, he was in charge of the first public screenings of the Cinematograph at the Grand Café in Paris.

Louis Lumière to Victor Planchon[1]

[Lyon, Monplaisir] 5 November [189]5

My dear Monsieur Planchon,

Please forgive my not replying to your earlier letter. I have been very busy. We are very keen to receive the supplies to which you refer and we hope there is no further delay as we wish to take stock of our current experimentation and, as soon as we are absolutely certain everything is in order, to start selling.

As regards the photo-jumelle,[2] the matter is of interest provided that, as you suggest, the use of metal frames to hold the photographic plates is no longer a requirement.

One matter which is potentially of great importance is the question of rolls of film for the 'Cinematograph'. Please look into it and send us, as soon as you can, samples of sensitive film. It will need to be very strong to guard against snapping and the emulsion will need to be laid in a very even coat. As far as the raw material is concerned, the specimens you showed us seemed very good, although perhaps too easily torn. It would be instructive to try and run a little through the machine. Laying emulsion on to American film is very difficult.

I am relying on you to look into this matter as soon as you can and to send us a few metres of something similar.

Yours ever,

L. Lumière

<hr />

1 This letter follows on naturally from the preceding. 'We wish to take stock of our current experimentation and as soon as we are absolutely certain everything is in order, to start selling,' writes Louis Lumière. This shows the extent to which Planchon was to become a crucial partner in the Lumière operation: he was to receive precise instructions from his clients in Lyon as to how film should be delivered – in rolls, not in strips – how strong it should be and so on.

Victor Planchon (1863–1935), educated at the Ecole Lavoisier, was assistant to Bardy, a leading chemist. Himself a chemist and a keen photographer, he established at Boulogne-sur-Mer, in 1890, a factory to make film destined to supplant photographic plates. This was the first factory in Europe to sell photographic chemicals on an industrial scale. The Lumière family were established clients as they purchased the ingredients for their famous Blue Label plates from Planchon. They now turned to him for help in experimenting with film for the Cinematograph.

2 Known as the jumelle Carpentier, which Carpentier had patented in 1892, the photo-jumelle was a stills camera that looked like a pair of binoculars. It allowed photographers to hold their camera at eye-level, using a viewfinder placed beside the lens. The camera contained a set of various photographic plates. It achieved a deal of success.

Auguste Lumière to Van Neck

7 November 1895

Monsieur Van Neck
Antwerp

Thank you for your letter of the 4th of this month. It is most unfortunate that your request should reach us at this late stage because we have only one machine at our disposal and prior engagements which prevent us from giving you satisfaction. The person[1] who is to perform a demonstration of our 'Cinematograph' in Brussels must return immediately the session is over in order to fulfil other, earlier commitments.

We hope you will be able to come to an agreement with the Association regarding the guests whom you wished to invite and we hope to be able to help you in this matter at a later date.

Yours sincerely,

A. Lumière

<hr />

1 Charles Moisson.

Louis Lumière to H. Véra

7 November 1895

Monsieur H. Véra
Paris

Thank you for your letter of the 6th of this month.

Eclair have made various proposals concerning our 'Cinematograph' directly to us and we have had to disappoint them as we are currently unable to make any firm commitments regarding this device. We are nevertheless most grateful to you for your information on the subject.

Yours sincerely,
for L. Lumière
Monsieur Paris

Jules Carpentier to Louis Lumière

Paris, 9 November, Saturday evening

My dear friend,

I expect you received machine no. 1 yesterday and I am sure it is going to be a great success in a little while.

I am sure you have noticed that it was returned with a counterfeit nut. The original is in the hands of a manufacturer who is to supply our cabinet-maker with copies.

In my letter dated the 4th, in my haste, I wrote somewhat confusedly about the shutter and consequently you did not comprehend my meaning. Referring to variations in the speed of cranking, I did not mean that such variations were a desirable method of altering exposure; I realize, as you do, that in principle the number of frames per second should remain constant; what I intended to say was that, however undesirable, such variations were inevitable, and that under the circumstances any attempt at controlling aperture was doomed to failure; I wonder therefore whether there is any merit in complicating the machine with a mechanism which can only make it more expensive. You have spoken: the matter is decided.

Our work continues apace. We have not run into any hitches. The assembly line has, however, taught us that certain details will, in the future, need rethinking. The small mirror, for instance, that presses down on the film, is not appropriate for manufacture in quantity. It is relatively difficult and slow to assemble. In fact, in its present form, it is fragile. On Wednesday, just as we were about to send the machine off to you, we noticed that one of the corners of this little mirror had snapped off. We had to start all over again, which slowed us up. Similarly, the metal bin into which the film spools, though cute, costs us a pretty sum. Consequently, the price of a pair of spare magazines is forced up, and that will hinder sales of these accessories which, I am convinced, are essential. It is imperative that we manage to simplify.

I have relaunched work on my machine for perforating film.[1] I need it for my 'Cinegraph'[2] which I have abandoned in order to look after your 'Cinematograph'.[3] A proper manufacturer will always sacrifice his own inventions! In any case, altering a few minor parts will easily adapt the perforating machine for use on your films.

Speaking of your films, I must report a conversation I had yesterday with one of my colleagues in the Société d'Encouragement which left me dumbfounded. We were discussing you, which, in itself, is not surprising. I was explaining all that you had done to launch the manufacture of good quality film. My colleague interrupted me and stated that your firm only affected to be involved in the business of laying emulsion on to film; that all you in fact did was to send your emulsion to Boulogne where Monsieur Planchon coated it on to film, using machines of his own invention; that, in the end, your firm was no more than a customer, in the ordinary commercial way. I wanted to deny it, but I thought better of it as the information came from Monsieur Planchon[4] himself; I merely said I would look into it. I should be grateful if you could let me know exactly what the facts are, in order that my friendship for you is not embarrassed again.

As soon as you know when you are coming please let me know. I shall probably have to go out of Paris for a few days next week and I do not want to miss you.

All the best.

J. Carpentier

1 The existence of this project suggests that Carpentier's Cinegraph (see next note) was probably at an advanced stage of conception.
2 A device invented by Jules Carpentier, who patented it on 30 March 1895. It was designed to project film-based photographs of moving scenes. These photographs were driven by the teeth of an intermittently rotating dispenser and not by a continuous sprocket system.
3 A generous man. Carpentier's Cinegraph might easily have proved a dangerous competitor for the Cinematograph; but Carpentier admired the Lumière brothers and served them well.
4 Planchon, as we have seen, played a part in Louis Lumière's experiments. But to say that Lumière was merely a customer in the ordinary commercial way is hardly an accurate representation of events. Lumière's replies of 11 and 12 November put Planchon politely in his place.

Louis Lumière to Jules Carpentier

Lyon, Monplaisir, 11 November 1895

My dear Monsieur Carpentier,

I want to enlighten you about the film business immediately. Monsieur Planchon[1] has got some cheek – as they say at the Elysée[2] – to be telling Monsieur Bardy (for I assume he is the person to whom you were speaking) such tall stories.

We asked Monsieur Planchon to look into the matter of this film stock, in order to take the burden off us and in the hope that it would obviate the need to buy American supplies. I referred to this in my recent letter to you when I said that we were envisaging another solution. But this has not prevented us from trying, and carrying on trying, to coat American film with emulsion, because, although we have asked Monsieur Planchon to look into the matter, we do not intend to rely solely on him for our supplies of sensitive strips.

There is no doubt that his equipment (he possesses big glass tables which he can use to lay the emulsion on to film) and his experience of gum printing may induce us to entrust him with a portion of our supply contracts, but so far he has not produced anything of use. We are currently sending him emulsion (this is between us) to be laid on to auto-tensile film. Transporting this to Lyon on sheets of glass is causing us no end of breakages and other trouble.

This is the truth of the matter.

In any case, we manufacture the emulsion and that surely makes us somewhat more than 'a customer in the ordinary commercial way'.

Could you tell me by return of post whether we could meet on Thursday morning? I intend to travel on Wednesday by the two o'clock train. I have a couple of points to make about the way the bin is made.

Yours ever,

L. Lumière

1 This letter relates to some untimely remarks of Planchon's. An active man, he was not always prudent, though he soon proved himself worthy of trust. After some initial hesitation, the Lumière brothers commissioned him to manufacture the film their equipment required.
2 Translator's note: The palace of the President of the French Republic.

Louis Lumière to Victor Planchon

[Lyon Monplaisir] 12 November [189]5

My dear Monsieur Planchon,

We have been informed of a conversation in which you apparently said that we were 'merely customers in the ordinary commercial way'.

We are most surprised at you and hope you will now be more discreet since no one has been told of the way we are working together on auto-tensile and other types of film.

Having said which, your 6.5 x 9 sample looks like working. But isn't fixing it to cardboard over-complicated? Send us the finished film as soon as you can, since we have sent you a fair amount already and received nothing in return. Perhaps it would be best to ensure a regular flow of supplies in order to avoid accounting problems and cover us for the risk we are taking in sending you emulsion.

I am off to Paris tomorrow and I am not certain that I shall have time to see you because I must be back here on Sunday. If I find a spare moment, I shall send you a telegram from Paris asking you to lunch or dinner.

We are awaiting rolls of film and anxious to test what you have put together.

Yours ever,

L. Lumière

Auguste Lumière to E. Demole

12 November 1895

E. Demole
Geneva

Thank you for your letter of the 11th of this month. As far as the 'Cinematograph' is concerned, we are committed to performances in Paris and so cannot currently satisfy your request. This is most disappointing and we hope to be more fortunate on another occasion.

Our colour photographs by the indirect method[1] are in circulation, but they are spoken for over the coming weeks, until 15 December inclusive. We shall not be able to forward them to you until after this date.

We are entirely devoted to your instructions.

Yours sincerely,

A. Lumière

1 This letter clearly indicates that the Lumière brothers had abandoned the 'interferential' method discovered by Lippmann and started research into colour photography by the indirect method pioneered by Charles Cros and Louis Ducos du Hauron (see his letter of 17 June 1895).

Auguste Lumière to R. Rousseau

14 November 1895

Monsieur R. Rousseau
Jambes

Thank you for your letter of the 11th of this month. We abandoned colour photography by the Lippmann method some months ago. A number of the prints we had managed to make were lost by a railway company while on their way home after being lent out. As we consider the remaining prints to be of historic interest, and are attached to them, we have decided not to allow them to travel before new ones are made – if ever we decide to take up that method again.

We are sorry we cannot assist you in this matter and hope to be luckier on some other occasion.

As far as the 'Cinematograph' is concerned, we are fully booked for the coming weeks. We will bear your request in mind as soon as we are in a position to grant it.

We are most touched by your congratulations, and very grateful to you for writing to us.

Yours sincerely,
A. Lumière

Auguste Lumière to A.Molteni[1]

14 November 1895

Monsieur A. Molteni
Paris

Thank you for your letter of the 13th of this month.

Monsieur Louis Lumière is currently in Paris and no doubt you will see him at the start of term session at the Sorbonne next Saturday. He will give you all the information you require in person.

Yours sincerely,
A. Lumière

1 The Lumière brothers' Cinematograph was illuminated by a lamp called a Molteni lantern. Alfred Molteni was, with Dubosq, the acknowledged expert in the field of light projection. He was the agent in France for Beale's Choreutoscope. A manufacturer of lamps for projection, in 1895 he launched an oxyether lamp called Securitas. It was used in the Joly-Normandin Cinematograph which set fire to a crowd at a charity bazaar (Le Bazaar de la Charité) on 4 May 1897. Molteni was nicknamed 'projection incarnate'. He manufactured and distributed Robertson's fantascope, as well as plates for the Choreutoscope under the brand name Wheel of Life. His apparatus came with top-grade achromatic lenses and functioned either by oxyether torch or by arc-light. The brothers Lumière opted for the latter.

Auguste Lumière to Jos. Maes[1]

14 November 1895

Monsieur Jos. Maes
Antwerp

Thank you for your letter of the 11th of this month. It is most kind of you to be so complimentary. Our 'Cinematograph' is, as you say, under construction in Paris and we do not yet know when it can be made available to the market. We are very sorry that previous engagements prevent us from agreeing to your request for demonstrations in your various departments.

We should very much like to be able to grant your request, but we cannot at present take any firm decision on the sale and presentation of our machine. It has been expensive to develop and we therefore intend to arrange paying demonstrations for a few months, before launching it on the market, in order to recover our costs and also advertise the invention.

We are most grateful to you for your suggestion; it shall not be forgotten and perhaps we will call on you in the future.

We are unable to fix a sale price as we do not yet know how much it costs to build.

We apologize for being unable to satisfy your request at present and we hope to be more fortunate at a later date, for we wish to be agreeable to you in every way.

Yours sincerely,
A. Lumière

1 This letter is a reply to one of many demands from all over the world to participate in the business of selling an invention whose reputation had spread like wildfire, well before the first public screening on 28 December 1895, because of articles appearing in the specialized press and a few private or semi-private demonstrations. Maes would appear to have been some kind of impresario; he was to become the Lumière franchise holder for Antwerp, once the Cinematograph appeared on the market in 1896. This letter provides important evidence

that the Lumière brothers were unwilling, in 1896, to sell their camera-projectors to compensate for the capital outlay involved in developing the machine. They insisted on managing their operation as an integrated business, offering a complete show. This consisted of films, projectionists and projectors, all of which were for hire and not for sale. One advantage was that the mechanics of the camera-projector would be harder to copy. It was not put up for sale until February 1897 (to franchise holders) or May 1897 (to the general public).

Auguste Lumière to Hector Colard

16 November 1895

Monsieur Hector Colard
Brussels

Thank you for your letter of the 13th of this month. Regarding our colour prints, made by the Lippmann method, we are sorry to say the majority of them were lost in transit, after exhibition. We have put in a complaint to the Railway Company and are awaiting the results. One consequence is that we are most attached to our remaining prints and no longer willing to loan them out, for the time being.

Monsieur Louis Lumière is currently in Paris with a set of colour prints made by the indirect method. As soon as he returns, we will examine the possibility of agreeing to your request at the date you suggest.

Yours sincerely,
A. Lumière

Louis Lumière to Fuerst Brothers,[1] London

[Lyon, Monplaisir] 19 November [189]5

Dear Sirs,
I am writing for information as follows:
We are about to set up a plant for the manufacture of very long, light-sensitive film, destined for use in our 'Cinematograph'. Before we do so, we are wondering whether it would not be possible to reach agreement with Blair Co., either to be given a licence to manufacture according to Blair processes, or to be supplied with large quantities of Blair stock at a price which would enable us to sell it on at a reasonable margin.

The first of these options is preferable if it is acceptable to the gentlemen in question and providing their demands are not exaggerated.

We should be most grateful if you could reply by return of post, advising us whether you feel such a proposition might be received favourably. If so, we should be grateful if you would put us in touch with the managing director of Blair Co.

Yours sincerely,

L. Lumière

We are told that Blair Co. produces clear film as well as translucent. Could you perhaps send us a sample?

1 This letter relates to the letters Louis Lumière sent Jules Carpentier and Victor Planchon on 5 November. Even though he had described the prospect of applying to the Blair Co. for film, the venture with Planchon was not yet up and running. In any case, he had been indiscreet. Louis Lumière therefore applies to this London firm, either for supplies of American film, or for a licence to manufacture it. This latter solution was considered preferable. The Lumière brothers wished to control the entire production process, for technical and experimental reasons as well as commercial ones. A letter published on 20 November 1896 in *Amateur Photographer* (London) suggests that, from the start, it had been anticipated that Lumière franchise holders would only be so for a limited time: 'Sir, you will pleased to hear that, as exclusive agents for the Lumière Cinematograph for Great Britain, the colonies and the United States of America, we are able to take orders for machines designed to produce moving pictures. Such requests will be taken on a first come first served basis; the machines will be delivered in May next. All interested parties should contact us soon. Yours, Fuerst Brothers, 17 Philpot Lane, London EC.

Auguste Lumière to Marquent

20 November 1895

Monsieur Marquent
Rouen

Thank you for your letter of the 17th of this month. Regarding the plates to which you refer, we suggest you contact Monsieur Balagny,[1] 11 rue Salneuve, in Paris. He will be able to provide you with information about the process you wish to try.

As you request, we are sending you a copy of our brochure which includes instruction on how to use our orthochromatic plates. We are at your disposal for any further information you may require.

Our new device, the 'Cinematograph', is currently under constuction in Paris and we are unable to say when we shall be in a position to put it on the market. Nor do we yet know what the sale price will be. We will let you have this information as soon as we are able.

Yours sincerely,

A. Lumière

1 Georges Balagny (1837–1919), chemist, Fellow of the Société de Photographie, friend of A. Londe, director of the photographic department at the Hospital for Nervous Diseases of the Salpêtrière in Paris. On 7 May 1884, he presented transparent silver gelatine paper on to which a coat of gelatine had been applied. It was very firmly stuck, before exposure, and easy to peel off afterwards. He provided Marey with 90mm celluloid film up to 1.10m long. On 5 March 1885, he signed a contract with the Lumière company for the manufacture of a new product: supple film.

Lieutenant-Colonel Jungblutz[1] to Messieurs Lumière

Brussels, 20 November 1895

Sirs,

I have been instructed by His Royal Highness Prince Albert of Belgium to thank you for the delightful photographs which you were gracious enough to send him and to let you know how grateful he is for your kind attention.

His Royal Highness was most impressed with your 'Cinematograph' and is deeply interested in that remarkable invention. The photographs you were good enough to send him have further increased his admiration for your superb discoveries and I have been asked to inform you of this fact, with thanks.

Aide-de-camp
Lt Colonel Jungblutz

1 Prior to its launch, the following year, the Cinematograph acquired prestigious backing. A first showing was organized at the Palais du Midi in Brussels on 10 November 1895 for the fellows of the Association Belge de Photographie. A second screening took place on 12 November before members of the Artistic and Literary Club in what is now the Cercle Gaulois, in the park, in Brussels. This letter suggests that a further screening took place, perhaps before 10 November, in the royal palace. Thus the Cinematograph entered the world of politics, after its forays into scientific and artistic circles. Since all these different establishments endorsed it, it was possible to say that, henceforth, the Cinematograph was in fashion.

Louis Lumière to Fr. de Walque

25 November 1895

Monsieur Fr. de Walque
Louvain

Thank you for your letter of the 20th of this month. We are delighted at the enthusiastic welcome which the Louvain section of the Association Belge de Photographie gave our Cinematograph and we are most grateful to you for it. We are also pleased to have been able to be fulfil your request on this occasion.

We are sorry to say, regarding our colour prints by the 'direct' method, that most of our prints were lost after they had been out on loan. We have made a complaint to the Railway Company and we are still awaiting the result. We are anxious to preserve the few remaining prints until such time as, either the lost prints reappear or we decide to make new ones, which we are not at present considering.

We are therefore unable to make any commitment in this area.

Yours sincerely,

L. Lumière

Louis Lumière to Jules Carpentier

[Lyon, Monplaisir] 25 November [189]5

My dear Monsieur Carpentier,

My father, on his return, informs me that the matt paper I had given you did not work well. I am surprised because it works very well here. Perhaps you were missing the right instructions for use. Here are the important ones:

Developer:

Water	7000
Anhydrous sulphite of soda	20
Diamidophenol (hydrochlor.)	5

The picture should develop in thirty to forty seconds.

Are your products free from impurities?

As soon as you have completed a machine, I should very much like to try one out.

I have made many attempts at coating American film, but I am not making much progress.

Planchon's solution may work. I've just tried a sample of the Cromet.

On the other hand, we have started talking to Blair Co. Perhaps we can come to some agreement.

We must get out of this misery somehow.

In order not to interrupt the manufacturing process, you can start on one or two hundred because, once we launch this business, we want to be ready for very rapid expansion.[1]

50

Please send my regards to your wife.
Yours ever,
L. Lumière

My brother sends you his best wishes.

1 Lumière is ordering one or two hundred machines before a single public projection had confirmed that the Cinematograph was going to be a popular success.

Louis Lumière to Victor Planchon

[Lyon, Monplaisir] 25 November [189]5

My dear Monsieur Planchon,

We have received your first set of auto-tensiles. They work. There is just a slight lessening of sensitivity, compared to our glass plates, but the difference is insignificant. One thing I advise is that you watch the thickness of the emulsion carefully. It tends to be on the thick side, which can provoke coloured fog.

We urgently need sample sets of two or three plates, enough so we can send out to all our clients. We want to do all we can to encourage this business. Current demand is almost nil.

I have tried the sample you sent of long strips of film. It is not bad. I think you will eventually produce something excellent and there will be considerable demand for it. I do have a few important comments, crucial in fact, with respect to use with our Cinematograph. Here they are:

1) The film is too supple. Too much glycerine. (By my reckoning, 150 grams of glycerine should be enough.)

2) The gum base is too thin. It should be 9 or 10 hundredths of a millimetre.

This over-suppleness made it difficult to experiment with the Cinematograph. Rewinding in the machine will require a certain degree of stiffness, a certain elasticity, which the film you sent lacked.

As to the purity of the base, it is only a matter of care and installation. Small defects are unimportant once the film is developed. The adhesiveness is adequate, but only just.

I beg you to do everything you can immediately to hurry these trials and to send us as soon as you can new samples which take into account the comments mentioned above.

The film is beautifully transparent which should lead to a magnificent series and if we bring it off, I promise you there will be a large number of orders.

And there is not a minute to lose.[1]

Will you manage 15 or 20 metre lengths?

We have just accepted two of your bills. We would be most grateful if you did not issue any more as long as the outstanding debt is not paid off because it might lead to trouble and bother.

I look forward to hearing from you, my dear Monsieur Planchon.

L. Lumière

1 Planchon seems to have won back his clients' trust. Financially, he does not seem to be in particularly good shape, since he has to pass on two bills to Lumière, which is not much appreciated. Furthermore, the quality of his product is insufficient and Louis has to request improvements: too supple, too thin, it seems like a rushed job. Which is hardly surprising, since the competition is hot on their heels . . .

Louis Lumière to the Photographic Club of Lombardy

26 November 1895

The Vice-President
The Photographic Club of Lombardy
Milan

Thank you for your letter of the 24th of this month. Our new device, the 'Cinematograph', is currently under construction in Paris and we do not yet know exactly when it will be ready. To our regret, we are not therefore in a position to grant your request. We shall however bear it mind and we hope to be able to be agreeable on another occasion.

We are most grateful to you for the interest which you have shown in our new invention and as soon as it is on the market, we shall let you know.

Yours sincerely,
L. Lumière

Jules Carpentier to Louis Lumière

27 November 1895

My dear friend,

Since your father left us, we have produced more prints with the new paper and it has worked very well. Our initial failure was certainly caused by some error in the exposure time. Despite this, your instructions will be most useful.

We shall have completed a machine today[1] and we shall send it to you tomorrow. We shall not send a base as we are still waiting for the hinges; we shall just give you the board that rests on the base, together with three screws so that you can fix it to the base you already have. Examine the machine thoroughly, and try it out as quickly as you can, to see if it meets its requirements. The idea is that it should serve as a model for all future products. We shall only be able to start the quick and reliable manufacturing process once we have a model *ne varietur*.

Make sure that the bin is just right: we have stopped producing its sisters because of your criticisms. The first series of machines will be equipped with mirrors similar to yours, as they are already made; but the machine we are sending is equipped with a mirror of our design. It will be much easier to make and much less fragile. We hope you will agree to its future use. We are ready to start rapid production on the two hundred machines which you want but only on condition, as I say, that there are no alterations once we start. Take a brief look at the inscription[2] engraved on the machine and let us know whether its text, its size and its position are agreeable.

I hope that, one way or another, you will soon be in a position to guarantee supplies of film. My perforating machine[3] is going to need greater alteration than I originally thought in order to fit your strips. I cannot tell you when it will be available for your use.

Will you finally resolve, my friend, to supply good quality fine-grained slow plates for use in printing positives on glass?[4] Why do we have to go on using Ilford plates? We use 24 x 30, 6.5 x 9, 6 x 6 and 4.5 x 6. I know lots of amateurs would follow our lead and use these plates if you were to put them on the market.

I enclose a small 6.5x9 negative to which we are very attached. Please enlarge it up to one metre in length so it can be used at the Cycle Show which is due to open any minute at the Palais de l'Industrie.

Finally, I remind you that you promised to grant my friend Richard's brother, Monsieur Albert Richard, a licence to sell your products in the small shop he is opening at Menton for the winter season. Monsieur Albert Richard will contact you himself about this matter, but I want to thank you for accepting my recommendation.

Best wishes to you all.

J. Carpentier

1 The machine is question is no longer a prototype, but the first industrially manufactured

Cinematograph. All the modifications and improvements decided on during the course of the next few weeks of correspondence will relate to this machine. They will produce an industrial product of such quality that even today surviving specimens are in perfect working order, whereas most of the competing cameras and projectors of the day are not. 'There were other similar devices at the time,' admitted Louis Lumière, 'but they were just toys.' The Lumière device was light, reliable and solid.

2 This brass plate mentions the Cinematograph, followed by the names of its inventors, and then that of its manufacturer (Carpentier himself). It will be placed on the front of the camera-projector (see Louis Lumière to Jules Carpentier, 4 December 1895)

3 Lumière had already, with Charles Moisson, constructed a protoype perforating machine of his own but it would seem from this letter that Carpentier's model, constructed for his Cinegraph, was in some way preferable.

4 The system referred to consisted in projecting a negative image on to a glass plate in order, subsequently, to print it up on paper: the offset principle.

Jules Carpentier to Louis Lumière

Paris, 28 November 1895

My dear friend,

Your machine has gone off.

In yesterday's letter I said that the mirrors for the next twenty-four machines were already made. I was wrong. The metal frames that hold them are made, together with fixtures. Under the circumstances, I urge you to give up your shape for the mirror and accept mine. This would be a wise decision and I would rather reshape the frames rather than be constrained to use them.

I should point out that the shutter discs are made of thin ebonite. This is another considerable improvement.

In its compartment, the photographic lens should focus on 12 metres. To photograph anything closer, pull it out a little.

Best wishes.

J. Carpentier

Auguste Lumière to Robert William Paul[1]

28 November 1895

Monsieur Robert W. Paul
London

Thank you for your letter of the 25th of this month.

We do not manufacture kinestoscope[2] films but we are shortly to put a new machine on the market, called the 'Cinematograph', for which we

54

shall be making films.
    Yours sincerely,
    A. Lumière

1 Manufacturer of scientific instruments, established in 1891 in Hatton Garden. He rapidly perfected a copy of Edison's kinetoscope and produced about sixty of these copies in 1895 for fairground entertainers, calling them 'theatrograph' or 'animatograph' (marketed by a firm called Paul's Animatograph Ltd.) With Birt Acres, he made films for his customers who were unable to obtain Edison's films because he only supplied these to people who bought his kinetoscope.
2 This letter suggests Paul ordered kinetoscope films from the Lumière brothers, perhaps in the hope of by-passing Edison. It also shows that a decision had been taken by the Lumière brothers to produce their own films.

Louis Lumière to Edison's Belgian Kinetoscope

29 November 1895

The Director
Edison's Belgian Kinetoscope
Brussels

Thank you for your letter of the 27th of this month. We wish to inform you that we do not manufacture kinetoscope films.

We are shortly to put our new device, the 'Cinematograph', on the market and we shall then be selling films for this.

    Yours sincerely,
    L. Lumière

Louis Lumière to Jules Carpentier

[Lyon, Monplaisir] 29 November [189]5

My dear Monsieur Carpentier,

    It was unforgivable of me to have forgotten the slow plates[1] I promised you and I apologize profusely. We are today sending you several dozen sets of the various formats you have asked for; please let us know what you make of them when you have had them tried.

    The enlargement you asked for is ready. I think it looks well. We shall send it to you as soon as it is mounted on canvas.

    We await the machine which you say is on its way with some impatience, and as soon as we can certify that the new mirror you have installed performs the same function as the old we shall let you know. More than likely, it does.

We shall use our perforating machine until something better turns up, but we should be grateful if you could let us have yours if you follow up your idea of altering it to suit our strips.

With best wishes.

L. Lumière

Will my photo-jumelle[2] be ready soon? Thank you in advance.

1 See note to Jules Carpentier to Louis Lumière, 27 November.
2 See note 2, letter from Louis Lumière to Victor Planchon, 5 November 1895.

Louis Lumière to Jules Carpentier

[Lyon, Monplaisir] 30 November [189]5

My dear Monsieur Carpentier,

We have just received the machine and I put it to the test immediately. You are going to find me irritating, but never mind. Here are my remarks:

The fit between the moving parts is really quite loose, between the axle and the frame, between the shaft and the hole that serves as a bearing. The consequence is that the machine is noisy and that the claws do not move with the same precision as before. I know that this first model was built by an exceptionally skilled worker, but I should be grateful if you would look into the matter of this play with some care.

The rewind seems to me to operate very well. The magazines (the wooden ones) seem excellent as they are.

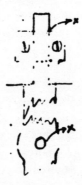

The weather was not good enough for us to try using the machine to take photographs. We shall do this as soon as possible and then I shall give you

56

my final verdict.

I wanted to let you know the above difficulties as soon as possible so you could mend them if it is possible.

A thousand pardons for being so boring.

Best wishes.

L. Lumière

A few additional points:

The leather[1] cushion for the fork had been forgotten.

Don't forget to nickel-plate the grooves inside the bins.

Nor must you forget the strips of cloth[2] that need to go on the lower board for stability and as a safeguard against vibrations from the crank.

The hole in this same board through which strips of negative pass during printing needs to be garnished with velvet or cloth. You probably think I am being pernickety.

1 A bit of leather serving to cushion the fork in order to avoid excessive friction and wear. The fork is part of the drive mechanism consisting of two prongs which dig into perforations in the film and drag it forwards.
2 Serve the same purpose: situated on the G-shaped board.

Jules Carpentier to Louis Lumière

Paris, 2 December 1895

My dear friend,

You are not to say that you are being irritating, boring or pernickety when you point out flaws that need correcting or improvements that need introducing to the machines we are constructing.

You may rest assured that these machines do not need to be made by exceptional workers to be above reproach. In that sense, everyone here is exceptional.

As far as the play to which you refer is concerned, there is one which does not surprise me: the lengthwise play of the shaft. It does not surprise me because I have just noticed that the worker who assembled the machine, by an oversight, forgot to place a small steel ring which fits into the grooves at the base of this shaft. The looseness between the axle and the frame is more worrying: there is no sign of this problem in similar parts now in the workshop.

Metal bins: nickel-plating the interior grooves is well-nigh impossible. What would be the point? To protect the surfaces from rust? The machine is put together in such a way that this channel can be opened, and thus cleaned, which is the best defence against rust; four or six screws need undoing, then the part they hold in place is removed, and the groove is got at and cleaned. It could not be easier. So no nickel-plating. Production of a battalion of bins is underway, according to the model provided.

Leather cushion: Did not seem necessary. We will reinstate it.

Strips of cloth: Deliberately removed. Appeared to be the cause of vibrations as observed. Two well-made wooden surfaces ought to provide a much more stable foundation. I have made room for the back gate to open. This arrangement seems worth keeping.

Garnishing the exit passage: We will stick some velvet in. Are you satisfied with the way the film is released forwards?

Please reply by return of post. As soon as you have been able to complete your observations, please return the machine so we can alter it as necessary.

All the best.

J. Carpentier.

Auguste Lumière to Edison's Belgian Kinetoscope

3 December 1895

The Director
Edison's Belgian Kinetoscope
Brussels

Thank you for your letter of the 1st. We confirm our previous letter in which we stated that we do not manufacture film strips for kinetoscopes.

Our 'Cinematograph' is currently under construction in Paris and we do not know when it can be launched. Nor do we know what the sale price will be. As soon as we can furnish you with this information, we shall certainly do so.

Our machine is designed to produce negative strips, print positives and project them.

Yours sincerely,

A. Lumière

Auguste Lumière to Jos. Maes

3 December 1895

Monsieur Jos. Maes
Antwerp

Thank you for your letter of 30 November past.

We are quite overwhelmed by the demand for demonstrations of our 'Cinematograph' and as, at present, we have only one of these machines available, we are unable to satisfy very many people. It is absolutely impossible for us to make any commitments at present.

We have taken note of your interest and as soon as we are able to respond, we shall let you know.

Please do not hesitate to contact us again. We will do our very best to satisfy you.

Yours sincerely,
A. Lumière

Louis Lumière to Jules Carpentier

[Lyon, Monplaisir] 4 December [189]5

My dear Monsieur Carpentier,

This morning, we exposed and developed a positive print. When projected it gives a good image, but not as sharp as we managed to achieve with the previous machine. Here are some observations which I take the liberty of submitting to you:

Play: I have mentioned this before. Please try the following experiment.

Bring the fork up as far as it goes, and take hold, between the two sprockets, of that portion of the frame which supports them – without obstructing the axle – and you will see that the maximum extension of the claws varies considerably. The same is true at the lower end, and the consequence is that the gap between the extremities is plus or minus 20mm. I realize, of course, that you cannot completely eliminate this looseness, but could it not be very much reduced?

We have fitted a small ring to the end of the shaft and this reduces the play lengthwise.

Mirror-plate: Your improvement is excellent but the top edge will need to be rounded off because at the moment it really scrapes.

Shutter-discs: Ebonite is brittle. The top disc should be fixed in an invariable position so that only the other disc moves, because this will reduce exposure time and thus the likelihood of error.

Forward release of negative: Excellent. Much better than before.

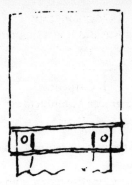

Bin: Works very well. I probably failed to make myself clear about nickel-plating: I meant the inner surface of the tube where it comes into contact with the rubber. Copper sulphurizes very fast, and the fit will loosen very quickly. As to the groove through which the film passes, it works fine but I would have preferred velvet on the side affected by emulsion because silver bromide will leave a deposit in two places, and the deposit will harden, scratching the film and leaving black lines on the photograph if it is not cleaned every time. Obviously, frequent cleaning is a possibility and if push comes to shove we can drop the velvet idea.

Board: Your observation about two well-fitted bits of wood is true enough, but only for a few days. Wood warps. I would suggest limiting the magazine to a breadth of two 10–15mm strips, slightly raised (and without the cloth) so as to spread the point of contact over a smaller surface. What do you think?

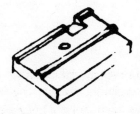

Lenses: Good and well-fitted.

Plate opening: Now gives slightly smaller images, separated by about two-thirds of a millimetre. It may be all for the best and I suggest we keep these dimensions. But the velvet should be cut back (as you will see we have done, because it was fraying and threads were marking the pictures). Could not the edges be crimped? Probably not easy. As is, only a fraction is

compressed by the glass but our experience tells us a tiny surface is enough.
Inscription: Please alter as follows:

Cinematograph
Auguste and Louis Lumière
Patented S.G.D.G.

— — — — — — — —

J. Carpentier
Engineer-Manufacturer
Paris

(It may be a little long, but for certain reasons which we'll go into later, we prefer it that way.)

Finally, it will be essential to manufacture some little winding machines in order to facilitate the gathering up of the unspooled film and rewinding it. You know the somewhat makeshift tool we designed. Perhaps it would do.

We're returning the machine to you today. When can we have two or three?

Please forgive this long scrawl.

Best wishes.

L. Lumière

I was forgetting: when the crank is turned, the feet twist. Can this be remedied by fitting appropriate cross-bars to the feet?

Louis Lumière to Victor Planchon

[Lyon, Monplaisir] 6 December [189]5

Monsieur Planchon
Boulogne sur Mer

We are happy to confirm our recent discussions.

The large strips of coated film[1] which you brought us are close to perfection. The pictures we have produced using our 'Cinematograph' are wonderfully transparent and much better in this respect than any other film we have had at our disposal. The emulsion is pure, intense and very fast. But you have seen, as we did, that the emulsion does not adhere to the film sufficiently strongly. You must look into this critical factor as quickly as possible in order to obtain the best adhesion you can, at least as good as in your previous samples.

Having said which, we are anxious to inform you that we are sure to be able to order large quantities of this product as soon as you are able to make it in lengths of not less than 15 metres; but it is crucial this happens immediately because if there were any delay we would have to resort to other arrangements.

We know of sufficient demand for our 'Cinematograph' to be sure that there will be considerable demand also for supplies of your film, without which the 'Cinematograph' cannot work. Since you ask for a figure, we estimate a requirement for some hundred strips per day, in other words, fifty square metres' worth. We cannot in any sense be bound by this estimate, but we regard it as a low target amount which will soon be met, and soon be superseded.

Also, the tests we have conducted concerning the auto-tensile strips you sent us originally are satisfactory. The business of laying emulsion on to film at a distance, as it were, now seems perfectly resolved. We shall launch a vigorous marketing campaign and first send out samples to all our customers. We need a large number of boxes of samples as soon as possible.

We are convinced that the products you are now manufacturing have considerable business potential for both of our enterprises. That is why I have developed a notion for a new contract between us, which you and I have already discussed.

As a token of our high opinion of your business, we promise to assist you in forming the new company which you are going to establish. When you are able to inform us of the statutes of this company, upon which we have already advised you, we intend to subscribe 100 shares, or in other words, 50,000 francs. This undertaking cannot be binding until it has been agreed to by our board, but we are sure this authorization will be forthcoming. In any case, the matter will be decided next Monday and we shall let you know immediately afterwards.

We regret that we cannot, upon reflection, accept your offer that one of us should sit on the board of your new company. Quite apart from the problem of distance, we feel that the situation would give rise to complications.

As to the advice and information which you say you would need, you may be sure we will provide them to the best of our ability.

One of the executive directors,

L. Lumière

1 Planchon improved the quality of his product. The formula of his emulsion is now lost and in order to retrieve it we would need to have a supply of unexposed negative for analysis. It

has never been matched. The 'light' of the original Lumière films is legendary. This letter is evidence of an alliance between Planchon and the Lumière firm. Planchon will later be given a great deal of responsibility within the Lumière business, including, in 1903, running the 50–acre photochemical plant at Feyzin outside Lyon. In 1907, the film manufacturing plants at Monplaisir and Feyzin will be merged under the Société des Celluloses Planchon, with a capital of 3 million francs and a large Lumière family holding. Planchon branched out into synthetic fabrics like artificial silk (invented by Chardonnet in Besançon in 1878). Both products are made of nitro-cellulose and both require similar manufacturing techniques. The Lumière family will sign an agreement with Cinès, a company in Rome, to manufacture film in Italy according to the Planchon process. Louis Lumière and Victor Planchon will sit together on the board of Cinès. But first, as this letter shows, a merger in the form of a Lumière family stake in the Planchon business, is underway, and Planchon is going to move from Boulogne to Lyon.

Jules Carpentier to Louis Lumière

Paris, 9 December 1895

My dear friend,

As soon as your instrument reached me, I looked into the matter of this looseness of fit. No complicated experiments were required to note that there was a tremendous amount of sideways play about the main axis. This is the result of a mistake by the worker who assembled the camera-projector, a mistake which, needless to say, he scarcely broadcast and which, in my haste to get the thing sent off to you, I had overlooked. The worker in question has been given a rocket and it won't happen again. I was deeply ashamed when I saw it.

The mirror will have its edges rounded off and it will be polished up to optical standards.

Ebonite, it is true, is brittle for a shutter. But it is also light, flat and perfectly adapted for this use. Is the shutter not safe? One of the discs should be fixed, that is agreed.

Now the question of nickel-plating is decided: you shall have your way. As to inserting velvet in the passage, I quite see the point but it will not be very convenient. We shall do our best.

As to the board, we will work up a joint best suited to resist the potential for warping.

When we cut the velvet round the shutter, we were careful to burn the edges. Apparently, that was not good enough. I do not think crimping is an option. We will widen the opening, as you indicate. The inscription will be amended as you suggest. We shall do what we can to solidify the base without resorting to something over-complicated. I do not think I can come up with a solution for this series.

As soon as we have a machine of our own that we can use, we will work up the little winding machine so that it fulfils the requirement, which we shall then understand. We cannot do this until we have had a chance to work with film strips, and so far we have hardly had any.

I intend to deliver a few machines before the end of the week. You will receive, within the next two days, machine no. 2, amended and brought up to date. You will understand that these alterations, which I admit are inevitable, none the less hold us up and bring production to a halt. Thus the bins, which were still awaiting a go-ahead, can now start up again, though the question of the velvet (albeit essential) is going to make us tread warily. The same is true of a few other details. How I wish we had a definitive model so we could take your order for two hundred cameras by storm.

Thank you for the enlargement which you made for us.[1] It is very fine. Unfortunately, the edges are slightly over-cropped and an important figure in the cycling world no longer appears. If I could be so bold, I would ask you to make up a second print as quickly as possible: then I'd have enough for two large panels, one to put where people who know Monsieur X pass by and another to put where they don't know him.

Best wishes.

J. Carpentier

1 An enlargement of a photograph of the finishing line of a bicycle race, in the presence of official personalities. The 'important figure' who was cropped must have been in the foreground. Such photographs were often enlarged and framed to flatter the people they showed.

Louis Lumière to Fournier

9 December 1895

Monsieur Fournier
Lyon

Please supply us urgently with twelve 6 ohm 15 amp rheostats[1] with switch below (similar to the ones you sent us with the Brown dynamos) [see illustration].

Please make them up with nickel silver, as ferro-nickel is fragile and these rheostats are destined to undergo a great deal of transport.

Please also let us have the first few immediately, and bill Messieurs Auguste and Louis Lumière.

We anticipate that you will give us a bulk discount, particularly as we are likely to order further large quantities.

Yours sincerely,

L. Lumière

1 A rheostat is an electrical device which controls the current in an electrical circuit. An important element in the marketing of the 'Cinematograph', since electrical current had only recently become available and supplies were unpredictable.

Auguste Lumière to A. Molteni

9 December 1895

Monsieur A. Molteni
Paris

Please supply us with the following, as soon as you can and of the highest quality:

Twelve projection lamps, no. 7, similar to those you supplied us with on 29 July last.

Please send us the first few immediately and bill Messieurs Auguste and Louis Lumière.

Bearing in mind the size of this order and the fact that we are certain to have to order further large quantities, we anticipate that you will grant us a very substantital discount.

Yours sincerely,

A. Lumière

Louis Lumière to Jules Carpentier

[Lyon, Monplaisir] 10 December [189]5

My dear Monsieur Carpentier,

I have just received your kind letter for which I thank you. The benevolence with which you have greeted my comments entices me to make fresh ones. Just as one reckons one has dealt with something, something else crops up. I am certain we are all but home and dry now.

I have just noticed a serious difficulty. I was projecting a new film strip, made very supple by dampness, when the strip in question was damaged in the holes. Examining the problem, I discovered that although the strip was flat in the passage, it tended to rise with the fork, whose sprockets now rise above the surface of the velvet in their ascent. The nap of the velvet is probably worn. In any case, it seems most essential that we reduce the length of the sprockets by about 0.5 or 0.6 in to ensure that this sort of accident never happens. They will be long enough at that length. If they could be set yet further back, and still dig in to the same extent, it would perhaps be better. But perhaps this would be too complicated. What do you think? Could you look at the backward pull of the sprockets in the machines you have under construction to determine whether they really pull out of the way? And I would urge you to bear in mind that the velvet wears easily.

This change in the condition of the velvet has obliged us to diminish the thickness of the corners that bear the mirror: the pressure was no longer strong enough to maintain the film in position when the claws were in. Also, please diminish the size of these small mirrors or increase the size of the.frame so that they sit deeper in the plate.

We have amended our perforating machine so as to approach the spacing between the successive holes of the sprockets. We have, however, maintained a very slight difference, still, in order to prevent stretching of the film as it is pulled along. You were right to say this would be best.

Once the two minor alterations mentioned above are taken into account, I am sure that it will be perfect and that it we will have the definitive model we need to make proper progress.

I hope we shall be able to send you the enlargement tonight; we have redone it as quickly as we could.

Please send my regards to Madame Carpentier.

Yours ever,

L. Lumière

Louis Lumière to Victor Planchon

[Lyon, Monplaisir] 11 December [189]5

My dear Monsieur Planchon,

The new measures which you propose are completely different. On reflection, our view is that it would be far preferable to maintain the old arrangements, as I am not sure we would be allowed to use ether[1] in a residential district without provoking complaints which would force us to shut the plant down as soon it had opened. This is a serious consideration.

My father tells me that he plans to call on you, but I have not written to him as I assume he will be in Boulogne before this letter reaches you. Perhaps you would raise this matter with him and tell him of my concern. Is our original scheme unworkable?

I am very anxious to receive your first samples and, although it is probably superfluous, I urge you to work as fast as you can on that front.

Please take another look at the prospects of our first plan and let me know what the outcome is.

In haste . . . a cordial handshake,

L. Lumière

1 This probably refers to the problem of what kind of projection lamp to use in the Cinematograph. As we have seen, some of them used oxyether lamp torches. The Lumière brothers always refused this, because of the fire risk. They had probably tried it experimentally. The terrible fire of the Bazar de la Charité in Paris on 4 May 1897, which seriously compromised the prospects of the nascent French film industry, was caused by someone lighting a match too close to a bottle of ether. It is, however, conceivable that the ether referred to in this letter relates to the composition of the emulsion. In 1903, the removal of one of the Lumière manufacturing plants from the inhabited district of Monplaisir to a new industrial suburb, Feyzin, was occasioned by complaints about ether vapour. Planchon, as mentioned above, was to be director of this new plant.

Auguste Lumière to A. de Maroussem

11 December 1895

Monsieur A. Maroussem
20 boulevard Poissonière
Paris

Thank you for your letter of 9 December. We do not manufacture films for Edison kinetoscope but we shall be making them for our 'Cinematograph'.

As regards this device, it is currently under construction in Paris and we are as yet unable to say when exactly we shall be putting it on the market.

Nor we do yet know the sale price, since we have not established the size of our outlay.

As soon as we are able to give you the information you request, we shall not fail to do so.

Yours sincerely,
A. Lumière

Auguste Lumière to V. Calcina[1] et Cie.

12 December 1895

Messieurs V. Calcina et Cie.
Turin

We have the pleasure of enclosing a letter from *Il Progresso* of Turin requesting a photograph of our Cinematograph. We are sending you this photograph today and we would be grateful if you could forward it to the newspaper as soon as it reaches you.

Thank you in advance.
Yours sincerely,
A. Lumière

Would you also be good enough to send us a sample of 13x18, or other size, Morgan bromide paper, of your most commonly employed quality? Many thanks.

1 V. Calcina subsequently held the Cinematograph franchise in Turin and became a film-maker.

Auguste Lumière to Rostaing-Biéchy

13 December 1895

Monsieur Rostaing-Biéchy
Grenoble

Thank you for your letter of 11 of this month. We have not yet taken any firm decision as to how we will manage sales of our 'Cinematograph', but we feel we ought to to inform you that we are currently in talks with several large corporations.

Nothing, however, is yet settled and we shall let you know as soon as it is. We are most grateful to you for your offer and we shall certainly bear it in mind.

Yours sincerely,
A. Lumière

Jules Carpentier to Louis Lumière
Paris, 14 December 1895

My dear friend,

I was about to send you your machine, complete with alterations, but your letter has just arrived: I shall make the various changes you ask for and, I hope, still manage to send it off tonight.

Regarding the length of the sprockets, you may recall that we originally intended that they should be shorter. On one of your trips to Paris, you asked me to lengthen them. Following on from your comments, I shall shorten them, but only on the leader of our little flock, at least for today, so you have time to consider whether this alteration really is desirable. I wonder whether the tear you have discovered is not the consequence of some other unnoticed cause. Secondly, you speak of altering the sprockets, moving them back while maintaining the same hold on the film: this is a quite a business, a major alteration, and I do not believe that it is particularly useful. Think it over.

We will diminish the size of the presser mirrors so that they stand out more.

All the best.
J. Carpentier

Thank you for rushing a new enlargement through. Your father has just looked in on me. He has just left.

Louis Lumière to Jules Carpentier
[Lyon, Monplaisir] 14 December [189]5

My dear Monsieur Carpentier,

I enclose a note which sums up the points I must raise and which, I am sure, will be the last.

As soon as you have some finished machines, would you be good enough to send them to us?

Thank you again. All the best.
L. Lumière

The mechanism of the machine we have just received is now perfect. I feel there is something criminal about my having taken the liberty to make alterations in a machine constructed by you! I hope you will forgive me and put it down to our haste.

The length of the claws is correct. Do not alter it.

The velvet, which at first seemed too thick, should be left untouched: it is fine. But the passage through which the negative runs during printing positives should be enlarged as follows: diminish the thickness of the fixed element marked X in such a way as to bring the surface marked cd level with the surface marked ab. I suggest the enlargement of this portion of the run because film strips will have to pass through here after repair.

70

For the same reasons, we must round off as much as we can, following round the sharp point at X and planing down the succession of projections around the top of the gate by giving it a long curving shape corresponding to ef. (I altered the machine we have just received in the way outlined above after I had ripped several film strips and it now works perfectly.).

The velvet at the mouth of the bin prevents scratching but it also makes it hard for the film to get inside, because of the succession of tight corners that it is required to negotiate: the tip of the film strip touches the velvet and makes passage difficult. For this reason, I fear we may have to forgo the velvet, unless your considerable ingenuity finds some trick.

Please shape the sprockets which hold the end of the film strip in the bin as illustrated. Rewinding is flawless.

The ebonite discs would have been fine, but unfortunately the heat of the arc-light twisted them in the most horrible way. I regret to say that I do not think we can use this material. Would vulcanized fibre work? That is what we used before.

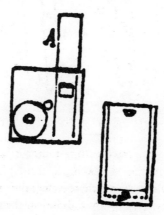

When you come to build new magazines, please put the opening on the opposite side (A) and diminish the height of B, because getting the film into the slit as it is is made awkward by B.

I have conducted many experiments over the last few days and I think I am in a position to say that Saturday's improvements and today's bring us up to scratch.

Would you be kind enough to let us have a few machines, complete with the above alterations, as soon as you can. I leave the matter of the shutter discs up to you. We will put them to the test and I am confident that they will turn out to be our definitive models.

I hope you are feeling better. I look forward to hearing your good news.

Yours ever,

L. Lumière

Louis Lumière to Jules Carpentier

[Lyon, Monplaisir] 15 December [189]5

My dear Monsieur Carpentier,

A new problem has cropped up.

In order that the film strips run properly through the last machine we have received – machine no. 1 – during printing, the two strips must be perforated to exactly the same dimension: 20mm apart. But not all our old negatives are identical. Some were deliberately perforated at 19.8 or 19.9. The shape of the tip of the claws will not tolerate this variation because of the steepness of the curve that connects the tip to the body of the cylinder. Under these conditions, the film strips will wear very quickly, even in projection, and I am writing to ask you to make us, as quickly as possible, so that this matter can be settled once and for all, a new sprocket-piece identical in proportion to that which is in machine no. 1, but with this difference only, that the tips, instead of being shaped, as at present, thus:

are shaped thus:

in other words, that they are finished with a flat edge about 1.2mm in diameter. I hope you can let us have this piece as soon as possible. I think it

72

will enable us to ignore variations in perforation (so our experiments with the old machine lead us to believe, anyway) because the film will slip into place if the sprockets do not fall exactly into the holes, something which cannot happen at present.

I am sorry to be going over old ground – I think this was the original shape of the sprockets – and, naturally, we shall bear the costs of amending the machines which are already built, as soon as we have established that the proposed alteration works by examining the part you will send us.

Everything else is fine except for one small point:

Even though machine no. 1 has hardly functioned at all, the passage through which the shafts move as the sprockets rotate back and forth is badly worn. The left-hand surface should be plated but that is clearly not practical. There was was much less wear in the first machine we received (I shall call it machine no. 0 since it was un-numbered).

Do you think the small rod marked X can be reinforced without affecting its cylindrical shape? This might be the simplest solution if you think it will work.

I am relying on your kind sympathy to ensure that we receive the part mentioned above as soon as possible.

Yours ever,

L. Lumière

A Monsieur Terme called on us yesterday.[1] He is an employee of the municipal tax office here in Lyon. He asked us for a strip of film on the grounds that he had invented a Cinematograph and that you were building it for him. Naturally, we refused because it seemed too obvious that we would be encouraging a competitor's experiments by furnishing him with results of our labours. Which is not to say we want to stop the progress of ideas – that would be absurd – but it seems only natural not to work for 'the king of Prussia'. Does this not seem right?

1 One of the innumerable amateur inventors – French and foreign – who from May 1896 were to try and copy or improve upon the Cinematograph. Terme is ahead of the game and probably well-informed as to what the Lumière brothers were up to. He is going to try and

pass himself off as a partner of Carpentier's. Could he have been one Jules Terme, who took out a patent for a reversible camera on 9 March 1896, or Joseph Marie Terme, who, on 15 July 1896, invented the cinematerme?

Auguste Lumière to A. Molteni

16 December 1895

Monsieur A. Molteni
Paris

Thank you for your letter of the 12th of this month. We do indeed refer to lens-less lanterns, double condenser, hand-held directional lamp and spring release.

As far as the lanterns you are going to manufacture are concerned, you can indeed make the chimney and casing in varnished canvas instead of in copper, but if this alteration involves any delay, please send us the lanterns you have in stock as soon as you can, as they are.

We look forward to receiving these goods as soon as possible.

Yours sincerely,
A. Lumière

Auguste Lumière to E. Touzet

18 December 1895

Monsieur E. Touzet
Paris

Thank you for your letter of the 16th of this month.

Regarding Paris performances of our 'Cinematograph', we have already made arrangements and the business is to be launched shortly. We are consequently unable to do anything further in that respect.

Projections will take place in the dark. The images will be projected in various sizes, two metres in breadth being the largest attainable. The projector may equally be placed either side of the screen.

Yours sincerely,
A. Lumière

Auguste Lumière to Count de Saint-Priest

19 December 1895

The Count de Saint-Priest
Paris

Thank you for your letter of 18 December last.

Our new machine, the 'Cinematograph', is currently under construction and for the time being we have only one example available. Consequently, we are sorry that we are unable to grant your request that we send a 'Cinematograph' to Saint Petersburg.

Yours sincerely,
A. Lumière

Louis Lumière to Jules Carpentier

[Lyon, Monplaisir] 20 December [189]5

My dear Monsieur Carpentier,

Thank you very much for responding so quickly to my request for a new part. It arrived at 11 this morning. I tried it out immediately and the results are conclusive: this shape is right and I would ask you to adopt it from now on.

Could you also slightly diminish the tension in the springs that hold the small mirror in place, as its new shape has increased the area of the point of contact between it and the velvet and it is now on the hard side. A 50% reduction should be quite enough, either by altering the shape of the blades or by using thinner steel.

L. Lumière

Auguste Lumière to A. Molteni

20 December 1895

Monsieur Molteni
Paris

It is our pleasure to confirm our recent letter ordering lanterns and we should be most grateful if you would immediately deliver to us those which you have in stock.

75

Contrary to what we stated earlier, we require short-stemmed condensers not long ones.

Yours sincerely,

A. Lumière

Jules Carpentier to Louis Lumière

Paris, Sunday 22 December 1895

My dear friend,

I have been so busy I have not had a chance to answer your letters of the 14th and 15th of this month. You know, however, that our work has not suffered; we have marched on as fast we could and I am pleased to say that, apart from the bins, work on which was delayed by all the tests conducted, our first series was completed the evening before last. The new specification for the fork will inevitably delay delivery by some few days. I have started my teams on the new forks, since they cannot be obtained by modifying the ones currently in place, because we had shortened them by some 0.5mm after your letters of the 10th and 14th of this month. I will make sure the new parts are made as quickly as possible. I have not entirely given the old ones up for lost because I believe that a very minor alteration will enable them to do the job they were designed for. What have you got against them? If I understand you correctly, they are too stubby for you, and so they rip the film unless the perforations fall exactly at the right point, instead of tugging the film back into place. Why not simply lengthen the tip, and do away with the flattened end you requested? Try this on the part you rejected. You have enough room to play with and can lengthen the tip without affecting the straight-sided section which marks the limit of how far the fork can dig into the film. I am certain you will find this gives a satisfactory result.

In this small test part I sent you, the little drive rod has been strengthened as you requested. We shall do the same for all other, similar pieces. You have been somewhat overhasty in your worries about wear. Such wear is inevitable between two new parts that meet only at a single point but it quickly reaches its limit as new surfaces are made; there is, in fact, much less wear than you would think.

When you warned me that our ebonite discs were hideously deformed, we had finished manufacturing all the shutters. I threw them out and started again, using thin, blackened brass. Fibre is useless. The new shutters

76

will naturally be more solid. They will also be heavier, which may not be a drawback.

The shafts have been altered as you said.

The velvet for the bins was ready. I will keep it on hand but will not install it. I will try to think of a satisfactory solution.

The film hooks in the bins will be as you suggest.

We will shift the opening of the new magazines to the opposite side. It will not be easy to lower the threshold.

In your letter of the 15th, you refer to a certain Monsieur Terme and stories he told you. I have never heard of Monsieur Terme and he has not sought out the honour of my services. I take this opportunity of informing you that I would never undertake to build a Cinematograph for someone without first letting you know. I welcomed you – indeed invited you – here because I was attracted to the idea of a connection with the Lumière family. I have done all I could, and I shall do all I can, to give you all the loyal support that I can. Thus, I laid my own system, the basis of which I have discussed with you, to one side in order to apply myself fully to the manufacture and improvement of your devices. In this way, I intended to show you what I meant by friendship and hospitality. As a result, I believe I have earned your affection; I am glad of this and I know I shall never regret it. I do not allow any Tom, Dick or Harry to enter my premises. Monsieur Terme has not yet knocked at my door.

I learnt recently that Monsieur Marchand, who manages the Folies Bergère, intended to organize a Cinematograph performance on stage. He even had someone tell me he would be delighted to see the apparatus I was engaged upon building. I went to see him, as though to spare him the bother of coming to me, but actually to find out what was afoot. I shall pass over the details of how those people receive one: the most elementary manners and courtesies are totally foreign to them. I did, however, find out that the show they intend to put on in January comes from Cologne and it is indeed some sort of Cinematograph performance. The artiste who organizes these shows all over Europe claims to represent *life-size* moving figures.[1] Monsieur Marchand would have liked to see our 'number' so he could compare it with the one he is expecting. I informed him that if he wished to come and see the Lumière Cinematograph on my premises, he must first obtain permission from Messieurs Lumière. I expect he has written to you. You must respond as you wish.

I saw your father yesterday. He mentioned the beginnings of some arrangement with Monsieur Planchon. I told him that if there was any point in my participation, I was prepared to subscribe, with the same guarantees that I am sure you are obtaining for yourselves. Let me know.

I must stop here. This letter is too long and it is time to send the post.

Yours,

J.Carpentier

1 The Skladanowsky brothers, variety artists based in Berlin, organized moving picture shows at the Weingarten from 1 November 1894 onwards, by means of a bioskope. Max Skladanowski invented the bioskope. It projected two films running simultaneously past two lenses, alternately revealed by a half-moon-shaped shutter. The films were perforated and the perforations protected by metal rivets. The title of each film was projected on to the screen by means of a magic lantern. The whole system was clumsy and complicated; the results were uncertain. However ingenious, the bioskope could never have been propagated round the world. In Berlin, however, the eight films of the bioskope repertoire commanded more attention than the Cinematograph did in Paris. In December 1895, the Skladanowski brothers came to the end of their contract in Berlin and so offered their show to Marchand, of the Folies Bergère in Paris. They were not successful because he was more interested in the Lumière Cinématograph. Indeed, at the first public screening, on 28 December, in the Grand Café, he tried to buy it (see below).

Louis Lumière to Jules Carpentier

[Lyon, Monplaisir] 23 December [189]5

My dear Monsieur Carpentier,

⌈I have just received your most friendly letter.

We were not in the least bit surprised that the charlatan Monsieur Terme should have informed us that you were building him a machine. What you say merely confirms your frankness and friendship. It makes the warm feelings you express towards us even more invaluable and we are most proud of them.

You may be certain we feel the same way towards you and that we are entirely devoted to you because we know how you took us in and all the friendly things you have done for us. Thank you once more for the kind terms of your letter. Concerning the shape of the forks which I asked you to alter, you are right to consider that their tips are too stubby. I am not sure that we can use the old ones because I think I find that there is not enough of the cylindrical length left if the tips are lengthened – particularly if you take wear into account, which has reduced the run a fair bit. But one cannot tell without accurate measurement, which I have found difficult.

⌊The reinforced elements are quite strong enough now.

⌈ Had the mirror-spring of machine no. 1 been altered, in relation to the rounding off of the edge? If the answer is yes, then I would ask you to whittle this edge down still further because, though it works very well with new film strips, the same is not true when the strips have been repaired. Obviously, such mending is occasional, but it does allow use of film damaged by some clumsiness. Apart from that, and you see it is not much, all is well.]

It is unfortunate that the ebonite discs had to be sacificed but I must admit I much prefer the radical solution you have adopted.

Yours ever,

L. Lumière

I was forgetting to thank you for subjecting yourself to an interview with the director of the Folies Bergère. We have had someone tell the chappie he can see what we've achieved at the boulevard des Capucines[1] in a few days' time. He had written to us. I would still be curious to see the German machine. I wonder if it will be possible to arrange.

I believe that the Planchon business may well turn out to be of interest. We shall know in a few days' time. Perhaps today. I shall let you know, unless you hear from my father first. He is in Boulogne.

1 The name of the street, in Paris, where the Grand Café is situated, and thus where the Cinematograph was to be put on public display for the first time.

Louis Lumière to Victor Planchon

[Lyon, Monplaisir]23 December [189]5

My dear Monsieur Planchon,

I received your kind letter, together with the samples it contained. The film is much harder after heat treatment. Furthermore, I believe that it is not so easy to rip: it is more solid and more like American film. The white spun cotton is probably all right. The sample, however, is easy to rip. Can that be due to anything but the cotton?

I am very keen to receive the roll of emulsion film which you say is coming.

Have you tried, in order to maximize adhesiveness, adding acetic acid to the emulsion? It is true that it takes longer to dry, but on flat sheets of glass that should not be too inconvenient and you know that it does not affect sensitivity.

Please let me know the results of your experiments using an undercoating of acetic acid. I am sure it is of interest.

You must be in a terrible state, at the time of writing. I hope you find a good and rapid solution and I hope to see you soon in Lyon.

As soon as we have been able to test our latest film, I shall let you know the result.

Cordial handshake.

L. Lumière

Auguste Lumière to Major Daireux

23 December 1895

Major Daireux
Chairman of the Liège Section of the Association Belge de Photographie
Liège

Thank you for your secretary's letter about the 'Cinematograph'.

We cannot at present make any commitments with regard to demonstrations of this machine; indeed it is probable that we shall organize public shows as soon as we have a sufficient quantity of machines available.

We are honoured at your request and only regret not to be able to respond favourably. Unfortunately, as I say, we can make no engagements now, because we do not yet know exactly when the machines currrently under construction will be delivered.

We are very sorry not to be able to grant your request and we shall certainly bear it mind in the hope that we will be more fortunate on another occasion.

Yours sincerely,

A. Lumière

Auguste Lumière to Edmond Marchand

23 December 1895

Monsieur Ed. Marchand
Paris

Thank you for your letter of the 20th of this month.

Regarding our new device, the 'Cinematograph', we are unable to say when it will be available and we cannot at present give you any information on this subject.

As to how the machine works, you will be able to see for yourself from

Wednesday 25th onwards, boulevard des Capucines, where we shall be organizing public performances.

Yours sincerely,

A. Lumière

Auguste Lumière to Monsieur Bouvrais

23 December 1895

Monsieur Bouvrais
Planzolles

Thank you for your letter of the 21st of this month.

Regarding photographic reproduction of colour, to which you refer, you will find the relevant description in the bulletin of the Académie des Sciences, for March or April of this year.

In the 15 December issue of *Revue Générale des Sciences*, you will find an article which gives precise information about the current state of affairs in this matter.

As far as our new machine, the 'Cinematograph', is concerned, we cannot give you the date on which we intend to start selling it because it is still under construction in Paris. Nor do we know what the sale price will be. We shall bear your interest in mind and as soon as we are able we shall let you have the relevant information.

Please find enclosed an issue of *Nature*, which contains a description of the 'Cinematograph'.

Yours sincerely,

A. Lumière

Auguste Lumière to Eugène Trutat[1]

26 December 1895

Monsieur E. Trutat
Toulouse

On 28 November last, we sent you various illustrations relating to an article which you were kind enough to write about our new device, the 'Cinematograph'.

As these photographs are in demand by various publications, please return them as soon as you have used them.

Thank you in advance.
Yours sincerely,
A. Lumière

1 Author of a work entitled *La Photographie Animée*, published 1899, on the eve of the Universal Exhibition (Paris, 1900), which describes in detail the various systems currently employed for cinematographic projection.

Antoine Lumière to Jules Carpentier

Paris, 28 December 1895

Monsieur Carpentier
20 rue Delambre
Paris

Dear Monsieur Carpentier,
I shall make sure that everything is ready by six o'clock. Please come to the Grand Café with as many people as you wish. A handshake.
Lumière

Auguste Lumière to Léon Gaumont et Cie.[1]

28 December 1895

Messieurs L. Gaumont et Cie.
Paris

Thank you for your letter of the 25th. Regarding sales of our 'Cinematograph', we can only confirm what Monsieur Véra said: we do not yet know whether we are going to market it ourselves, or whether we shall entrust someone else with this task. We have not reached any decision about this.

We are most grateful to you for your offer; we shall certainly bear it in mind if the occasion should arise.
Yours sincerely,
A. Lumière

1 Léon Gaumont (1864–1946) started out at the age of sixteen as a book-keeper with Jules Carpentier. In 1893, he became the manager of an establishment called Comptoir Général de la Photographie (General Photographic Supplies) and in 1895 he established Léon Gaumont et Cie., with backing from, among others, Gustave Eiffel. He marketed Demenÿ's chronophotograph from 1896 on and, from 1902, the chronophone, the first attempt at talking pictures. He founded the first film studios in France, at the Buttes Chaumont, in

1906, and produced a large number of films there with directors like Emile Cohl, Henri Frescourt and Louis Feuillade. In 1911, he established studios and laboratories at Flushing, New York. In 1912, he invented the chronochrome, a first attempt at colour movies. He contributed a great deal to the distribution of French films abroad.

Jules Carpentier to Louis Lumière

Paris, 30 December 1895

My dear friend,

So now your 'Cinematograph' has entered a new phase[1] of its life and your first night[2] was a tremendous success. Unfortunately, I was not there. The only warning I had was a printed circular, received the day before, and I was unable to cancel previous engagements. At the last minute I did beg the favour of an invitation for my brother-in-law, Monsieur Violet, and for Monsieur Cartier, and these two friends gave me their first impressions which were, like those of everyone else in the audience, excellent.

They were a large number of people. Which is not surprising. I would have hesitated to overload this première, even if I had been told of it on time, by asking a large number of my friends and acquaintances to be admitted, though it would have been pleasant enough for me to invite them. I have been told that at my colleague Monsieur J. Richard's, invitations were available for the asking. Many people gained admittance by this route, even though it might perhaps have seemed more natural for me to invite them. The person who told me about that did not exactly warm my heart, I can tell you. I am sure you understand my feelings.

Our new forks will be finished tomorrow night; we will fit them in when work re-starts in 1896. It will not take long and I shall then deliver the

83

machines according to your instructions.

Do we have a definitive model now? Can we start on the order for two hundred?

As this letter will reach you, my friend, on New Year's Eve, I take this opportunity of sending you and your family my best wishes for the coming year.

J. Carpentier

1 The Cinematograph was perfected and advertised by a series of semi-public demonstrations which made it famous throughout the world during the course of 1895, but it did not expand commercially until 1896, when it spread over the five continents.
2 The Cinematograph was launched at the Salon Indien of the Grand Café, 14 boulevard des Capucines, in Paris, on 28 December 1895 (see drawing by Leopold Maurice; the place no longer exists). The room was covered in bamboo, and elephant tusks provided the exotic touch. A few photographs by Clément Maurice hung on the walls. Access was by a spiral staircase. The decision to hold the launch over the Christmas–New Year holidays was a judicious one: stalls offered passers-by toys and sweets; people strolled the avenues of Paris, looking for something to do. A number of the best scientific columnists in town had been invited to a 'dress rehearsal', together with theatre owners and managers, such as Georges Méliès who ran the Théâtre Robert-Houdin. It was probably like a cocktail party. Clément Maurice and Antoine Lumière met the guests; Charles Moisson, Francis Doublier and Jacques Ducom were in charge of the projection. Neither Louis nor Auguste Lumière nor Jules Carpentier were in attendance. It was such a success that Georges Méliès and others offered enormous sums of money to buy the machine. Antoine Lumière refused all offers.
The first few performances did not do much in the way of takings, not even covering the cost of the location. Almost no mention was made in the press, other than *La Poste* and *Le Radical*, who both deplored the rebarbative name with which the invention had been baptized. This state of affairs did not last. Clément Maurice was to describe how success eventually came. 'What I remember as being typical was some passer-by sticking his head round the door, wanting to know what on earth the words Cinématographe Lumière could possibly mean. Those who took the plunge and entered soon reappeared looking astonished. They'd come back quickly with a few friends they'd managed to find on the boulevard. By afternoon, people were queuing all the way to the rue Caumartin, a quarter of a mile away.'
Some days, they took as much as 2500 francs, which meant huge profits. There were twenty sessions per day from 10 in the morning to 1.30 in the morning, with two breaks, one from noon to 2p.m. and one from 7p.m. to 8p.m.

Louis Lumière to Jules Carpentier

[Lyon, Monplaisir] 31 December [189]5

My dear Monsieur Carpentier,

We were most put out, my brother and I, to hear what you had to say about last Saturday's performance. You may rest assured that it had nothing to do with us. My father tormented us into agreeing that he should be in charge of organizing these Paris performances and we were keen not to be involved in any way. Richard's probably got their invitations from Ducom,[1] since Ducom is a great friend of Maurice's and my father was anxious to involve him.[2]

Please accept our apologies for this ridiculous business.

I am confident we now have a definitive model and that you can start manufacturing the next two hundred machines. I should like to try out a few, or perhaps just one, of the finished machines and I should be grateful if you could send some. As soon as I have received them, I shall give you a definite go-ahead.

I am sorry that you got your New Year's wishes in first. We may be late, but rest assured that we are no less forthright and sincere in wishing you and your family our best wishes.

Yours ever,

L. Lumière

1 Jacques Ducom was Charles Moisson's assistant during the Grand Café performances. Normally in charge of general management at the Lumière works in Lyon, he was responsible for sending out Antoine Lumière's invitations to the 'dress rehearsal' at the Grand Café. A film called *Fire Ballet* shot by him in 1896 with one of Demenÿ's chronophotographs appears in the Gaumont catalogue.
2 Clément Maurice was the man who showed Antoine Lumière the Edison kinetoscope. He had been Antoine's assistant, and then moved to Paris where he set up as a photographer. This in turn had put him in touch with artistic and show business circles in the capital. He was put in charge of running the Paris Cinematograph operation and organized, with Antoine, the Grand Café performances. Later, Dr Doyen commissioned him to film his operations, in order that his students could use them as examples. The medical profession went to law to prevent these films being shown.

Jules Carpentier to Louis Lumière

Paris, 31 December 1895

My dear friend,

In an attempt to please you and to please your father too, whom I saw just before his departure and who seemed disappointed at not being able to carry a Cinematograph home with him, I have got the workshop to sprint home and complete three machines. They have just finished them. I am sending them to the station. You will receive them tomorrow with your presents. I hope that, despite the rush to make the changes, we won't have forgotten anything this time.

Kind regards.

J. Carpentier

P.S. I delivered your revised photo-jumelle to the station this morning. I trust you will find it entirely satisfactory.

Auguste Lumière to T. Aldow[1]

31 December 1895

Monsieur T. Aldow
Brighton

Thank you for your letter of the 29th. Our new device, the 'Cinematograph', is easily transportable. It produces negative strips of animated subject matter, turns them into positive prints and then projects them.

This machine is currently under construction in Paris and we do not yet know when it will be available for sale. Nor we do yet know what the sale price will be. We shall bear your request in mind and as soon as we can give you the information you request, we certainly shall.

Yours sincerely,
A. Lumière

1 Tom Aldow and Miss Theo were 'electrical clowns and musical parodists, quick to undress and instant painters' according to an advertisement in a Burgundian newspaper, *Le Progrès* (19 May 1896).

Louis Lumière to Victor Planchon

[Lyon, Monplaisir] 2 January [189]6

My dear Monsieur Planchon,

I have just rceived your kind letter together with the sample it contains. It is much more adhesive as you say. I am sure it will work. The base, however, still scratches fairly easily.

I was not able to give you the results of our tests on the last large strip. We had taken our cutting and perforating machines to bits for major alterations which have proved entirely successful.

We only tried the strip today. The adhesiveness is poor. The emulsion is still coated much too thickly, despite what you told me. But since you have brought further promising improvements, this test is no longer significant. We have analysed American film stock: it contains acetanilid.[1] The proportion is roughly 12% of the total, according to our initial testing. We are doing a second test now and I shall send you the results tomorrow morning. But there is no doubt as to the nature of the product: we purified it and identified it as commercially available acetanilid. In addition, there would appear to be a very slight quantity of some resinous oil, probably linseed oil.

It might be an idea to adopt this ingredient, since American film is much tougher than your samples.

Please keep me informed. Try to come to Lyon before the 15th. I have to take my wife and my daughter to La Ciotat[2] and we cannot wait or the weather will turn bad.

Thank you for good wishes and we in turn wish you a very happy New Year, trusting that this year will see the start of period of well-deserved prosperity for you.

Yours ever,

L. Lumière

1 A substance which protects film emulsion against scratching.
2 Small town on the Mediterranean coast where Antoine Lumière had established a family house.

Messieurs Lumière to Clément Maurice

2 January 1896

My dear Maurice,

This is to confirm the telegram we sent you today in which we requested that you return the damaged films to us as soon as you have received the ones we are sending you in exchange.

We would be extremely grateful if you could indicate the cause of damage as it is very important that we should know. Please be kind enough to let us know exactly what happened concerning these accidents.

Please also return the film entitled *La Voltige*[1] which needs repairing, although there will need to be drying time after the repairs.

We have no print of *Les Forgerons*[2] to send you today but we will make one very shortly.

We look forward to hearing from you.

For Messieurs Lumière

R. Paris

1 Translator's note: *Trick-riding*.
2 Translator's note: *The Blacksmiths*. These two films were among those shown on 28 December 1895. Apparently, the film stock was somewhat frail.

Auguste Lumière to Balagny[1]

Lyon, 2 January 1896

My dear Monsieur Balagny,

I should like to take this opportunity of wishing you and your family a happy New Year.

I should further like to address the following points relating to our situation with respect to you, since these points have been raised, as a misunderstanding between us is to be avoided.

We have been informed that you seemed to be unhappy at the Cinematograph performance arranged by my father on Saturday; we have also been been informed that you laid some claim to sales of films designed for use with this machine. The agreement which I reached with you two years ago has also been criticized. I stated that I knew you were incapable of unfair demands and I am certain I am right.

Allow me therefore to be entirely frank with you, and also to ask you to answer certain questions:

You know what results we have so far achieved in our venture with you: you negotiated an agreement with my father under which we have been dealing with film stock. This business has to date brought us a deficit of 80,000 francs. I have the figures before me, and there are a large number of items which have not been put on the account.

Is that the result?

Shall we ever make up for this deficit, by means of the methods which you have brought to us and the processes we have brought to bear on them? I do not believe so.

Obviously, if ever anything came of this business either from your patents, or arising out of the research and comments which we have made while working on them, we should do it with you, but we should also recognize that not very much is likely to come of it.

At one point, we thought that, short of manufacturing Planchon film in our workshops here, we could at least coat them with our own emulsion; but we had to abandon even that and now we send off our emulsion to Monsieur Planchon.

Apparently you asked my brother, in compensation for this business, for a royalty of 5% on our turnover. Is that fair? None of this business relates to your methods; we are paying for it alone, without you; it is costing us money; it is not about to bring in a profit; and you expect to be the only person to make something out of it. I am sure that by merely listing these facts I can dispel the misunderstanding.

We shall certainly find ourselves in a similar situation regarding long strips of film. We are going to have to look for help elsewhere, buy patents or supplies of ready-made film. Do you believe that, in the circumstances, you have any claim on us?

I am certain your answer will be in the negative and we will not even have to appeal to your sense of fairness, which will in any case force you to the same conclusion.

I take this opportunity of pointing out that our little agreement is ambiguous on several points. So far, material obstacles and instances of force majeur have prevented various other clauses from coming into play.

May I give you my opinion and my earnest and true desire on this agreement? Between honest people who claim to behave fairly, as far as is possible, these sorts of compromises have nothing but disadvantages. Trust us as we trust you. Let us cancel this agreement and I assure you, you will have no regrets. It will also have the advantage of negating all the criticism and rumours that are flying about.

If my brother and I promise to do our personal best to satisfy you, either with regard to manufacturing film paper, or in some other fashion, we are certain you will not lose out by cancelling this agreement.

And if, one day, we can benefit in any way, either by using your patents or by working with you, or by any observations we may have made while working with you or arising out of such collaboration, you can be sure that we would never try to squeeze you out in such an instance and we are certain you would not do us the insult of doubting this statement.

You are aware that we are, *at last*, approaching the end of the road in the matter of film paper. If you could come to Lyon, you would see what sacrifices we have made to obtain the desired result. Do not ask for any more, Monsieur Balagny, it would not be fair.

As a matter of fact, the photographic plate business is expanding enormously; and the question of photographic paper is also giving us a lot of work. Aside from film paper, which we are determined to see all the way through, we have resolved not to deal with film at all.

Whatever is achieved in this field won't be achieved by us.

You can rely on us.

Yours sincerely,

A. Lumière

1 A joint venture between the Lumière works and Balagny for the manufacture of photographic paper had been negotiated by Antoine Lumière but had apparently gone wrong since there was a deficit of 80,000 francs. Balagny was demanding a percentage on sales of

Cinematograph films. Hence the misunderstanding which Auguste is trying to sort out. See his letter to Marquent, 20 November 1895.

Auguste Lumière to the Society of Photography of Savoy

4 January 1896

The Treasurer
Société Photographique de Savoie
Chambéry

Thank you for your letter of 1 January. We shall not be in a position to assist with the performance to which you refer because we still only have one machine.

Furthermore, we have a large number of demands around the time you suggest and we have committed ourselves to a certain number of engagements to which we must stick.[1]

We regret that we are therefore unable to grant your request. Indeed, we are very sorry and we hope that we shall do better on another occasion.

Yours sincerely,
A. Lumière

1 The Treasurer must have been eloquent, for a performance was aranged in Chambéry on 1 February 1896, which is one of the earliest performances in provincial France. As a matter of interest, 'one projection was reserved for pupils of the free schools, the orphanage and the day school; and another, at the municipal theatre, was specially for pupils at the Lycée, the teacher training college, girls' and boys' community schools, active and honorary members of the Society and their families'.

Auguste Lumière to Wladimir Woulfert

4 January 1896

Monsieur Wladimir Woulfert
Moscow

Thank you for your letter dated 15/27 December last.[1]

As we informed you earlier, we should be delighted to let you have some of our colour prints together with a note on how they were produced. Perhaps you would let us know when you expect your Exhibition to open so we can arrange matters.

As far as our 'Cinematograph' is concerned, we are sorry to have to say that we are not at present able to grant your request. The device is currently under construction in Paris and we do not yet know exactly when it will be available to us. The only machine we have is in Paris and, because of previous engagements, we cannot let you have it.[2]

We should have been delighted to have been able to satisfy your request for which we are particularly grateful and we are very sorry that this is not possible.

Yours sincerely,

A. Lumière

1 Russia before the revolution used the Julian calendar, by now some twelve days behind the Gregorian used in the West.
2 This letter gives useful background. By 4 January, the other two hundred Cinematographs had not yet been delivered. Also, in this letter, as in others, the fact that enquiries regarding colour photography and cinematography come jointly suggest that in many people's minds, it was simply all part of the general progress of photography which was acquiring two new characteristics, motion and colour.

Louis Lumière to Jules Carpentier

[Lyon, Monplaisir] 4 January [189]6

My dear Monsieur Carpentier

We received last night only the three machines you were good enough to finish ahead of the rest and I tried them out this morning. They are all right, but I am afraid I have some more comments.

The slipway through which film drops into the bin is too tight, particularly towards the top. Please widen it considerably, therefore, at aaa . . . bbb . . . in such a way that it is never less than 1mm wide.

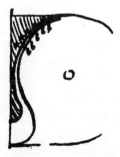

We have made this minor alteration on the bins of machines 2, 3 and 4; the film strips used to tear and now they no longer do. The beak, B, of the wooden magazines is slightly too thick which means the bolt of the metal door must be forced closed; in one case, closing it is impossible.

I think one comment about the mirror-spring has been forgotten. This part now hardly touches the velvet and is held in place by springs that are much too rigid. Could you see to it, because it is causing trouble? The shape of the mirror is perfect now.

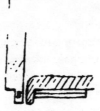

I have found the slight inconvenience which we discussed with respect to machine no. o in Lyon: cranking backwards provokes some kind of click that then prevents cranking forwards. I think this is because the edge of the fork which is responsible for provoking this click should have been whittled down. The crank needs to fit more loosely into its hole: at the moment, it is a strain and the helicoidal grooves no longer prevent cranking the wrong way.

Finally, here is a point which needs careful consideration. The fork is not effectively activated by the rods on the drum. The claws dig in mainly because of the shock of the front end which makes up the rods with lateral stems (the ones I asked you to reinforce; it works very well now). At normal speeds, this shock makes a noise; it also means that the claws dig in too suddenly, which may cause damage. We noticed this very clearly thus: we removed the shutter discs, whitened the tip of the fork and, when the machine was put into action, the persistent image on the retina was b or c instead of a.

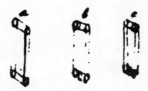

It works, of course, but it would be better to mend this slight defect.

I apologize for writing at such length, such gibberish, together with these horrible sketches.

Best wishes.

L. Lumière

I have just received my photo-jumelle. It is a wonderful instrument and I am sincerely grateful to you for sending it.

Louis Lumière to Jules Carpentier

[Lyon, Monplaisir] 5 January [189]6

My dear Monsieur Carpentier,

I now know that the comment I made about the crank fit is only half-true: I cleaned the hole thoroughly, as well as the crank (they were both thickly coated in oil) and I found it worked. Please ignore that comment, therefore. I am sorry I made it.

As regards the gearing between the fork's lateral stem and the front end of the rods – a problem which only occurs at a certain speed – we have managed to deal with the problem we mentioned by placing on the three prongs of this fork rings designed to absorb any lateral play. We used 3/10mm rings to the front (a) and 6/10 to the rear (b). Have we got the right idea?

In other words, there is very little to worry about and you can quite happily launch the next two hundred machines we have ordered.

I look forward to hearing from you.

L. Lumière

When you have finished a few machines with the above modifications (wooden magazines, bins, mirror-spring) perhaps you could send them to us? Thank you in advance.

Messieurs Lumière to Imbert

7 January 1896

Monsieur Imbert
Chambéry

Thank you for your letter of the 6th of this month. We should certainly like to satisfy your request, and also the fellows of the Society of Photography of Savoy and in principle we can certainly agree to a presentation of our 'Cinematograph'. The problem is that, concerning the date of this event, we are quite unable to make any kind of commitment at present because we are unable to say when machines currently under construction will become available to us.

Please apologize to the Fellows on our behalf and inform them that we very much regret that we cannot immediately satisfy their wish.

Thank you in advance.

Yours sincerely.

for Messieurs Lumière

who apologize for not replying in person and send you their compliments

Monsieur Paris

Auguste Lumière to Delaroche

Lyon, 8 January 1896

My dear Monsieur Delaroche,

When we approached you the other day regarding our 'Cinematograph', it was not, you may be certain, out of personal interest.

The thing did seem to be of interest to you once upon a time and we wished to be agreeable so we thought we ought not take measures to establish this business in Lyon without first referring to you.

We have made you several propositions, asking in return only what you were pleased to grant us. We are sorry that you have received these propositions in such a fashion and that you appear to hold things against us, quite unjustly.

My father has held no dinner for the press. He has, it is true, dined with his friends Sylvestre, Goetschy, des Houx and so on over the last month.

His close friendship with these people stretches back long before the interview to which you allude and is a perfectly good explanation for the article in *La Dépêche*.

We have always done our best to be agreeable to you and the offers we have just made prove this fact.

The scant interest which our business seems now to hold for you, and various other reasons too, have induced us to abandon the idea of overseeing it personally and, as of last night, we have handed it over to a representative who will henceforth take care of things.

Despite all this, we are at your disposal and we would be happy to be of service to you if the situation should arise.

Yours sincerely,

A. Lumière

Messieurs Lumière to Count des Fosses[1]

10 January 1896

Count des Fosses
Paris

Messieurs Auguste and Louis Lumière have received your letter of the 9th of this month. They apologize for not replying in person but they are extremely busy just at present.

We have already arranged for performances of our 'Cinematograph', which is on show to the public every day at the Grand Café, boulevard des Capucines.

Consequently, the machine will be well known by the time of your 1 March session and it will have lost its novelty. We had thought, as you suggested when you called on us, that this session would take place during October and we would have been delighted to satisfy your request by showing the fellows of your Society our device.

If we come up with any interesting novelties between now and the day appointed for your session, we shall be pleased to let you know.

Yours sincerely,

for Messieurs A. and L. Lumière

Monsieur Paris

1 A somewhat surprising letter, addressed more than likely to member of a photographic society. The demonstration to which it refers seems to have lost its purpose, since within two months the Cinematograph will long since have ceased to be a novelty. 'It'll last six months or more' had been Louis Lumière's prediction to the cameramen he sent all around the world.

Auguste Lumière to the Anglo-Continental Phonograph Co.

Lyon, 10 January 1896

The Managing Director
The Anglo-Continental Phonograph Co.,
London

Thank you for your letter of the 7th of this month. We do not manufacture film strips for Edison kinetoscopes, but we are about to produce and distribute film strips for a new device of our invention, 'The Cinematograph'.

Yours sincerely,
A. Lumière

Thomas Alva Edison to Messieurs Lumière

January 1896

Would Lumière welcome an offer[1] to sell Edison a fully equipped plant for the manufacture of cinematographic films and send an expert here to set it up?

Edison would furnish buildings and material.

Payment in cash after the factory is up and running.

Edison

1 This offer was not taken up. See note to letter of 19 October 1895.

Auguste Lumière to A. Molteni

Lyon, 10 January 1896

Monsieur A. Molteni
Paris

It is our pleasure to inform you that we have received the lamps you sent us.

The condensers are still too long. Also, we would like the remaining lamps to be delivered to have lenses 25mm thick.

We look forward to hearing from you.

Yours sincerely,
A. Lumière

Auguste Lumière to Simon et Cie.

Lyon, 11 January 1896

Messieurs Simon et Cie.
15 rue de la Fontaine au Roi
Paris

We are pleased to inform you that we intend to arrange performances of a new device of our invention, 'The Cinematograph'. For this purpose, we are searching for premises in the rue de la République and we wondered whether you might be able to let us have part of your premises in the rue Président-Carnot, on the corner of the place de la République.[1]

If you were to agree, perhaps you would be good enough to let us know your terms.

You may be interested to see the device in question. It is operational at the Grand Café, boulevard des Capucines, in Paris.

We look forward to hearing from you and thank you in advance.

Yours sincerely,

A. Lumière

1 As it happens the next Cinematograph to open to the public was indeed in the rue de la République, but this one was in Lyon not in Paris: 1 rue de la République, at the Empire Theatre. The projectionists at the première were Perrigot, Mesguich and Trewey. The first public screening took place on 26 January 1896.

Auguste Lumière to A. Molteni

Lyon, 14 January 1896

Monsieur Molteni
Paris

We should be most grateful if you could speed up delivery of the apparatus which is still to come, as we shall be needing it.

Thank you in advance.

Yours sincerely,

A. Lumière

Auguste Lumière to Violette

Lyon, 15 January 1896

Monsieur Violette
Paris

Thank you for your letter of the 14th of this month.

Please do not hold the fact that we have not been sending you notes or brochures against us; we did not wish to importune you and we dared not ask you to publish such communications. We are most grateful to you for your offer and we shall certainly make use of it in the future.

As regards the 'Cinematograph', we shall chase up the pictures which go with the description and soon as we have got them back, we shall forward them to you.

Yours sincerely,

A. Lumière

Auguste Lumière to A. Molteni

Lyon, 15 January 1896

Monsieur Molteni
Paris

Thank you for your letter of the 13th of this month and for the lenses which you have sent us.

This last model is indeed the one which suits our requirements and we should be grateful if you would use it for the apparatus which is still to be delivered.

Furthermore, we are returning four lenses. Please send us two of the same diameter as the ones we have just received.

We remind you that we are relying on you to manufacture the apparatus we have ordered as quickly as you can.

Yours sincerely,

A. Lumière

Jules Carpentier to Louis Lumière

Paris, 15 January 1896

My dear friend,

It has been so long since I wrote to you. I was beginning to miss it. But now: during the month of December, in order to be of service to some friends, I agreed to chair the committee in charge of arranging this year's Ecole Polytechnique ball. The original chairman had a death in the family which obliged him to resign abruptly and there was no one to replace him. So I sacrificed myself. I was told there was nothing to it. It's abominable! The dance is arranged for next Saturday, the 18th of this month and for the last three weeks I have done nothing but attend meetings, write letters, call on people and shop . . . Not a moment to myself. I am even neglecting my friends.

Your interests are being taken care of, however. You will receive the two machines which you requested as a matter of urgency. Please make sure that, this time, there is nothing wrong with them. The others will follow.

I have given instructions to establish a cost price. I do not have a proper figure yet, but I know that I was wildly inaccurate in my estimates. The machines, with their accessories, will cost considerably more than I had thought. I will let you know next week. In the mean time, I send you my best wishes.

J. Carpentier

Louis Lumière to Jules Carpentier

[Lyon, Monplaisir] 15 January [189]6

My dear Monsieur Carpentier,

We have run into a most annoying problem. The wood used to make the cases of machines nos. 2, 3, & 4 was unseasoned. It is now impossible to close them. The back gate has buckled leaving a 2mm gap at a; when the bin is in place, the cloth at d must be entirely removed and the point at c where the bin slides in must be widened or else it will not close at all.

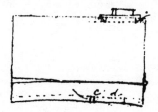

This dehydration has also distorted the ring at r where the lens rests, so that it is now impossible to unscrew the lens ring without using pliers.

These machines have scarcely been ill-treated. They have been kept in warm places, heated normally (15 to 18 degrees). What do we do if the same is true of the ones that are on their way?

I would be delighted to hear from you, my dear Monsieur Carpentier, because it is now some time since we have heard from you. Perhaps I am simply too dull with endless letters and all the remarks they contain. I trust you don't hold it against me because, like you, we want to come as near perfection as possible.

Monsieur Planchon is currently with us. The new business[1] looks like it is up and running; it is going to be interesting. We have conducted a fair number of experiments and I am sure that we shall soon be able to start making good film stock. The factory is to move to Lyon as soon as

Monsieur Planchon has settled up in Boulogne. His present company is going to become a limited company with a capital of 300,000 francs, and as soon as this is achieved, a further 200,000 francs will be subscribed to pay for new plant and to provide working capital. That's the idea. I will keep you informed. Would you still be interested in joining the board?

I leave tomorrow for La Ciotat where I am taking my wife and my daughter. Perhaps you could write to me at the following address:

L. Lumière at La Ciotat

(departement of the Bouches du Rhône)

Please give my regards to Madame Carpentier.

Your friend,

L. Lumière

1 Antoine Lumière went to Boulogne at the start of 1896 to supervise turning Planchon's little business into a limited company, the Société des Pellicules Françaises. Among the directors were Louis Lumière and Jules Carpentier, as well as one Bouchet, shipowner at Boulogne. This limited company built a new factory at 287 cours Gambetta in Lyon. It was managed by Victor Planchon. In fact, 1896 is a year of expansion for the Lumière firm which is organizing a network of supplies and taking a shareholding, often a majority shareholding, in all its various sub-contractors: Verrières de la Gare, a glassmaker at Aniche, in the Nord; Les papetries Montgolfier, a papermill at Annonay in the Ardèche; and La Société des Produits Chimiques, a chemical plant at Fontaines-sur-Saône, outside Lyon, near Buissons, where the family had a house.

Auguste Lumière to Fuerst Brothers, London

Lyon, 15 January 1896

Messrs Fuerst Brothers
London

Please be good enough to arrange to have manufactured and sent to us, as soon as possible, and most urgently:

20 new rolls of Blair film.

We would be grateful if you would speed up delivery of our last order and ensure that the packaging is clearly labelled 'light sensitive' and 'to be opened only in the presence of the recipient'.

Thank you in advance.

A. Lumière

Auguste Lumière to Victor Planchon

[Lyon, Monplaisir] 15 January [189]6

Monsieur Planchon
Boulogne sur Mer

In order to facilitate the conversion of your company, please note that my brother and I agree, on our own account, and up to a limit of 15,000 francs, to take responsibility for your company's debt towards the limited company for the manufacture of photographic plates and papers, and that in exchange for this amount, we agree to be repaid an equivalent in shares of the above-mentioned company.

Yours sincerely,
A. Lumière

Auguste Lumière to Calcina et Cie

Lyon, 16 January 1896

Messieurs V. Calcina et Cie.
Turin

We should be grateful if you would retrieve the pictures of the Cinematograph which we entrusted to you and if you could forward them to us as soon as they are in your possession.

Thank you in advance.
Yours sincerely,
A. Lumière

Auguste Lumière to the Marquis d'Osmond

Lyon, 16 January 1896

The Marquis d'Osmond
Paris

Following our discussion yesterday at our factory, we are pleased to confirm, as you suggested, the probable terms of an agreement between us, in the near future, concerning the proposal which you have submitted to us.

We should ask you to give us 40% of gross takings; we should provide you with two or three machines only to be used in Belgium. They would be handled only by our employees, and these employees would also be in charge of takings. They would be paid by you. All associated costs would be borne by you.

This is a rough indication of the terms we may be able to accept in a little while. We cannot make a firm commitment as of now.

Yours sincerely,

A. Lumière

Jules Carpentier to Louis Lumière

Paris, 17 January 1896

Monsieur Louis Lumière
La Ciotat (Bouches du Rhône)

My dear friend,

Our two letters of the 15th crossed. I expect you now know why I have been out of touch and you must never think that I tire of responding to a correspondent of whom I am so fond.

I am very put out by what you tell me about the casing. I am not quite as quick as you to accuse my cabinet-maker of supplying us with boxes made out of unseasoned wood. He is a conscientious, serious, careful man who has always done very good work. The boxes which are with us have not budged in all the time they have been here. But wood is wood and one must ask whether it is possible that a wooden box, frequently transfixed by a beam of electric light strong enough to fry film in a split second, is going to be capable of maintaining its equilibrium.

I shall be very pleased to go into business with you and I long to hear more about the Planchon factory. Please let me know the basis of the arrangement as soon as you can. I may be able to advise you before the matter is settled. On the technical side, I know your considerable competence will preserve you from any unpleasant surprises.

Yours,

J. Carpentier

Auguste Lumière to Servet de Bonnières

Lyon, 18 January 1896

Monsieur Servet de Bonnières
Paris

Thank you for your letter of the 17th of this month.

We are most grateful to you for the description of our Cinematograph which you intend to publish in *Le Monde Illustré*.

We do not at present possess any photographic print that has not been published. We enclose one which is almost unpublished and which has not been used by the Paris newspapers. If you prefer, we can certainly have a completely new illustration made up, but it is bound to take a few days and will thus delay publication of your article.

Please do not hesitate to apply for any further information you may require.

Yours sincerely,

A. Lumière

Auguste Lumière to Jules Van Grinderbeek

Lyon, 18 January 1896

Monsieur Van Grinderbeek
Louvain

Thank you for your letter of the 16th of this month.

Since we demonstrated our Cinematograph at the Belgian Association of Photography, we have not shown it to any other foreign Society. As we have a large number of requests from England, Italy, Germany, Russia and so on, we most certainly cannot make any kind of firm commitment regarding your 10 March session. We regret we cannot be of assistance in this matter, but we do not want make any promises we would not be able to keep.

Yours sincerely,

A. Lumière

Auguste Lumière to Abel Buguet

Lyon, 20 January 1896

Monsieur Abel Buguet
Rouen

Thank you for your letter of the 17th of this month.

Our board of directors recently discussed the matter of exhibitions. As we have recently taken part in a large number, and as we have nothing particularly new to show, other than our customary production of plates and papers, it was decided that we should not participate in any shows for the time being. You will understand, I am sure, that this is beyond our control and that we must abide by the decisions of our board. Nevertheless, as you are well disposed towards us and as we should like to be agreeable, we shall submit the matter to the board in the near future and we shall let you know what decision has been reached.

As regards our 'Cinematograph', we do not think we could be ready by the date you indicate. Before showing this device in Rouen, we want to show it in Lyon and perhaps in various capital cities. Furthermore, as we have only a very small number of machines available, we do not expect to have one free at the time of your Exhibition. We are really very sorry not to be able to be of assistance to you in these matters, but we would rather tell you the position frankly than make promises we should not be in a position to keep.

Yours sincerely,
Auguste Lumière

Auguste Lumière to Major Daireux

Lyon, 20 January 1896

Major Daireux
Liège

Thank you for your kind letter of the 17th of this month. We confirm what we wrote to you in our letter of 23 December.

We were most grateful to you for your suggestion and we should have been delighted to be of assistance, but numerous prior engagements concerning the launch of our 'Cinematograph' make it impossible we should grant your request on this occasion.

We have demonstrated our machine at the Belgian Association for Photography, and it has not been shown to any other foreign Society. We have had numerous requests from England, Russia, Italy, Germany and so on; we are obliged by the small number of machines in our possession to answer these requests in turn and in order.

We regret we cannot be of assistance and we hope to be more fortunate on another occasion.

Yours sincerely,
A. Lumière

Auguste Lumière to A. Molteni

Monsieur A. Molteni
44 rue du Château d'Eau
Paris

We need the lamps we ordered from you as a matter of urgency and we should be grateful if you would send all or part of the consignment as soon as possible.

We thank you in advance for doing what you can in this respect and we await prompt delivery.

Yours sincerely,
A. Lumière

Auguste Lumière to Balagny

20 January 1896

My dear Monsieur Balagny,

I have received your reply and I am extremely grateful to you for giving me the explanations it contains.

We were not, as you seem to think, encouraged by your directors; the principal reason for my letter was your demands in relation to the Planchon film business.

It is crucial for us to know whether you make any claim on films not manufactured by us, and whether any such claims would extend to other films purchased by us for use in our Cinematograph.

I have indicated the extent of our sacrifices in an attempt to be of assistance to you, and exactly how things stand at present. It is most important that we should have a very clear idea of your intentions, in order that we can match our behaviour accordingly. A further outlay is no doubt required, but we cannot allow it unless we know the exact circumstances.

I am in any case confident of your response; I know that the entirely unfair claims to which I referred previously will not be confirmed by you.

I think we are home and dry with your paper, and this time we are ready to manufacture. It is a lengthy process – it goes through the machine three times – and reasonably expensive; but the outcome will, I know, meet your expectations.

Yours sincerely,
A. Lumière

Jules Carpentier to Louis Lumière

Paris, 21 January 1896

My dear friend,

At last, the dance is over! What a relief! I can get back to work and live in peace, or as much peace as is afforded by the usual waters I sail through.

Monsieur Planchon came to see me on Saturday morning and I was delighted to make his acquaintance. He filled me in on the business he is starting up. As you know, I was in any case interested in this matter; now he has mapped out its future for me, I can only be even more involved and I am keener than ever to join you. All I ask is to see a copy of the statutes of the new company, or rather the re-established company, a copy of the contracts between it and the Société Lumière, and other essential documents. As regards the technical merit of the processes in which the company is investing, your positive appreciation is the only guarantee I need. I should however be delighted to come to Lyon to see the excellence of these new films with my own eyes. It would be a good excuse to come and see you!

I have to tell you that the pleasure of Monsieur Planchon's visit was somewhat compromised by something he told me and that is really the purpose of this letter. While discussing various products which will keep the new factory going, he mentioned continuous strips bearing at regular intervals cross lines of perforations designed to make the separation of prints easier.[1] I thought of this a long time ago and am currently conducting experiments with regard to a set of film binoculars, and a roll enlarger, both of which are merely applications of the idea. I was going to patent it. But if you have already thought of it, perhaps you have been quicker off the mark and staked your claim on this industrial territory? Have you taken out a patent yet? Can I carry on looking into the matter? Perhaps you would let me know as soon as you can.

Yours ever,

J. Carpentier

---

1 The idea clearly described in this letter is a crucial one; it would seem that Carpentier and Lumière reached the same goal by separate routes. This accidental competition did not in any way affect relations between the two friends.

Auguste Lumière to Servet de Bonnières

21 January 1896

Monsieur Servet de Bonnières
Paris

Thank you for your letter of the 19th of this month.

We are having a new photograph made up out of an unpublished Cinematograph film strip. As we informed you in our recent letter, we are certain that this illustration will not be ready for two weeks or so, being the amount of time required by firms in this line of business.

Yours sincerely,
A. Lumière

Messieurs Lumière to the Marquis d'Osmond

Lyon, 23 January 1896

The Marquis d'Osmond
Paris

Thank you for your letter of the 17th of this month.

Since your visit to Lyon, we have seen several people interested in establishing Cinematograph companies in Belgium and Holland. This outfit offers serious advantages, notably 50% of the gross takings.

Since, however, we have also received a recommendation from Monsieur Gravier, former Secretary-General of the Prefecture of the Rhône and from Monsieur Cerfi, we should prefer to treat with you. We are therefore writing to ask you to draw up an agreement on the following terms: in exchange for 50% of the box office gross, we shall supply you with two or three Cinematographs, together with films, for performances in Belgium. Two of our employees will accompany each of these machines, one in charge of the machine itself and the other responsible for the box office. Both of these employees shall be paid for by you, as well as all further production expenses.

We look forward to hearing from you.

Auguste Lumière to Paul de Montal

Lyon, 27 January 1896

Monsieur Paul de Montal
Grenoble

Thank you for your letter of the 24th of this month.

We have indeed just set up a moving picture theatre here. We now intend to show the thing in all the capital cities of Europe, before arranging performances in the larger French towns.

It is not therefore possible for us to grant your request, at least for the moment, but we shall certainly bear it in mind, as the occasion arises.

Yours sincerely,
A. Lumière

Auguste Lumière to S. Pozzy

Lyon, 27 January 1896

Monsieur S. Pozzy
Paris

Thank you for your letter of the 24th of this month.

A considerable workload prevents us from managing performances of our 'Cinematograph' personally and we have therefore granted exclusive rights for Paris.

Furthermore, for the reason given above, it would not have been possible for us to give the lecture to which you refer.

We are sorry we cannot be of assistance to you in this matter and we hope to be able to remedy this on another occasion.

Yours sincerely,
A. Lumière

Auguste Lumière to Paul Renard

Lyon, 28 January 1896

Monsieur Paul Renard
Paris

Thank you for your letter of the 24th of this month.

We have already received a number of applications for performances of our Cinematograph in France and abroad. Perhaps you would be good enough to let us know the terms you would be able to propose so we can study them.

Yours sincerely,

A. Lumière

Auguste Lumière to E. Ingold

Lyon, 28 January 1896

Monsieur E. Ingold
Lyon

Thank you for your letter of the 26th of this month.

From the point of view of its construction, our new device, 'The Cinematograph' bears no relation to the kinetoscope. It is not therefore possible to transform your machine in the way you suggest.

Yours sincerely,

A. Lumière

Jules Carpentier to Louis Lumière

Paris, 29 January 1896

Following your instructions, I started work some time ago on the two hundred cinematographs which you ordered.

I must charge you 360 francs each. This price breaks down as follows:

The device itself, together with two lenses	275
Set, single magazine	8
Double magazine	12
Metal bin	30
Base	35

My first estimates, as you see, were over-optimistic; but I know the outcome will seem reasonable. The things need to be well made, with a great deal of precision. Besides which, the accessories are relatively expensive and I had not initially taken this into account.

Even though the first order, which I have just completed, was weighed down with one-off costs arising out of the various alterations which we made during the course of manufacture, so that the unit cost of this first series is exceptionally high, I dare not charge you more than 360 francs, which we should call the mean rate. I am irritated enough as it is to have to admit to having got my initial estimates so wrong.

As a formality, I enclose details of your account with us as of today.

I should mention that I have retained machine no. 25 of the last series as a model. When you have an excess of successful, positive prints, I should be grateful if you could send me some so we can run the machine and see how it works.

I am impatient to come to Lyon for the Planchon business. When we meet, I want to tell you about a matter I looked into around 1882 or 1883, and that I have since done nothing about. I am sure that we could bring it off together. It is of interest; I shall be delighted if you like it. If you don't, just tell me without bothering to be diplomatic or polite.

Yours ever,

J. Carpentier

Auguste Lumière to Fuerst Brothers, London

Lyon, 30 January 1896

We should be most grateful if, as a matter of great urgency, you would make us:

20 rolls of Blair film.

We look forward to delivery soonest.

Yours sincerely,

A. Lumière

Auguste Lumière to François-Henry Lavanchy-Clarke[1]

Lyon, 30 January 1896

Monsieur Lavanchy-Clark

Paris-Passy

Thank you for your letter of the 27th of this month.

We take note of your interest and, as you request, shall without fail make an appointment to see you when we next travel to Paris.

Yours sincerely,

A. Lumière

1 A cameraman. He introduced the Lumière brothers to Demenÿ and presented the Cinematograph at the Swiss National Show in Geneva (1 May–15 October 1896).

Auguste Lumière to A. Molteni

31 January 1896

Monsieur A. Molteni
Paris
Very urgent

Thank you for your letter of the 30th of this month. Please amend the apparatus which you are sending us in the way you suggest. Please also send us all or part of this equipment as a matter of urgency and without delay; we await it impatiently. Please let us know your probable delivery date.

We look forward to hearing from you.

Yours sincerely,

A. Lumière

Auguste Lumière to Niewengloski

1 February 1896

Monsieur Niewengloski
Paris

Thank you for your letter of the 30th of this month. We are most grateful to you for your offer and we hasten to accept.

In order that the illustrations you require should match the articles you wish to publish, we take the liberty of requesting that you should have them made up yourselves at our expense. If this proposal suits, please send the bill to us here and we shall settle it.

In accordance with your suggestion, we are enclosing a portion of film strip, together with several recent articles[1] on 'The Cinematograph'.

Please do not hesitate to contact us if there is any further information you require.

Yours sincerely,

A. Lumière

P.S. Regarding the invitations to which you refer, we are writing to our Paris representative and he will forward them to you. We have none available here.

1 A very large number of explanatory articles on the Cinematograph, usually accompanied by illustrative sketches, appeared in the press between the spring of 1895 and the summer of

1896. National dailies vied with the scientific journals to analyse the 'scientific miracle'. Most of them made up in sincerity and enthusiasm for what they lacked in accuracy. Some of them are involuntarily hilarious.

Auguste Lumière to H. Véra

Lyon, 1 February 1896

Monsieur H. Véra
Paris

Thank you for your letter of 31 January.

You were quite right to send us the 'Crooks' tube[1] that you managed to get hold of and we are most grateful to you. We shall reimburse you the amount on Fontaine's bill, together with cost of postage.

Perhaps you would go to *La Nature* and *La Revue des Sciences* to obtain the photographs they used to illustrate articles on the 'Cinematograph'? When you have retrieved them could you forward them to Monsieur Frédéric Dillaye,[2] 8 rue St Joseph, who intends to write something for *La Science Illustrée*?

Thank you in advance.

Yours sincerely,

A. Lumière

1 A cathode ray tube, which generates X-rays. Auguste Lumière was a pioneer in the field. He produced the first X-ray of a fracture, reduced by Professor Ollier. X-rays had just been discovered and were the object of considerable public enthusiasm. In the *Revue Encyclopédique*, 28 March 1896, fun is poked at the 'Cafés on the boulevards who offer their customers cinema and radiography shows, and thus become annexes of the Faculty of Medicine' (in Eugen Weber, *Fin de siècle*).

2 Frédéric Dillaye was a scientific journalist, a photographer and – later – a shareholder in Gaumont. He wrote a column in *La Science Illustrée*, a popular journal, entitled 'Photography in motion'. On 2 May 1896, *L'Univers Illustré* wrote: 'It is with indefatigable energy and considerable ability that Monsieur Frédéric Dillaye does his best to assist the progress of photography. From his earliest writings onwards, he has insisted on one major notion: whatever its many applications, and the many applications yet to be discovered, photography is an art form. Since those days, a number of public displays in favour of the photographic Art have come to show us that he was not mistaken. It is hardly surprising that the works of Monsieur Frédéric Dillaye meet with such success and that this success compels him to continue, revise and perfect his output: *La Pratique en Photographie* by Frédéric Dillaye, 8vo, 400 pages, with 200 engravings including 13 photographs after the author's own photogravures. Price: 4 francs (published by Librairie Illustrée, 8 rue Saint-Joseph, Paris).'

Auguste Lumière to Frédéric Dillaye

Lyon, 1 February 1896

Monsieur Frédéric Dillaye
Paris

Thank you for your letter of 31 January past. We are writing, by the same post, to Monsieur Véra, our technical representative in Paris, in order that he may do what is required in relation to your request for electrotypes[1] for the article you intend to publish in *La Science Illustrée*.

Thank you very much in advance for this publication. We are at your disposal should you require any further information.

Yours sincerely,

A. Lumière

---

1 Electrotypes: here, photographs ready for printing which the Lumière brothers sent out as promotional material.

Auguste Lumière to Clément Maurice

Lyon, 2 February 1896

My dear Maurice,

We should be very grateful if you would forward a few invitations to Monsieur Niewengloski, editor of *La Photographie*, 45 rue Daguerre.

Could you also give Monsieur Véra a few portraits so he can make 30x40 bromide enlargements.

Thank you in advance.

Yours truly,

A. Lumière

Auguste Lumière to Madame Aveyron

Lyon, 4 February 1896

Madame Aveyron
Lyon

Thank you for your letter of the 3rd of this month. We intend to give free performances for all pupils in city schools and we shall be making arrangements shortly.

Yours sincerely,

A. Lumière

Auguste Lumière to Monsieur Dalbanne

Lyon, 4 February 1896

Monsieur M. Dalbanne
Lyon

Monsieur Perrigot[1] has forwarded to us your letter and the suggestions for advertising which you put before him. As soon as we are in a position to put our device on the market, we shall certainly need advertising and we shall not fail to take up your offer, but we are not, at present, ready to take it up.

Yours sincerely,
A. Lumière

1 Like the Lumière brothers a former pupil of La Martinière in Lyon, Perrigot was the technical and marketing manager of the Lumière works. As soon as the Cinematograph was invented, he took over responsibility for marketing it, and then took charge of the permanent Cinematograph theatre situated in the rue de la République in Lyon where, with Mesguich and Trewey, he arranged the first public projection. Later, with Promio, he was also given charge of training cameramen-projectionists for the Lumière organization (see note 2, letter of 8 February 1898). A few years later, he is to be found managing the autochrome colour photography plant.

Auguste Lumière to Albert Guisman

Lyon, 4 February 1896

Monsieur Albert Guisman
Lyon

Thank you for your letter of the 1st of this month. The idea you have been kind enough to put before us is indeed most interesting and we should already have attempted to put it into practice if we had the benefit of larger premises for our Cinematograph.

Regarding the offer you have made, we should certainly have wished to take you up on it and assist you in this matter, but the small number of machines we have available prevents us from making any firm commitments for private showings. We shall be arranging demonstrations in the main capital cities, and our few machines will thus be engaged.

We much regret not being able to be of assistance to you and we trust we shall be more fortunate another time.

Yours sincerely,
A. Lumière

Auguste Lumière to the Marquis d'Osmond

Lyon, 5 February 1896

The Marquis d'Osmond
Paris

We have just seen our friend Monsieur Thomas, who tells us that you are anxious for a response following our recent discussions.

I cannot at present travel to Paris as I had hoped and we do not wish to keep you waiting any longer.

Having examined the matter carefully, my brother and I, we have decided not to make any kind of commitment, at present, as my father intends to manage performances himself.

We regret not to be able to be of assistance to you.

Yours sincerely,

A. Lumière

Louis Lumière to Jules Carpentier

[Lyon, Monplaisir] 6 February [189]6

My dear Monsieur Carpentier,

I am sorry to have been so slow in responding to your recent letter: I have only just returned from La Ciotat.

We note your price for the Cinematograph. I have remarked that the shutter should be left open as wide as possible when obtaining the negatives: this prevents a jumpy effect when representing sudden movement. We should therefore not hesitate to allow only a fixed shutter disc, giving an invariable setting. The exposure time can be varied according to the lens diaphragm. We need to be able operate at approximately $f/12.5$, $f/18$ and $f/22$.

I shall, however, be letting you know an alteration regarding the metal opening. Also, the perforations are not always opposite the sprockets. I have been working on this because of a certain amount of trouble with the film strips, in our performances at Paris and Lyon, arising out of a lack of pressure from the mirror-spring. The mirror rests on its bevelled edges and after a time ceases to press against the film. In this respect, I should be grateful if you could have some mirrors cut thicker than the rest, by some one or two millimetres in order to ensure that the pressure on the film is sufficient.

The alteration in the opening to which I refer above will not involve altering the basic model, but it will mean having a rectangular opening. I shall send you a sketch as soon as it has been thought out.

We have had no news on the Planchon front for some days now. The limited company should be established by now. Monsieur Planchon is expected in Lyon towards the end of next week. I expect he will call on us.

We shall be delighted to look into the matter to which you refer when you come to our fair city.

Needless to say, if you took it into your head to come some time now, we should be absolutely delighted and perhaps we could, with your advice, come up with a definitive model for this machine which you have already been asked to alter so many times, and about which you have been so patient.

Yours ever,
L. Lumière

I should be grateful if you would agree to wait a few more days before your bills are paid so that we may avoid liquidating investments.

Louis Lumière to Fuerst Brothers, London

Lyon, 6 February 1896

Thank you for your letter of the 4th of this month.

Monsieur Lumière[1] is due to travel to London shortly to make arrangements for our Cinematograph. We cannot however tell you exactly when he is going, though it will be soon.

Yours sincerely,
L. Lumière

P.S. We confirm our telegram of yesterday ordering Blair film and we should be grateful if you could reply by the same route as soon as you are able.

1 At this point, Antoine Lumière was travelling the length and breadth of Europe to establish a network of Cinematograph franchises in the principal cities. On 17 February, the silhouette artist, Trewey, a great fried of Antoine Lumière's, demonstrated the Cinematograph for the first time at the Royal Polytechnic Institute.

Louis Lumière to Niewengloski

Lyon, 6 February 1896

Monsieur Niewengloski
Paris

Following our recent letter to you, we are pleased to enclose a print taken from one of our film strips. We remain at your disposal if there are any further documents or information you should require in relation to the article which you intend to publish.

Yours sincerely,
L. Lumière

Louis Lumière to the *British Review.*

Lyon, 6 February 1896

The Editor
British Review
Paris

Thank you for your letter of the 4th of this month. We are most grateful to you for the article about the Cinematograph which appeared in your journal. As soon as we are in a position to put our device on the market we shall certainly want to advertise it and we shall then bear your offer in mind.

Yours sincerely,
L. Lumière

Auguste Lumière to Emile Bary

Lyon, 7 February 1896

Monsieur Emile Bary
Parc Saint-Maur

Thank you for your letter of the 4th of this month. We are most grateful to you for your article. We should very much like to be of assistance to you in return, but we cannot make up the two enlargements which you request because the originals are no longer in our possession. We very much regret this. If you have any other interesting photographs which you would like enlarged, we would be pleased to do so up to whatever size you suggest.

Yours sincerely,
A. Lumière

Perrigot to Y. Rabilloud[1]

8 February 1896

Monsieur Rabilloud
Lyon

We should be very pleased to learn what has happened with regard to an American patent[2] for the Cinematograph as we are already receiving proposals for performances in the United States.

We should therefore be very grateful if you could let us know how things stand and undertake any necessary steps to find a solution as quickly as possible.

Thank you in advance.

Yours sincerely,
for Monsieur Perrigot
Monsieur Paris

1 An employee of the Lumière firm involved in the Cinematograph sales campaign.
2 The American patent for the Cinematograph was not taken out until 30 March 1897.

Messieurs Lumière to Charles Rossel[1]

8 February 1896

M. Charles Rossel
Paris

We enclose an entry book relating to the machine which is currently in Paris.[2] Please fill in the entries for takings to date and then keep it on a daily basis. The counterfoil should be completed every day and mailed to us, with the specified information.

Yours sincerely,
for Messieurs Lumière
Monsieur Paris

1 One of the Lumière representatives in Paris and a projectionist, under Maurice, at the Grand Café.
2 A member of the team was required to fill out a counterfoil to ensure that headquarters staff were kept informed of box office takings. The Lumière organization was entitled to 50%.

Messieurs Lumière to H. Véra

8 February 1896

Monsieur H. Véra
Paris

Thank you for your letter of the 7th of this month. Please convey any photographs of the Cinematograph which you have in your possession to Monsieur Dillaye and ask him to select whichever ones he requires for the article he is writing.

Thank you in advance.
Yours sincerely,
for Messieurs Lumière
Monsieur Paris

Messieurs Lumière to Fuerst Bros, London

Lyon, 9 February 1896

Thank you for your letter of the 6th of this month. For the time being, 10 rolls of Blair film per week should be enough for our requirements. If, in due course, we discover that this quantity is no longer sufficient, we shall ask you to increase the amount.

Yours sincerely,
pp Messieurs Lumière
Monsieur Paris

Messieurs Lumière to Fuerst Bros, London

Lyon, 11 February 1896

Thank you for your letter of the 8th of this month enclosing a bill for forty rolls of film. We are crediting this sum to your account. Regarding payment, we authorize you to draw a bill on our name, as you request.

Yours sincerely,
pp Messieurs Lumière
Monsieur Paris

P.S. We note that in your recent consignments of film, the emulsion is thinner and thinner. The results obtained are no longer satisfactory. The negatives are woolly, and do not suit us. Please therefore urge Blair Co. to deliver regularly coated film, similar to the first consignments we received, which gave much better results than these last.

Messieurs Lumière to Charles Rossel

12 February 1896

Monsieur Charles Rossel
Paris

A few days ago we sent you a notebook regarding performances of the 'Cinematograph', asking you to fill out a daily counterfoil with the day's takings. We also requested that you complete counterfoils for every day's performance since the opening. As we have not yet received any counterfoils, we are obliged to renew our request.

Since you are our representative in Paris, and since we do not overburden you with demands for information, it would be appreciated if you answered such demands when they came.[1]

In short, please complete the counterfoils for the past weeks, since the première, and forward them to us without delay. In future, we shall expect to receive a daily counterfoil on a daily basis, without interruption.

Yours sincerely,
for Messieurs Lumière
Monsieur Paris

1 Managing the box-office was not easy. It implied a degree of commitment on the part of franchise holders which was not always there. Clearly, this letter is a reminder. Because the company wished to maintain centralized accounts, book-keeping became increasingly complicated. Disputes often broke out. For instance, in an unpublished letter from Milan, the cameraman-projectionist Pierre Chapuis complains, on 12 October 1896: 'the chief representative wrote to Calcina that two days before he had omitted at least 180 tickets for the Cinematograph.' Head office replied: 'Don't control everything and get on everyone's nerves.' Chapuis then writes to his family: 'It's tough seeing people steal before your very eyes and not even be allowed to mention it.'

Such problems, and the burden of an increasingly complicated accounts system, may explain why the Lumières decided to leave management of Cinematograph performances to others, by selling machines outright to franchise holders in February 1897 and to the general public in early May of the same year.

Perrigot to J. Ferrero

12 February 1896

Monsieur J. Ferrero
Geneva

Thank you for your letter of the 10th of this month. We were far more astonished to learn that we had agreed a franchise for performances of our Cinematograph at the Swiss National Show in Geneva, as we have made no firm decision about this matter as of yet. We have come to no arrangement, either with you or with anyone else. The information you have been given in this respect is absolutely erroneous.

We are returning the plan which you were good enough to send, as you requested.

We should add that our 'Cinematograph' has no connection whatsoever with Edison's kinetoscope. For this reason, we shall never agree to showing our device on a stand set aside for Edison's inventions. This is not meant to denigrate that great American inventor's well-earned reputation, but you will understand that it is quite impossible for us to conceive of placing our 'Cinematograph' on an Edison stand. If there were a Marey stand, then perhaps we could, more appropriately, take refuge under its roof.

If you see any other solution, other than this stand, please let us know your offer, although we cannot, as of now, make any commitment as to whether we shall be able to accept it or not.

Yours sincerely,
for Perrigot
Monsieur Paris

Messieurs Lumière to Clément Maurice

14 February 1896

My dear Maurice,

We confirm what we wrote in a previous letter. We would be most grateful if you could send a few invitations to Monsieur Niewenglowski, editor of *La Photographie*, 45 rue Daguerre. We promised them to him several days ago.

From now on, the film strips you receive will be rolled backwards, emulsion on the inside, and the start at the heart of the spool.

Yours truly,
for Messieurs A. and L. Lumière
Monsieur Paris

Perrigot to Louis de Beaufort[1]

Monsieur Louis de Beaufort
Paris

Thank you for your letter. We are not quite sure what you mean by doubling the number of poses. Our machine is designed to take up to 100 frames per second. We only photograph at 15 frames per second because it is absolutely sufficient and we cannot see what benefits would acrue from increasing this figure.

We are, none the less, most grateful to you for your kindness; we are always delighted to receive any information which you are pleased to send us.

for Perrigot
Monsieur Paris

1 This inventor produced, like the Lumière brothers, a machine to view rapidly moving images. Because the number of frames per second was greater, the duration of the film was shorter. The maximum length of a film strip was 17m, which, at the originally stated Lumière speed of 15 frames per second, was to give a minute's entertainment. Louis de Beaufort's images were too fast, his films too short.

Messieurs Lumière to H. Véra

15 February 1896

Monsieur Véra
Paris

We should be grateful if you could obtain a series of photographs of sketches of the 'Cinematograph' and have about ten electrotypes of each made. As soon as you have got a set, please forward it, with a picture to illustrate a portion of film strip, to Monsieur Brunel, editor of *Nouvelles Photographiques*, 2 rue Boulard.

The other sets should be sent to us here.

for Messieurs Lumière
Monsieur Paris

Messieurs Lumière to Clément Maurice

17 February 1896

My dear Maurice,

Thank you for your letter of the 15th to which we reply by return. We have appointed, for each of our machines, a member of staff who knows how to operate it and who is in charge of doing so. Monsieur Charles Rossel is indeed your employee. His job is to inform us of every detail of the operation which concerns us, and to send us, on a daily basis, a counterfoil indicating the day's takings. He is, if we can put it this way, a collaborator of ours attached to you and our representative with you.

This employee is naturally remunerated by the franchise holder who employs him and his wages are fixed at 10 francs per day + some small commission.

We are most surprised that Monsieur Lumière senior omitted to explain this arrangement to you in detail, as it is the same as we have adopted with all organizations similar to yours.

Yours truly,
for Messieurs Lumière
Monsieur Paris

Messieurs Lumière to Paul Lacroix[1]

17 February 1896

Monsieur Paul Lacroix
Hotel Mathis
London

We have the pleasure of informing you that we are today sending you a book of counterfoil slips to be filled out with the daily amount of box office takings for the 'Cinematograph'. The slips should be filled out daily and sent to us on a regular basis. We rely absolutely on your being punctual.

The no. on the book does not correspond to the no. of your machine, but this is unimportant.

Yours sincerely,
for Messieurs Lumière
Monsieur Paris

[1] Paul Lacroix occupied the same function in London as Charles Rossel in Paris.

Perrigot to L. Garchey

17 February 1896

Monsieur L. Garchey
Lyon

Thank you for your letter of the 13th of this month. Regarding the Cinematograph franchise in the area to which you refer, we know that Monsieur Lumière senior[1] is discussing this matter in Paris and we believe that he is about to make a definite commitment. If this were not to be the case, we shall consider your offer and, in any case, we are bearing it in mind.

Yours sincerely,
for Perrigot
Monsieur Paris

[1] From 28 December 1895 and the Grand Café on, Antoine Lumière regarded the marketing of the Cinematograph as his own special field. This activity soon extended, with the assistance of Promio and a few others, to all the main cities in France and abroad. 'Antoine Lumière is in charge of spreading the Cinematograph abroad, of setting it up wherever he can. People are clamouring for it all over Europe . . . Travelling is his relaxation, and business travel his pleasure.' Interview with Antoine Lumière, by Adolphe Brisson, *Le Temps*, 7 April 1896.

Messieurs Lumière to Gallois

17 February 1896

Monsieur Gallois
Nice

Thank you for your letter of the 15th of this month. We shall get hold of a turnstile immediately and forward it to you. We have no objection to your having posters made immediately to advertise the forthcoming opening of our exhibition.[1] We advise you always to use the words 'Auguste et Louis Lumière' after the word 'Cinematograph' on all printed matter, as this is an essential component of copyright.

Yours sincerely,
for Messieurs Lumière
Monsieur Paris

[1] The word projection was not yet used. In practice, the first cinemas used whatever was to hand: theatres, abandoned churches, back rooms in cafés and so on.

L. Violet to Louis Lumière

Dear Sir,

Upon receiving your telegram of 28 February, I telegraphed you that you could keep the last example of an amended Cinematograph, and that the information in our possession sufficed to enable us to undertake the construction of the series we are currently engaged upon. Unfortunately, we now notice that one of the points in your last letter requires further elucidation. Here is a copy of your sketch.

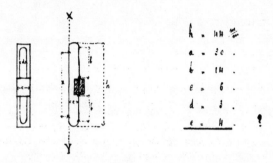

You request that the surface marked XY should be just less than flush with the interior surface of the door in such a way that the springs are kept off the film when the film is not pushed away by the claws. And you suggest that if this is done then the rods at (e) will be 4mm apart. We do not understand. If (e) is 4mm, since the plate is only 3.5, the spring will be out by 5/10 plus its own thickness, which is 2/10. From your letter, it would seem that you want the spring to remain back from the frictional surface as long as the claws are not pushing the film.

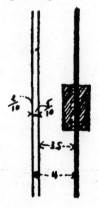

I should be grateful if you could send me an explanatory note.

I received your letter of 28 February this morning. I am having 25 double magazines made. I have already informed you that I have had 12 centimetre projection lenses made. I expect the model to be with me shortly.

Yours sincerely,

pp J. Carpentier

L. Violet

Louis Ducos du Hauron to Antoine Lumière and his sons

Algiers, 19 June 1896

Monsieur A. Lumière and his sons
Lyon-Monplaisir

Dear Sirs,

My brother has just completed a lengthy work entitled *Three Tone Colour Photography and Printing, Louis Ducos du Hauron's System of Photochromography, New Theoretical Description and Practical Application to General Advances in Photography, Optics, Photomechanical Printing and Associated Arts*. This work describes all my research, over the last thirty years, into means of achieving this three-tone system[1] in various different forms and it reveals important discoveries hitherto unpublished.

We have just reached agreement with Gauthier-Villars, booksellers and publishers,[2] who are to publish the book shortly. Publication will be timely. One thing is certain: the current excessive popularity of black photography [sic], which is practically everyone's hobby these days, has encouraged a number of amateur and professional photographers to want to achieve that prestigious grail, so much more demanding and complex, which is known as Colour.

You, gentlemen, have understood the force of this longing and you have encouraged it.

You have encouraged it not just by creating special plates which are appropiate for the execution of interferential chromophotography[3] devised by Monsieur Lippmann, but still further and more recently by launching a beautiful process of printing reversible tones, which comes under the heading of three-tone colour photography.

For our part, in the above-mentioned book, we describe this process with care, but we also, my brother and I, provide a detailed account of all the other printing methods by which science and industry currently encompass the reconstitution of our three colours. I have studied these printing processes in some depth. Some are available to amateurs. Some necessitate full-scale industrial means.

Coming at a time when polychrome projection and tinted printing are carried out almost everywhere in Europe and America, using the equivalent principles of colour separation and reconstitution, there is no doubt that this publication will precipitate matters.

In the circumstances, I beg you, gentlemen, to pay careful attention to what I have to say:

Whether they want to or not, anyone who, in one form or another, by high-speed photomechanical printing or by slow amateur printing, is going to want to make three-colour polychromatic photographs, will be forced to abandon their inconvenient and cumbersome triple dark rooms, advocated either by myself until very recently or by various manufacturers, in favour of a new device which I have invented and patented under the name 'Chromodialytic Polyfolium': a thin book consisting of interleaved coloured film screens and sensitive film which print through each other, the lot contained in the negative compartment of any ordinary dark room.

The book which we are about to publish contains a detailed description of this arrangement.

I have conducted detailed experiments. It works perfectly. It provides an immaculate trio of the three phototypes, one corresponding to blue-violet light, the second to green light and the third to red-orange.

Since the three film types are not commercially available, ready made, I have had to make do with Planchon film as marketed by your firm: I removed the silver bromide from two of these films and substituted the desired emulsion; the third – corresponding to red-orange – I left as was. A modest amount of pressure on the book from the frame guarantees three fine images.

When I wrote to you, gentlemen, last autumn, about this polyfolium, I had not yet conducted thorough experiments. A single article in a journal brought a number of letters from amateurs asking me for said polyfolium. What will it then be when the book is published? And how many more requests will flow on the day when you match this advertisement with your immense renown, if we come to an agreement! . . .

Now, gentlemen, I wish to disclose something which I am sure will not leave you indifferent.

Many years ago, I imagined not only the theory but every detail of that wondrous art the theory of which was later presented to the world by Monsieur Mareten France, and the practice, in America, by Edison, in a defective form, only to be taken up and improved by you; I have been careful to guarantee, by legal means, all my rights of seniority, my property over this invention.

Circumstances did not allow the realization of my system.

It lies absolutely within my brother's intention to publish a pamphlet establishing, at least as far as honour is concerned, my rights as inventor: the notes I used to keep will provide you, should the need arise, with weapons against the so-called improvements brought about by Mr Francis Jenkins, for I described minutely his system of allowing both continuous movement and constant lighting. But over and above the notes I have kept and the improvements proposed by Mr Jenkins, my meditations on this subject, which has been so familiar to me for so long, have induced me to simplify and to advance where he cannot dream of going.

I am ready, gentlemen, before contacting anyone else (and before settling in Paris, with my brother, which is to be expected shortly) to give you the benefit of my special knowledge and the documents in my possession. See, gentlemen, on what terms you could encourage me to speak openly with you.

There is a particular passage in the manuscript which has been delivered to Messieurs Gauthier-Villars (a passage which refers to my past work) which is to be cut or altered according to the response which you choose to give me and which I await soonest.

Yours sincerely,
Louis Ducos du Hauron
Inventor

1 See letter of 17 June 1895.
2 Gauthier-Villars: co-publisher with Cinéopse of *A History of the Lumière Cinematograph* by Georges Coissac. Mainly a bookseller specializing in scientific works; apart from the work referred to, he also published, from 1905 onwards, annual Lumière diaries containing information about advances in photography and Lumière products, both photographic and pharmaceutical.
3 See Lippmann to Lumière, 2 August 1891.

Chancellery of the Marshal of the Court
to Monsieur Lumière

Belgrade, 9/21 July 1896[1]

Monsieur Lumière
Manufacturer of Photographic Equipment
Lyon

Sir,

When your representatives Messieurs Carré and Girin[2] visited Belgrade, they were kind enough to allow His Majesty the King the use of the chamber in which the Cinematograph was displayed to the public. As a result of a mistake on the part of employees at the Chancellery, for which I apologize, Messieurs Carré and Girin were not remunerated the agreed sum before their departure.

Not knowing where your representatives now find themselves, I am pleased to forward the enclosed cheque for 300 francs directly to you. I should be grateful if you would acknowledge receipt.

Yours faithfully,
for the Marshal
His Majesty the King's Secretary

1 Like Russia, Serbia used the Julian calendar of the Orthodox church.
2 Lumière projectionist-cameraman and assistant respectively; they were in Belgrade on 30 May 1896. They set up the Cinematograph in a room of a former restaurant now used for exhibitions and meetings, Aux Croix d'Or. The press showing was on 5 June with *Entry of a Train into the Station at La Ciotat, Demolishing a Wall, A Children's Dance, The Fish Market* and *Sea-Bathing*. On 16 June, the King and the Queen Mother attended a screening in this room. The Cinematograph remained only about twenty days in Belgrade before moving on to Bucharest, Romania. The same team returned to Belgrade on 28 February 1897, performing at the Grand Hotel.

Etienne-Jules Marey to Messieurs Lumière

Paris, 12 September 1896

Dear Sirs,

Your success has impelled a whole army of researchers, all of whom dream of emulating your projection of moving pictures.

For other reasons, I have myself attempted to improve my chronophotograph by eliminating its defect which is the irregular interval between images.

I have managed to obtain pictures as large as one wants, at strictly regular intervals, by removing the vibrating parts of my old machine. The film is not perforated. In addition, for the purposes of projection, I have had to allow for retracting the film in the developing bath and I have achieved this by employing a variable roller controlled by a screw.

Finally, I have obviated the need for complete darkness when the picture is moving by using a translucent disc instead of an opaque one.

I have received offers for the commercialization of my patents. Before opting for one camp or another[1] I have the pleasure of letting you know the circumstances in case you wish to reach agreement with me.

Rightly or wrongly, I believe that large-scale, lengthy projections will prove necessary. I doubt whether the current devices designed to make massive animated projections of extended motion can provide the desired conditions and I believe that people will turn to the solution I have patented.

I am in Paris four days more. Please do not hesitate to contact me for futher information about my new machine.

Yours faithfully,
Marey

1 What seems to be behind Marey's technical concerns is that the synthesis of motion, operated by – among others – the Lumière Cinematograph, is the exact opposite of what he, who described himself as a 'physiologist of motion' was doing. 'The true quality of scientific method,' he says in his preface to Eugène Trutat's *Photographie Animée* (1899), 'is to supplement the senses where they prove inadequate and to correct their mistakes.' F. Dagognet expands on this when he says, 'Marey's somewhat rigidly scientific approach kept him apart from this invention . . . indeed, he preferred to account for the world through a series of graphs rather than the reverse; he had no enthusiasm for the artifices of fictional animation.' (In *Etienne-Jules Marey*, Hazan, Paris, 1987.) See also Count d'Assch to Lumière, 26 July 1892.

Antoine Lumière to the Federation of Stockbrokers of the Paris Bourse

Lyon, 24 September 1896

The Chairman and Members of the Federation of Stockbrokers of the Paris Bourse

Dear Sirs,

We are pleased to request a listing on the Paris Bourse for shares in the Société Anonyme des Plaques et Papiers Photographiques A Lumière et ses fils[1] with a capital of 3,000,000 francs; registered office, Lyon, Monplaisir,

rue Saint Victor 25. We enclose the usual documents.
Yours faithfully,
for the Board of Directors
The Chairman
Antoine Lumière

1 Translator's note: A. Lumière & Sons, Photographic Plates and Papers Ltd.

the Prefect of the Rhône[1] to Auguste Lumière

Lyon, 26 October 1896

Monsieur Lumière Auguste
Manufacturer
County Delegate for the 3rd Ward of Lyon

Dear Sir,

It is my pleasure to to inform you that, on 14 October last, the Departmental Council for Primary Education which must, under article 65 of the law of 30 October 1886, entirely renew the county delegations, has appointed you a member of the delegation appointed to supervise schools[2] and special schools in the 3rd ward of Lyon for the years 1896, 1897 and 1898.

I venture to hope that you will agree to undertake this task. The Council is relying on your devotion to public service and the interest which you have shown in all matters concerning primary education.

The first meeting of the delegations is due to take place on Sunday, 8 November next.

The delegates will gather at the town hall of the county town, at a time stated by the mayor responsible for organizing the meeting. They will elect a chairman who will ensure that I receive as soon as possible the minutes of this meeting, which must include a distribution of delegates among the various schools of the county . . .

Yours sincerely,
Prefect of the Rhone
G. Rivaud

1 In each of the French departments the Prefect is a career civil servant who represents the central authority of the state, as opposed to elected officials who theoretically represent regional interests. The Rhône is the name of a department, by far the largest city of which is Lyon.
2 It is characteristic of the French Third Republic that schools were supervised by leading

personalities whose human qualities were supposed to equal their professional status: Auguste Lumière, a scientist and philanthropist, was in much demand.

Auguste Lumière to the Stockbrokers' Company

Lyon, 29 October 1896

The Administrator
The Stockbrokers Company
6 rue Ménars
Paris

We are pleased to enclose, in this registered letter, various documents which you request in your letter of the 17th of this month:

1. An example of the Tax Inspector's printed report
2. A list of dividends distributed by our company since its foundation
3. A list of board members
4. The reference number for the last coupon paid out together with gross and net earnings for this coupon
5. Two copies of the original statutes
6. A copy of the minutes of the extraordinary general meeting which modified these statutes.
7. A specimen example of the company's shares, together with repayment stamps for repayments up to date, including a repayment of 100 francs made on the 15th of this month.

Yours faithfully,
Auguste Lumière

Enclosed: A list of directors:
1. Claude Antoine Lumière, father, 21 rue Saint Victor, Lyon Monplaisir
2. Auguste Marie Louis Nicolas Lumière, son (same address)
3. Louis Jean Lumière, son (same address)
4. Auguste Thomas, businessman, Asnières (Seine)
5. Jean-Emile Girod, businessman, Paris, rue de la Trémoille, 26
6. Louis Pradel, manufacturer of chemical goods, Lyon, 21 cours de la Liberté
7. Francisque Vial, manufacturer of chemical goods, Lyon La Mouche, 40 chemin de la Scaronne

Auguste Lumière

Telegram from General E. Ponzio Vaglia
to Messieurs Lumière

Monza, 18 November 1896 at 8.10

Their Majesties[1] thank you and are pleased to accept the festivities which you are kind enough to offer in Rome on the 20th of this month.
  General E. Ponzio Vaglia

1 King Umberto I and Queen Margareta of Italy. Kings and queens and heads of state frequently requested private Cinematograph performances. The projectionists tried, on such occasions, to show films of the people concerned, or at least of their nations. The official or artistocratic aspect of these events made excellent publicity for public screenings. An unpublished letter by Pierre Chapuis, projectionist and cameraman, to his brother, Marius, also in the Lumière organization, dated 29 December 1896, gives an account of a picturesque performance for King Umberto I: 'You are surprised that there were three of us for the royal performance. I'll tell you why. Promio, as you'd expect, was at the projector; he told Genty to attend to the lamp; and I thought to myself, you've got it now, and indeed I had. My job was to hand over the spools and rewind them. Genty had never handled a lamp or practically not anyway. His coals were not ready and, you said it! Promio would yell, Put that lamp away, Genty, for Christ's sake! Turn up the resistance! Not knowing how the lamp screwed, he couldn't put the coals away. Promio was screaming, the resistance was creeping up over 40 amps. At last, Promio puts me on the lamp. Things were a bit better then, but the screws were burnt out . . .'

The Automobile Club of France to Messieurs Lumière

Paris, 20 November 1896

Messieurs Lumière
Lyon

Dear Sirs,
  In the name of all my colleagues who are still under the spell of the excellent evening which you have given us, I write to thank you.
  Monsieur Clément Maurice, as your representative, gave us the honours of your wonderful machine, the Cinematograph, which, with its gracious and fascinating subject matter, was a resounding success.
  We are most grateful to you.
  Yours faithfully,
  The Chairmen of the ACF
  Baron de Zuylen de Myrel
  Comte de Dion[1]
  The Technical Secretary of the ACF
  Comte de la Valette

1 An aristocrat who entered into partnership with a mechanic, Georges Bouton, who specialized in making scientific models and toys. Among their numerous patents is a rapid explosion engine. The De Dion-Bouton company brought out its first petrol-engined vehicle in 1899. In 1898, Comte de Dion founded the Aeroclub of France, and the Automobile Employers' Federation; in 1900, he founded the periodical, *L'Auto*, now called *L'Equipe*. He also held political office, as a member of Parliament from 1902 to 1923, then as a senator until 1941.

Auguste Lumière to O. Diradour[1] and Co.

23 November 1896

Messieurs O. Diradour and Co.
Constantinople

We should be most grateful if you could return to us the illustration we sent you to acompany the article you were kind enough to publish on our 'Cinematograph'. We need it in order to be able to reply to numerous expressions of interest.

Thank you in advance.

Yours sincerely,

A. Lumière

1 O. Diradour came into contact with the Lumière brothers as a photographer. He wrote occasional articles in scientific and popular journals, and was the author of articles which spread the reputation of the Cinematograph in Turkey.

The Imperial Polytechnic Society of Russia to Messieurs Lumière Bros.

St Petersburg, 6/18 December 1896

Dear Sirs,

The photographic section of the Imperial Technical Society [sic] of Russia has approached Monsieur Mathieu[1] with a request to be allowed to admire your Kinematograph [sic] which is so deservedly admired and famous.

Your representative here graciously accepted our invitation and demonstrated the Kinematograph at a session of the above-mentioned section on 29 November past.

A numerous audience was quite taken with your invention which it rightly admired. I have been charged to communicate our appreciation to you and it is with pleasure that I perform this task.

    Yours faithfully,
    President, Vth Section
    Imperial Technical Society of Russia
    S. Smirnoff

1 Monsieur Mathieu was Lumière's cameraman-projectionist in Russia, first with Marius Chapuis, then in a separate team. In 1897, he set up on his own account in St Petersburg with a machine to which he brought some improvements of his own and which won him the favours of the Imperial family.

Albert Lebrun[1] to an unknown Member of Parliament
Paris, 27 December 1896

My dear friend,

    You were good enough to inform Messieurs Lumière of the President of the Republic's wish that the terminally ill children of Ivry[2] should be allowed to enjoy a performance of the Cinematograph. I am now writing to ask you once again to speak to Messieurs Lumière on his behalf, but this time to thank them for the speed with which they answered his appeal and the gracious assistance they provided to give these unfortunate children of Ivry a few moments of pleasure, despite their suffering.

    You will tell Messieurs Lumière, won't you, how much the President of the Republic appreciates their gesture to assist him in accomplishing this good deed.

    It occurs to me that you may wish to be the bearer of this message of thanks, since you first interceded with your friends on behalf of the Elysée, after the President's visit to Ivry. That is why I am writing to you, which also gives me the opportunity of thanking you too.

    Yours sincerely,
    Lebrun

You will no doubt have seen that I have arranged to have a few newspapers report Messieurs Lumière's session at Ivry, which is one way of paying tribute to them for their gesture.

1 Albert Lebrun, (1871–1950) A graduate of the Ecole des Mines, one of the prestigious grandes écoles, sat in Parliament with the Democratic Left (1900), Minister for the Colonies between 1911 and 1914, then Minister for the Blockade and for the Liberated Regions,

1917–20, President of the Senate, 1931 and President of the Republic (1932–40). He resigned after the armistice and the formation of the Vichy government (July 1940). Arrested by the Germans, he was deported to Germany (1944–5).
2 A hospital for children outside Paris.

Constant Girel[1] to Messieurs Lumière

Paris, 14 March 1897 (Monday night)

Dear Auguste and Louis Lumière,

This is to confirm the telegram I have just sent you. I saw Monsieur Mascart[2] again at his residence to show him the pictures in question and to study your note on the matter.

Around the 25th of this month, Monsieur Mascart will give a lecture in Mulhouse on colour. He would be very pleased to have some prints and indeed is relying on you. I almost promised them on your behalf.

At two in the afternoon, I met Monsieur Carpentier and Monsieur Mascart at the Institut. Waiting for three o'clock to come round, we saw Monsieur Chaplain in his studio, who was ecstatic about your work, almost jealous of science on behalf of art. He made me promise to show these prints at the Academy of Fine Art. I could not refuse, since Messieurs Mascart and Carpentier also put pressure on me. It is to take place on Saturday.

Soon it was three o'clock. The stereoscope[3] stood majestically in the middle of the room. The fellows crowded around, queuing up to see the new wonders. They were unanimous in their appreciation of the results; then Monsieur Mascart gave his talk in which he emphasized all the advantages of this method and so on.

A fair number of members of the press were there, they took all my descriptions off me. Monsieur de Parville – who is quite charming – Monsieur Charlier, Cosmos and so on. Some of these gentlemen requested the use of the stereoscope for few hours' private usage.

Monsieur Carpentier wishes to present it at an electricians' dinner on Wednesday night. Monsieur Mascart wants it for Thursday and so on.

As my mission is almost over, I should be most grateful if you would let me know whether I can stay a few days longer (mainly for Saturday at the Académie des Beaux Arts). A telegram, for instance.

If the answer is yes, I should be even more grateful if you could add extra funds to enable me to complete my visit.

If I may say so, I believe that you should come and spend a few days in Paris yourselves. Everyone is very keen to see you.

Monsieur Violle of the Institut, who also wishes to give a lecture on photography, asks me to request a few colour photographs to be projected, including, if possible, some Lippmanns. He needs these for Monday next, at the Conservatoire National des Arts et Métiers.

This, in a few words, is the result. In short, enthusiasm and congratulations everywhere.

Yours truly,

Girel

1 In a letter of Pierre Chapuis', dated 5 December 1896, Constant Girel is mentioned as a projectionist employed by Calcina and the Lumière brothers in Pierre Chapuis' team in Italy. According to this letter, he would seem to have risen from the ranks since he appears to be charged with important work by the Lumières: installing machines, marketing, press.
2 Eleuthère Mascart (1837–1908) physicist, astronomer, succeeded Regnault as Professor at the Collège de France. Studied ultra-violet light and made an electrometer that was more accurate than Thompson's. In 1895, he was elected Chairman of the Société pour l'Encouragement de l'Industrie Nationale (Society for the Advancement of National Industry). In the name of this Society, he invited Louis Lumière to give a lecture on the photographic industry and Lumière products.
3 In 1832 the English physicist, Charles Wheatstone, discovered the principle by which two slightly different drawings, each one seen by a separate eye thanks to a stereoscope, would give an impression of depth or relief. He published this discovery in 1838 and tried, unsuccessfuly, to replace his drawings with daguerrotypes. In 1849, David Brewster perfected the process by the addition of two eye-piece lenses and by using transparent images on glass. This device, shown at the Great Exhibition in London in 1851, was very successful. The invention described here is a new, colour stereoscope developed by Lumière.

Gabriel Lippmann to Monsieur Lumière

Paris, 7 July 1897

Dear Sir,

I am writing on behalf of the Société Française de Photographie to thank you warmly for the magnificent donation which you have been good enough to make us. Your Cinematograph was demonstrated at the last session by Monsieur Davanne who, concurrently, informed the Fellows of your generosity. His words were greeted with the unanimous applause of the assembled company, who gave it thanks with cheers and charged its Chairman with the duty of transmitting them.

It is my pleasure to perform this duty today and to compliment you, in my own name, on the ingenious solution which you have found to this problem.[1]

Yours sincerely,

The Chairman

G. Lippmann

1 This is probably a reference to improvements to the Cinematograph as a result of the terrible fire at the Bazar de la Charité on 4 May 1897. A note by Auguste Lumière in *Bulletin de la Société Havraise de Photographie* (2 June 1897) says clearly: 'The terrible catastrophe of the Bazar de la Charité has drawn the public's attention to the terrible danger latent in handling a Cinematograph. The concentration of luminous rays on film can overheat it. But the danger is avoided in our machine because the light source is an electric arc-light. 800,000 performances of our machine have been given without a single accident, which is proof of its safety.' In order to increase that safety, the manufacturers offer to 'replace the optical condenser in the projector with an ordinary wine-glass filled with water. After an hour's continuous usage, the water boils without causing inconvenience. As a precaution, slip a lump of coke into the glass, suspended by a thread, as this prevents the water from boiling too rapidly.'

The President of the Republic to Antoine Lumière and his sons

Paris, 30 September 1897

Dear Sir,

Thank you for your letter of the 28th of this month. I have been asked by the Chief Private Secretary to inform you that the President of the Republic accepts your invitation to view projections of moving pictures on 7 October next, at Rambouillet,[1] if that is possible.

Your representative should contact the Elysée Palace and ask for Monsieur Le Gall in order to make the necessary arrangements.[2]

Yours sincerely,

The Secretary

1 Translator's note: Rambouillet is the country residence of the presidents of the French Republic, outside Paris.
2 Here is a report in the *Journal du Cher* which may suggest that this letter refers to a private screening and not a public première in the presence of the President: 'On Friday evening, guests gathered at the Elysée Palace to applaud Cinematograph views of the Tsar's coronation. The audience was fascinated by grandiose scenes full of life and movement before their very eyes. As the Member of Parliament for the Rhône, Monsieur Fleury-Ravarin introduced Monsieur Lumière to the President of the Republic who warmly congratulated the eminent inventor of the Cinematograph.'

The employees of the Lumière company to Antoine Lumière

Lyon, 2 October 1897

To Monsieur Lumière Senior

Dear Monsieur Lumière,

The staff employed in your offices and your works, profoundly grateful for the generous interest which you have once again this very morning shown them, writes to assure you that your words have been taken in, that your advice will be put into practice and that each of us will do his or her best to further the wise enterprise which you wish to establish in the interests and for the happiness of all.[1]

Please accept this expression of our gratitude and pass our thanks on to your sons, Messieurs Auguste and Louis, who are so well disposed towards us, and to the other directors, also, who have joined in your generous idea of contributing to such a degree to the future safety of those whose present existence you assure by the gift of work.

Yours,
Camille Roy
Barbier
Francis Doublier
Victor Vernier
A. Vernier
M. Paris
Pupier
J. Augier
Charles Moisson

---

1 This letter is an expression of the gratitude of the staff employed in the Lumière factory for a series of social policies which were considered highly innovative at the time, as this interview of Antoine Lumière by Adolphe Brisson shows: 'I have tried by every means to improve conditions for my workers. I am so bold as to believe that they are better treated than factory workers anywhere. First, by a free gift, I laid the foundations for each one to have a savings account, stipulating that they could only have the benefits of this account if they were dismissed or if they left of their own accord. At the end of the first year, most of them left me in order to have their money and I understood that my method was not right. So I found another. Someone drew my attention to the national pension scheme. I looked no further. That was the solution. If it was used more frequently, we should be spared much misery and many misunderstandings. This is what Monsieur Lumière did. He persuaded his partners to make a sacrifice. They gave each worker forty francs and they said: "We shall pay ten centimes per day into a pension scheme but only on condition you too pay in ten centimes per day. We shall arrange our behaviour according to yours. Be wise and have foresight. We shall reward you by matching your effort. But if you do not have the energy to levy this light tax on your earnings, do not expect us to help you." All of Monsieur Lumière's

employees, or most of them, followed his advice. At the end of the week, when the cashier hands over their pay, they spontaneously return a small sum which goes into their savings. At the end of the year, twenty centimes per day represents seventy-two francs; at the end of twenty or thirty yers, when a worker is invalided out, he has got an income to keep him out of poverty.'

Alfred Picard[1] to Monsieur Lumière

Paris, 3 December 1897

Dear Sir,

I am pleased to inform you that the provisional installation designed to provide the machine gallery with two hundred amp electrical current is now entirely finished and you can proceed, when you please, to conduct whatever experiments you wish.

The cables arrive in the middle of the machine gallery, on the first floor balcony, where you will find rheostats and measuring devices.

Please let me know when you intend to begin these experiments.

Yours sincerely,

The Curator

A. Picard

1 General curator of the Universal Exhibition of 1900. It was at his request that the Lumière brothers installed their widescreen projections in that exhibition. The Cinematograph was set up in the old Galerie des Machines at the Champ-de-Mars. The correspondence with Alfred Picard relates to these experimental screenings. A giant screen was built, 21 metres wide and 18 metres tall. The audience was placed either side. The screen was wetted, in order to make it sufficiently reflective. 'The projectionists lowered it at the end of each evening into a concrete pool under the floor of the room: half an hour before the first show, it was raised by a winch in the glass roof; during the course of the performance, streams of water washed the screen once more.' (1900 Exhibition, General administrative and technical report, Alfred Picard, Paris, 1903.)

Alfred Picard to Louis Lumière

Paris, 10 January 1898

Dear Sir,

Your assistance with the party for workers employed in the Exhibition on Saturday 8 and Sunday 9 January was invaluable. The performances so ably arranged by your engineer, Monsieur Moisson, were most successful. I have asked Monsieur Moisson to pass on my thanks and I should be grateful if you would let me know what reimbursements and fees are due to your firm for these two performances.

Yours sincerely,
The Curator
A. Picard

Alfred Picard to Louis Lumière

Paris, 18 January 1898

Dear Sir,

Thank you for your very kind letter but I cannot accept your offer and I insist that your firm should at least be reimbursed for any expenses incurred on behalf of the cinematograph performances of the 8 and 9 January (your engineer's travel costs, his assistant's travel costs, hire of equipment and so on). Otherwise I shall not be able to call on your services in the future and I should very much like to be able to do so. Please, therefore, let me have a figure for these expenses and allow me to thank you, once more, for agreeing to make your services available.

Yours sincerely,
The Curator
A. Picard

Felix Constantin[1] to Messieurs Lumière

[Battleship *Le Formidable*], Toulon, 8 February 1898
Messieurs Lumière
Lyon

Dear Sirs,

In the name of the Vice-Admiral, Commander-in-Chief of the Mediterranean Squadron and of the Committee of 19 February Ball, it is my pleasure to thank you for the generous assistance which you are pleased to grant us free of charge, by means of performances of the Cinematograph which will lend to our ball unexpected brilliance.

The film strips which Monsieur Promio[2] will shoot on board will no doubt increase the already considerable collection of views which your wonderful invention has already recorded.

The Vice-Admiral has ordered that Monsieur Promio should find on

141

board *Le Formidable* every assistance in the accomplishment of his mission.

Yours faithfully,

F. Constantin

1 A naval officer, from 1896, commander of the battleship *Le Formidable*. Lumière films catalogue nos. 809 and 812 to 829 were shot on board this ship.
2 A fan of the Cinematograph performances at the Grand Café in Paris, Alexandre Promio contacted the Lumière brothers via an old school friend of theirs from La Martinière and got himself hired. Trained by Louis Lumière and Charles Moisson, he represented the firm abroad and acted as an inspector. This meant a great deal of travel.

Henri de Parvile[1] to Monsieur Lumière

Paris, 22 March 1898

Dear Sir,

Thank you for your note in reply to mine. When your representative returns to Paris, on a Saturday, I should be grateful if you would ask him to come by the newspaper between three and five o'clock.

I have not comprehended your description sufficiently well to be able to give an account of it to daily newspaper readers. Certain points remain unclear. In short, I have not completely got the hang of it and I want to avoid getting it wrong.

Thank you, also, for thinking of *La Nature*'s collection of curios. We shall give the stereoscope[2] pride of place.

See you soon. Best wishes.

Parville

1 Editor of *La Nature*, science correspondent of *Annales* and *Débats*.
2 Louis Lumière had a persistent interest in 3D images. On 3 November 1900, he took out a patent for stereoscopic moving images but it was not until 1936 that he organized public screenings of 3D films.

Louis Lumière to Jules Carpentier

25 April 1898

My dear Monsieur Carpentier,

It has been ages since we have heard from you. I hope that you and your family are in good health and I should be glad of note to reassure me on this point.

We are as busy as ever here, which is why, on occasion, we postpone correspondence which should never be neglected. Please accept my apologies.

This letter is not disinterested either:

A chap[1] who is an old acquaintance of ours (everyone knows him in Lyon because of his size, two metres and sixteen centimetres[2] I think; he is known as the giant of Neuville) showed me a new kind of bicycle, of which he is the inventor and which he would like to have manufactured. As this instrument is propelled by a swinging motion of the pedals and a number of similar systems have failed, the manufacturers he has turned to all shut the door in his face. He has come to me in despair and shown me his machine which seems very clever to me in several respects, and well thought out. I thought that perhaps you would not refuse to take a look at this bicycle, which certainly uses muscular power with greater efficiency, and that its design might interest you because of your venture with Richard's Cycles. If you agree, would you let me know whether I may send you drawings, descriptions and perhaps even the machine itself? I should be grateful if you would give this matter the full brunt of your considerable expertise. Thank you in advance.

Will you be at the Planchon board meeting on Thursday? It would be very good.

A thousand regards to you and yours. I look forward to hearing you or seeing you soon.

A handshake.

L. Lumière

My inventor is named Bidault. He lives at 3 rue de Paris, Lyon-Vaise.

1 This letter suggests that the era was thick with inventors and new inventions, and that manufacturers watched their activity closely.
2 Translator's note: about 7ft 1in.

Jean Marie Casimir Ducos du Hauron to Auguste Lumière
Paris, 29 April 1898

My dear Sir,

My son Gaston, to whom, some time ago, with a confidence that has turned out to be amply justified, I entrusted the conduct of my family's complicated affairs, has just informed me of things which touch me beyond all expression. I learn that, upon his providing you with an account of our most recent financial embarrassment, which is the consequence of my brother's heroic labours, your princely intervention has once again put a stop to the cruel games which seem to make of us the plaything of misfortune. By this invaluable service, added to your previous help, you have managed to tear us out of the vagaries into which we were in danger of being plunged. Without any acquaintance with us you have acted towards us as the best of relatives and the most honourable of gentlemen. How can one acknowledge, Sir, the grandeur of your ways? I am not, I am sorry to say, up to the task which my gratitude imposes upon me. One thing at least is certain: in the account which shall be given, and published before long, of my brother's inventions, and his struggles, resounding homage will be paid to the role which your family has been good enough to play in the almost tragic events of mine. If it is true, and a sad thing it is, that the French Government has shown, to date, an indifference worthy of the dark ages towards the inventor and scientist that is my brother, it is also true that you have taken up the cause of this pioneer of French science and that, single-handedly, in this instance, you have done what the authorities should have done.

I thank you for him, Sir, kind Sirs. Thank you for him, for me and mine!
Yours truly,
Ducos du Hauron

Girel to Messieurs Lumière

Paris [1898] (Sunday morning)

Dear Auguste and Louis Lumière,

Appointments here are so difficult, the distances so large, that I did not see, yesterday, as many people as I should have liked.

No matter. Monsieur H. de Parville was delighted, enthusiastic about the result; he was charming and will publish next week a fine article on the subject, and also in *Débats* and the other publications where he writes.

I saw Monsieur Carpentier again. I am meeting him at his establishment on Monday and we are to go the Institut together.

I visited the Biograph[1] at the Casino de Paris which is pretty successful at the moment. Nothing really new except that the screen is huge, 4 metres wide, and there is slightly less flickering.

I'll be in touch again after the session. I'll send you a telegram on

Monday, as well as to the main newspapers in Lyon and elsewhere.

 Yours sincerely,
 Girel

1 American Biograph: originally launched in the United States as Dickson and Casler's 'mutoscope'. The first Biograph performances in America, in the autumn of 1896, provided the Cinematograph with serious competition. Mr Ramsaye gives a description of the workings of this machine: 'From a technical point of view, the Biograph gave the best picture ever. The quality of the image on the screen was much improved because it was enlarged eight times less than Lumière, Edison or Paul's. The Biograph consumed eight times more film and silver nitrate per frame than standard Edison film and was so expensive it was unlikely to provide much of a threat, except in large theatres where the cost was unimportant compared to the profit potential. Mechanical considerations further limited the Biograph projector's popularity. Film was driven by cogs and camshafts that escaped the constraints of Edison's patent, and were therefore subject to slippage which meant that constant supervision was necessary.

Girel to Messieurs Lumière

Paris, 31 [ ] 1898

Dear Auguste and Louis Lumière,

 I have just received a letter from Monsieur Mascart in Mulhouse asking me to inform you that your colour photographs were a huge success at the Town Hall in Brussels where they were shown in the presence of the Mayor. The results, he says, are excellent, and will provide a climax for his lecture in Mulhouse.

 I have not yet received the photographs and I await them with some impatience because I promised them to Monsieur Meyer and his friends for this evening.

 As I was saying yesterday to Monsieur Pradel, I shall have the honour of seeing you on Saturday morning early.

 Yours truly,
 Girel

Lieutenant-Colonel Renard[1] to Auguste Lumière

Chalais (Meudon), 4 January 1899

 Auguste Lumière
 Monplaisir, Lyon

Dear Sir,

 Upon his recent return from a mission, Major Hirschauer has given me an account of his conversation with you last month. I should first like to take this opportunity of thanking you for your kind welcome to this senior officer.

In brief, Major Hirschauer spoke with you about two matters:

The first and most important is the question of creating stockpiles in all the fortified towns of 18x24 autochromatic plates. You have agreed to take responsibility for making up lots, amounting to sixty dozen plates for each fort, starting with the four main forts in the East: Verdun, Epinal, Toul and Belfort.

These lots will be packaged by you, in waterproof crates, to be kept closed in the Engineers' stores in each of these forts, with every necessary precaution, and renewed every six months. Needless to say, all packing, transport and other expenses will be paid by the Ministry of War.

In other words, you agree to losing the usage of these stocks, without compensation. This generous solution pays testimony to your honour and your patriotism.

I am writing to thank you and also to establish the exact extent of your services, given free of charge, so that I can inform the Minister. I should be grateful if you would confirm this agreement.

The other matter discussed was our wish to embark upon cinemato-graphic research here at Chalais to study the motion of the new balloons at a distance. You were kind enough to tell Major Hirschauer that you would agree to loan us one of your machines. I willingly accept this offer and I should be most grateful if you would let me know where and when I could take consignment of this machine.

Yours sincerely,

Ch. Renard

---

1 Photographic invention was of considerable interest to the defence establishment and the army in general, because of the possible applications to topography and strategic observation. The Lumière brothers were often asked to collaborate with the armed forces and always agreed, but they refused ever to regard this activity as profit-making. See letters of 22 May and 4 June 1918.

Aimé Laussédat to Auguste Lumière

Paris, 4 February 1899

Dear Monsieur Auguste,

Your two large pictures[1] have just arrived. I am having them unwrapped and they will be in place tomorrow, but I do not want to lose a moment before thanking you for the speed with which you have consented to allow me to show your magnificent achievements to the public.

I must admit that it will be difficult to move pictures this large to the lecture theatre for Monsieur Wallon's lecture, but at least he will be able to invite his audience to look into the gallery where they are to be installed, which is indeed where they will be admired every day the museum is open to the public.

About our lectures, I can tell you that they are as successful as those we arranged in the winter of 1891–2 and that our great lecture theatre, which has a capacity for 700 people, has never been fuller. We are turning people away. Does this not at last provide evidence that we should be instituting a higher photography course? If this second attempt does not win the day for us, it will be very sad, but my conscience will rest easy: so should yours, and that of all the scientists and professionals who have been unstinting in the lectures they have given here.

Please give my kind regards and my wife's best wishes to your wife and your brother's wife, and shake your brother Louis' hand for me, and your younger brother if he is with you, and please all send my regards and all our wishes to La Ciotat.

Yours truly,

Laussédat

7p.m.: This letter will not go until tomorrow but I wanted to tell you that your two magnificent views of Egypt are in place and that they are most striking. In fact, I have been prevented from adding these few lines by interesting but ill-timed visitors.

1 No doubt giant photographs, illustrating the lecture on enlargement given Sunday 26 March 1899 by E. Wallon, physics teacher at the Lycée Janson-de-Sailly in Paris.

Camille Flammarion[1] to Louis Lumière

Paris, 4 April 1899

Dear Monsieur Lumière,

Returning to Paris on 20 March I took to my bed with 'flu. I think I caught it at the Gare de Lyon. There was an icy wind. Passengers were kept waiting half an hour before the Marseille train came in. Today is my first day back at work and my first task is to let you know how delighted I was to make the acquaintance of a scientist and artist such as yourself, and how pleased the Council of the Société Astronomique de France[2] is to count you among its founder members. As the April bulletin was not yet printed when I returned, we have inscribed you at the head of the list of introductions so that you can be nominated at the general meeting of 12 April next. It is pleasant to have men of spirit and men of heart at one's side.

I hope that your brother-in-law's condition has not worsened and that the attention he is receiving, together with medical science which has made such progress, will bring back the happy days of his lost health. I very much hope so because the little I have glimpsed of your family gave an impression of sweet harmony and luminous happiness.

I am sorry to write at such length, particularly as I know you receive hundreds of letters every day. I renew my sincere affection for you and shake both your hands.

Flammarion

You have probably received our volume for 1898. The list of founder members is at the head of the general list, p. 553.

1 A self-made man, Camille Flammarion entered the house of Le Verrier as a book-keeper's clerk in 1858. Interested in spiritualism, he rapidly started publishing works on the subject, before setting up a small observatory in Paris in 1882. He studied the comets, eclipses, sun-spots and went up in balloons. In 1882, he founded the *Revue Mensuelle d'Astronomie*. He was a talented popular scientist and his bestseller, *Astronomie Populaire* (1880), was the first success of his brother, the publisher. Flammarion is still one of the leading Paris publishing houses.
2 Nineteenth-century scientists and inventors gathered in highly active societies which provided a meeting place for men of very different backgrounds. In any case, astronomy provided a bridge between scientists like Flammarion and photographic experts, as is shown by the instance of the photographic revolver, invented by the astronomer, Janssen, for the observation of Venus.

The Director of Higher Education to Auguste Lumière

Paris, 1 August 1899

Monsieur Aug. Lumière
Correspondent of the Ministry of Public Education
Re: Notice of appointment
Enc: Details of function

Dear Sir,

I am pleased to inform you that, by a decree (details of which you will find enclosed), I have appointed you 'Correspondent of the Ministry of Public Education'.[1] This decision has been taken in consultation with the

Committee on historical and scientific research and it is my intention that you should be closely involved in its work.

I should be grateful if you would be kind enough to inform my services of anything which seems to you to be of likely interest to the various sub-committees of the committee. Allow me to express a wish that your information will reach us on a frequent basis and that you will annotate or comment upon your manuscripts, as this often facilitates comprehension of texts.

I should also be grateful if you would answer any requests for information which members of the Committee and members of my department may wish to send you. In this way, you will be of considerable assistance to us in our work and you will justify the Committee's confidence in you which led it to recommend you to me for appointment.

I trust, Sir, that your participation will be an active one. I know that you will want to justify the Minister and the Committee's confidence in your work and thus earn, in two years' time, a renewal of the office you are granted today.

Yours faithfully,
The Minister of Public Education and Fine Arts
for the Minister and upon his authority
The Director of Higher Education
Councillor of State
L. Hiaul

1 Auguste Lumière's new function is another example of the Third Republic's emphasis on education.

Etienne-Jules Marey to Messieurs Lumière

Paris, 18 August 1899

Dear Sirs and friends,

I regret that you have decided not to commercialize our device.[1] I should have been pleased to enter into closer relations with you, but I understand your reasons; perhaps I shall be able to interest you in some other invention one day.

I am most grateful to you for the generous assistance which you have been good enough to bring to the work of the physiological research station. The 10,000 francs which you have contributed will immediately be put to good use. When you are ready to transfer the funds, you may apply to the Crédit Lyonnais who will send the money to Branch A in Passy, where my account no. is 3127.

I am about to go on holiday for a few weeks' rest. Class XII[2] will not meet until early October. I hope to see you there and to have an opportunity of thanking you in person.

Marey

1 Marey's assistant, Demenÿ, had, a few years earlier, tried to interest the Lumière brothers in a system for driving film through a camera, known as the Demenÿ camshaft. They had turned down the offer, preferring their own claw system. Marey's chronophotograph was an earlier invention, but recent improvements had encouraged him to ask the Lumière brothers to take it up. They would appear to have softened the blow of their refusal by making a contribution to Marey's research costs – a tribute perhaps, to the fact that his chronophotograph was an ancestor of the Cinematograph.
2 A government committee at the Ministry of Industry, appointed to evaluate the merits of various technical and scientific research projects for the purposes of grant aid.

A. Perrin to Auguste Lumière

Lyon, 26 December 1899

Honoured Sir and Dear Colleague,

At the General Assembly of 12 October, Monsieur Marc Levy gave me the sum of five hundred francs for our Society and on your behalf. In the name of the Board, I am writing to thank you for this generous gift which will be of benefit to the unfortunates, deprived by nature and by providence, whom we support.

Thanks to your moral and material assistance, our young pupils will receive still further support. You shall have earned their thanks as well as ours. The Board as a whole was particularly touched by the extent of your solicitude for our blind and deaf-mute wards.[1]

Yours sincerely,
The Chairman
A. Perrin

1 There are innumerable letters testifying to Auguste Lumière's generosity. He was a great philanthropist as well as a doctor and researcher. For instance, during the 1914–18 war, he X-rayed his wounded patients at the Hôtel-Dieu hospital in Lyon at his own expense. This cost him the enormous sum of 200,000 gold francs.

Aimé Laussédat to Auguste Lumière

Paris, 8 May 1900

Dear Monsieur Auguste,

Your father and your brother Louis have informed me about your experiments in telephotography. I am particularly interested in this subject. If you had a specimen that you would authorize for inclusion in our exhibition on photographic measurement at Class XII, I should be most grateful. The point of the exhibition is to try to show this country's leading part in the various types of topographical photography. We were delighted, my wife and I, to catch a glimpse of you, if only for . . .

[*The second page of the letter has been lost.*]

Aimé Laussédat to Auguste Lumière

Paris, 18 May 1900

Dear Monsieur Auguste,

I am sorry that your experiments in telephotography do not yet seem worthy of public display but I understand that you, like the rest of your family, should only want to show perfect results. I have received the photograph of five pleasant colleagues which your father had promised me. Please thank him on my behalf.

We should be delighted, my wife and I, if you came to see us with Madame Auguste Lumière,[1] as you say you will.

Your old friend,

Laussédat

1 Marguerite Winckler (1874–1963), daughter of Léocadie and Alphonse Winckler. She married Auguste on 31 August 1893.

Etienne-Jules Marey to the Minister of Trade

Paris, 22 May 1900

Dear Sir,

If there is one name that everyone misses now that it is no longer on the list of the judges for Class XII, it is that of one of the directors of the Lumière establishment in Lyon, the most important [photographic firm] in France and even in Europe.

Messieurs Lumière are not merely manufacturers and businessmen of the first order, but they are also distinguished scientists.

They invented the Cinematograph. They have also made important discoveries in chemistry. They apply their fertile minds to most varied subject matter. It would be hard to find a more indisputably competent judge to appreciate the various products of Class XII.

In addition, the position of committee member to which you have been kind enough to nominate me is becoming something of a burden, because of the numerous duties which I have somewhat imprudently taken on.

As Chairman of a committee on hygiene and physiology, which will, all summer, judge physical fitness competitions, I shall often have to choose between conflicting obligations.

If, as permanent committee member, you were to replace me with Monsieur Louis Lumière,[1] you would be rendering a double favour. The committee would gain in competence; and I should be more free to serve the interests of Physical Education and Hygiene for which my research has better prepared me.

Yours faithfully,

Jules Marey

Fellow of the Institut

President of the Academy of Medicine and of Class XII and the Exhibition

1 Biographers and historians have suggested that Lumière and Marey quarrelled, but this letter is evidence of the good relations between them. They did not always make the same scientific choices, but both recognized that Marey's Chronophotograph was the ancestor of the Cinematograph and they held each other in high esteem.

Louis Ducos du Hauron to Monsieur Lumière

Charenton, 4 July 1900

My dear Sir,

I am writing to apologize most sincerely for not thanking you sooner for your posting me stiff film. I have just spent two weeks in bed with a fairly serious complaint, which is hardly surprising as, for the last year, my house has really been more of a hospital. I have been so hard at work over the last few months that I made myself ill and I am only just beginning to take things in hand once more.

Our colour plates have given us a great deal of bother. From one day to the next everything started going wrong. Failure is always in the details. The principle itself is perfect. Phew! Today everything is back to normal. With our 'Melans A', we obtain the three negatives of the one subject in a single exposure of 8 to 10 seconds, with just one lens. The resulting colours are splendid.

– the red screen frame uses your ortho B plates

– the green screen frame uses your ortho A plates (with a yellow screen when the negative is exposed)

– the violet screen frame uses your yellow label plates (but this screen is dispensed with when the negative is exposed)

Amateur photographers seem to be acquiring more and more interest in colour photography and I know that if we do not succeed, for lack of capital, others will triumph simply by taking over our business lock, stock and barrel.

The most recent machines are selling well; amateurs like knowing their efforts are definitely going to bear fruit.

The police department has adopted this machine for its anthropometric service, after a series of successful trials. It works not just for three-colour negatives but also for any type of printing, and for composite views too. Our modest display seemed to attract the interest of the judges. What will become of it all? I do not know. But I do know that we are receiving inquiries and orders from all over the place. We shall not be able to satisfy them because our works are simple and really just private. They will not cater for regular production.

I hope that, given all this, you will forgive my being so slow to thank you for your kindness. Your god-daughter is growing up very well and I am told she is very pretty (please forgive the father in me). As to my wife, her health still leaves much to be desired and you will understand that I cannot afford to send her to Switzerland again, which is what Doctor Richardière, who has been looking after her since the start of her illness, has recommended.

Yours sincerely,
L. Ducos du Hauron

Please pass on my regards to your brother, whose acquaintance I was pleased to make just recently.

Louis Ducos du Hauron to Monsieur Lumière

Charenton, Tuesday

Dear Sir,

It is with great pleasure that we see a time come when at last we shall have the pleasure of making your acquaintance. Please just send us a word, as you would with your own family, to let us know when you are coming, and to tell us what day you are lunching or dining with us.

Our establishment is simple but none the less comfortable and it would certainly be with pleasure that we should put you up.

We have a nice room for you and you would have the run of the house, only fifteen minutes from the centre of Paris.

Yours sincerely,

L. Ducos du Hauron

Etienne Jules Marey to Auguste Lumière

Paris, 3 January 1901

Dear Sir and friend,

Thank you very much for your good wishes and please accept my best wishes to you and your family. We had hoped to see your brother Louis at our last meeting of the committee for the Class XII, but he did not come.

I had been hoping for some time that one of you would come to Paris so I could bid you farewell until the spring. I am leaving for Italy in the middle of January with all my family and we shall remain in Naples until the beginning of May. I need a rest and a change of scenery. In any case, I am taking some work with me.

Your brother showed me a recording device which I am sure will turn out very useful if you can get it to run regularly.

My international committee is now up and running at the physiological research station. Its purpose is to invent or adopt the best instruments and to try to standardize physiological methods. If you manage to complete your blackened film-strip recorder, I know that it will be well-received.

Your letter led me to hope that I might see you and your brother before my departure.

Yours truly,

Marey

Etienne Jules Marey to Monsieur Lumière

14 June 1901

Dear Sir and friend,

The session of the Académie des Science was cancelled because of the deaths of Hermite and Chatin![1]

Consequently, Monsieur Gautier[2] was unable to present your note, as he had been meaning to do. He will present it tomorrow at the Académie de Médecine and will request that it is put before a committee consisting of himself and Tournier. On Monday 21st, Gautier will present the note at the Académie des Sciences.

I am off to Italy in two days' time and I hope to see you upon my return in two and a half months. Thank you for your interest in my work – your brother's and your own.

Yours sincerely,
Marey

1 Charles Hermite, Professor at the Collège de France, at the Faculty of Science in Paris and at the Ecole Polytechnique, President of the Geometry section of the Académie des Sciences from 1890. Gaspard-Adolphe Chatin, elected President of the Botany section of the Académie des Sciences in 1897, Professor of Botany at the School of Pharmacy, member of the Académie de Médecine and the Société d'Agriculture.
2 Emile-Justin-Armand Gautier, medical doctor and chemist, Professor of Medical Chemistry at the Faculty of Medicine, member of the Académie de Médecine. Elected President of Chemistry section in 1911.

Etienne Jules Marey to Auguste Lumière

Paris, 29 August 1902

Dear Auguste,

The study of hermophenyl[1] has put me in touch with my old friend Fournier. He told me five days ago that, at last, he was going to be able to conduct new experiments. I expect, therefore, that I shall have some results to communicate to you soon. As soon as I can, I shall call on him. Business is booming. I have been told that I am to get a decent annual grant. Which is precisely why I am running around for money to get my building finished and to equip it.

Hallopeau says that in any case there will be an election to the Professorship at the Faculty and that will give him his moment of free speech.

Perhaps Fournier will be in a position to give his opinion sooner than that.

We are all well here. My young niece is wonderful, a bit of joy in the house.

Best regards.

E. Marey

1 A cure for impetigo.

R. Dubois to Auguste Lumière

15 July 1903

My dear friend,

Congratulations on your excellent work,[1] which will be of real use since it clears the decks of a mass of cumbersome and erroneous documentation. Normally speaking, the organism's natural defences suffice to keep intoxication at bay, within reasonable limits of course. If nutrition was seriously affected by poisons or medicines, which usually amount to the same thing, would we be able to stand up to tobacco, coffee, alcohol and all the other drugs? It is only when natural defences are missing that medicines modify things, for better or for worse – often for worse. *Natura medicatrix*!

You are constructing a Villa Lumière and it is a great pleasure to see (this for Monsieur Louis, your learned colleague).

I am so sorry I was unable to attend the wedding Mass for Mademoiselle France[2] and Charles Winckler. Please pass on my regrets to your family.

Yours sincerely,

R. Dubois

Would you be kind enough to give me a line of introduction or to send a letter of recommendation to Monsieur Vidal, a landowner at Port-de-Bouc (Bouches-du-Rhône) who is, I think, a teacher at the Beaux-Arts in Paris (decorative arts, I believe), who knows you and is also a friend of your father's? I have some work to do on his land and his goodwill would be invaluable.

Yours.

R.D.

1 Auguste Lumière was, in his day, one of the great experts on anaphylaxia.
2 France Lumière (1863–1924) sister of Auguste and Louis, married Charles Winckler on 9

1 Antoine Lumière   2 his wife, Jeanne-Joséphine Castille
3 and their sons, Louis and Auguste

4 Louis Lumière

5 Auguste Lumière

6 & 7 The Lumière cinematograph: the camera on its wooden stand, the inside of the camera showing its circular shutter and . . .

8 . . . film winding through the mechanism.

9 Installing the cinematograph for a projection.

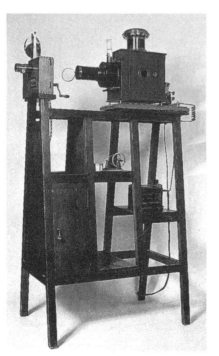

10 All set up and ready for projection.

11 A film can, with the Lumière name embossed.

12 A poster for the Lumière cinematograph showing *The Gardener Takes a Shower.*

13 A photogramme of *The Gardener Takes a Shower.*

14 A photogramme of the first Lumière film:
Workers Leaving the Lumière Factory.

15 A photogramme of *Lunch for Baby*, with Auguste Lumière,
his wife Marguerite and their daughter Andrée.

16 The Lumière house in Montplaisir in Lyons.

17 Henri Lumière during the First World War.

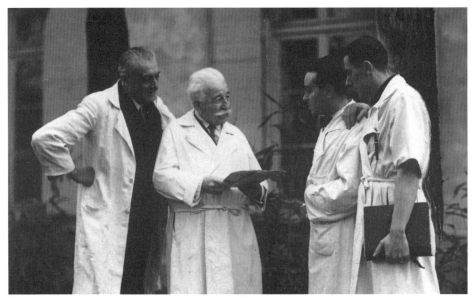

18 In the gardens at the hospital at Bon Abri: Doctors Vigne and Beaulaton with Auguste Lumière.

19 Louis and Auguste Lumière.

July 1903. After his sisters Rose and Marguerite, and his brother Jules, Charles Winckler was the fourth child of Alphonse Winckler, brewer in Lyon, to marry one of the children of Antoine and Jeanne-Joséphine Lumière.

Jules Nicolas[1] to Auguste Lumière

9 July 1904

My dear Auguste,

Thank you very much for the set of shelves which you and Louis were good enough to send me. It is superb and I am very pleased with it and I am sure that it will be doubly appreciated by my fiancée because it is so fine and because it was a present from a such a good and affectionate friend. You know, but I wish to reiterate it, how fond of you and devoted I am.

Please also pass on my thanks to Madame Auguste Lumière.

Yours truly,

Nicolas

1 A scholar of medicine and pharmacy, Jules Nicolas collaborated closely with Auguste Lumière on research into persulphate alkali, known as persodine.

Antoine Lumière to Isabelle [Petitrenaud][1]

Paris, 27 December 1904

My dear Isabelle,

Since you want to hear from me, here you are.

You say you are bored: well, then, look around you and it won't take you long in this day and age to find people more unfortunate than yourself. Don't complain about your fate, which would seem enviable to many people.

I hope this advice will give you some peace and that you follow it in the future so that life will be seem better to you.

I work as hard as I can to be able to honour those commitments I have and I don't complain though the years are starting to weigh down on my legs.

I have just been in America where I spent three months and where I have to return in a little while (about May).

I give you a big hug and shout: don't complain.

A. Lumière

Auguste Lumière to Claudius Poulaillon[1]

[Addressed to the factory at Burlington (USA)]

My dear Claudius,

We agree with you about replying to Monsieur des Garennes. Go ahead. About the lines of dots you have observed on the plates, are they caused by dripping from the emulsion tube? In that case, the emulsion filter system needs checking, as do the skins.

If, on the other hand, these dots do not correspond to where the emulsion outlet is, then you should check the glass rinsing – what about the brushes used to clean the glass? They get clogged up with CaFl,[2] and this can drop on to the glass. Another place to check is the sponging around the cylinders, and if necessary, replace it.

As to the unevenness of the warmer tones, that is hardly surprising. They don't keep well in Lyon, particularly in the summer. Only prepare what you actually need, and then keep it in a cool, dry place.

When you dry them, make sure the draught does not blow too hard . . . Too much air can affect the cleanliness of the plates. Every time the ventilation alters, there is a danger that particles of dust will be dislodged and cause spots.

The note about anti-trust laws which you have sent us is most interesting. Please keep us abreast.

Louis is at La Ciotat. I am in a hurry, so I shall not tell you any more just now. I was anxious not to hold up the information you are requesting.

A big hug, Claudius.

Aug. Lumière

I am having citrate and bromide paper sent off to you so you can decide whether there is any business in sending it off from here and selling it.

1 Manager of the Lumière factory at Burlington (USA).
2 Calcium fluoride.

Violle[1] to Messieurs Lumière

Paris, 25 January 1905

Dear Sirs,

Thank you for your study of the direct blackening effects on sensitive paper of scarcely refractible rays of the spectrum.[2] I am all the more grateful to you because I know that the operation is a difficult one. Did I tell you that the paper could be very slow, that it was an advantage if its surface was matt black, and that, consequently, it would be heat, not light, that affected it. This is in fact an exercise in actinometry,[3] exchanging paper designed, as far as possible, to absorb the energy of the sun's rays for a smoke-blackened thermometer.

Thank you.

Yours,

J. Violle

1 Physics teacher and researcher at the Conservatoire National des Arts et Métiers.
2 This tells us that the Lumière brothers were still conducting experiments in photochemistry as late as 1905. It is worth remembering however that though autochromes were patented in 1903, they were not put on the market until 1907 because of the difficulties involved in manufacturing them industrially.
3 An actinometer was a small instrument designed to measure the intensity of the sun's rays.

Mathieu Jaboulay[1] to Monsieur Lumière

Lyon, 10 September 1905

Dear Sir,

I am writing to abuse your extreme kindness and to ask at what time I may come to you in order to get my microscope photographs reprinted.

Yours sincerely,

Jaboulay

1 Inventor of neurosurgery, Mathieu Jaboulay (1860–1903) was appointed head surgeon at the Hôtel-Dieu hospital in Lyon in 1896.

Finance Office for Schools to Messieurs Lumière

Lyon, 30 January 1906

Messieurs Lumière and Sons
rue St Victor
Monplaisir

I write on behalf of the Committee for the Finance Office to thank you for the generous contribution which you offer in your letter of the 23rd towards the organization of festivities at the Town Hall in favour of our Municipal Charitable Office for Sending Children to the Mountains. Your generosity extends to all parts of our programme, to subscriptions and to the attraction of your wonderful Cinematograph.

The Committee expresses its gratitude and informs you that we shall let you know a week or so ahead of time the times and days when cinematographic projections have been arranged.

Yours, etc. . . .

Jacquinth to Auguste Lumière

Lyon, 23 November 1907

Dear Auguste Lumière,

I am taking the liberty of explaining to you in writing, which is easier for me, the particular situation I find myself in and the considerable request which arises out of it.

For the last five years, I have had intimate relations with Mademoiselle Chartier, currently at 18 rue d'Aguesseau and originally from Roanne. When I first met her, she was a seamstress in a factory; our relations were, at first, not out of the ordinary; they became closer about a year later, when her health began to fail her. Very nervous, although strong-willed, she could almost no longer bear to wear a corset or to sit at a sewing machine. She was only able to work intermittently. Very fond of her, I tried to help as far as I could, but I had no means, particularly not at that time. Out of my depth, I got into debt. Our problems reached crisis point when she became pregnant last year, and gave birth to a little girl, who is with a wet-nurse near Aix. Against my will, I decided not to marry her then, because of the financial straits I was in, and because of my family's hostility, which I could predict. For about a year, I was her sole support and my debts amounted to some 2000 francs. I have to say on this subject that when, just over a year ago, Monsieur Louis arranged for your father to lend me 500 francs, the explanations I gave were true, but I did not dare tell him the most serious part, which I am telling you now.

In short, I have about 1600 francs worth of debts; I am the father of a little girl nine months old; I should like to put my situation in order. I have hinted at the state of things to my family but the main obstacle is the sum of 2000 francs which I need to pay my debts and to get started in a basic way.

The object of this letter, as you have gathered, is to appeal to your kindness, to grant me the monetary means I need. If you would lend me the necessary amount, I should repay you whatever interest you named and I would undertake to return the debt by annual payments of 500 francs. You would be saving me from an oppressive situation, against which I have been struggling for more than two years, and you would be doing an inestimable service.

I am ready to give you, by word of mouth, any further information you may require. I should like to convince you that it would charitable to do this above all towards my friend and my child; to convince you, also, that if I have incurred debts for a woman it is not out of a taste for luxury or frivolous expenditure, but only out of duty and to provide her with the basics, though often not even that.

You know now the distress in which I find myself and the hope I place in you. Despite the amount, I do have hope that you will agree and above all that, if you are not able to provide me with the solution I desire, at least my confession, which I have made after many months of hesitating, will not lessen whatever little confidence or esteem I may inspire in you.

Hoping for a favourable response,

Yours truly,

Jacquinth

Society for Artistic Photography, Moscow, to Auguste Lumière

Moscow, 14/27 February 1908

Monsieur Auguste Lumière
Lyon-Monplaisir

Sir!

Wishing with all its heart to associate itself with the worldwide expressions of gratitude to your learned research which have so powerfully contributed to the advancement of photographic science, the Society for Artistic Photography of Moscow, following a vote of its general assembly on 23 January last, has the honour of inviting you to accept the title of Honorary Member, which is the highest distinction accorded in our statutes.

We hope, Sir, that you will accept this humble expression of our gratitude, which we are proud to offer you.

Yours sincerely,
The Chairman: C. Hipping
The Secretary: Mandesi

Secretary-General Van der Kindere and Chairman Van Bever to Auguste Lumière

Brussels, 1 April 1908

Monsieur A. Lumière
Lyon-Monplaisir

Dear Sir,

We have the honour of informing you that at its General Assembly last Sunday, the Belgian Association of Photography elected you an honorary member. We hope you will accept this title, which is attributable to any person who, by their work or their writing, has made a contribution to the progress of photography.

It was the desire of our Board to pay tribute to the eminent services which you have rendered photographic science by nominating you at the last General Assembly and our members unanimously ratified this proposal.

Yours faithfully,
The Secretary-General
Monsieur Van der Kindere
The Chairman
Alf. Van Bever

Camille Flammarion to Louis Lumière

Paris, 30 May 1908

Dear Monsieur Lumière,

Last year, after the magnificent *Illustration* lecture, you were kind enough to imply that you might this year agree to attend our Sun Fete at the Eiffel Tower. We have written colour photography into the programme, which is a splendid subject. Monsieur Moupillard has agreed to give the lecture and you were kind enough to offer him the assistance of your projectionist. I want to thank you on behalf of the Society. But I also wish to remind you of your gracious intention, as expressed last year, and invite you to our banquet. If you would not mind saying a few words to introduce our lecturer, and the invention, we would be delighted.

Our board includes, among others, Messieurs Deslandres, of the Institut, Director of the Observatory at Meudon who is the President; Baillaud, of the Institut, Director of the Observatory at Paris who is Vice-President; Count Labaune-Pleuinel; Puiseux; Lairaut; Bouquet de la Gyre; Poincaré; Lippmann; Caspari.[1]

The fete will take place on Saturday 20 June. Dinner is at 7p.m. precisely.

I hope, and we hope, that we shall have the pleasure of applauding two scientists and two brothers, at least by the presence of one of them.

Yours sincerely,

Flammarion

1 Edouard-Benjamin Baillaud (1848–1934), astronomer, participated in various research programmes, including one that produced a definitive topographical map of the sky. Directed the observatory at Toulouse, then Paris. Anatole Bouquet de la Gyre, hydrographical engineer, sent to Campbell Island (New Zealand) in 1874 to observe the passage of Venus. He failed to do this because of the mist. Started again at Puelsla, 1882. He established the parallax value of the sun for the Bureau of Longitudes. Edouard Cascara (1840–1918) Hydrographical engineer in France, Guadeloupe and Indochina. President of the Société Astronomique de France, 1905. Henri Deslandres (1853–1948) physicist and astronomer, studied the sun. Head of four expeditions to study total eclipses of the sun in Senegal (1893), Japan (1896), Spain (1900 and 1905). Director of the observatory at Meudon (1908) and Meudon and Paris (united) 1927.

Joseph-Simon Galliéni[1] to Monsieur Lumière[2]

Lyon, 27 June 1908

My dear Monsieur Lumière,

My daughter and her little daughter are staying with me. Remembering your kind offer, I am writing to ask whether you would mind photographing both, with my wife, according to your new colour process.

If my request does not strike you as indiscreet, tell me at what time, Monday or Tuesday morning, they could all three come to your studio, unless you would rather send a car for them. I will do my best to attend but I may not be able to do so because of my obligations.

I apologise.

Yours truly,

Galliéni

1 Prisoner in the Franco-Prussian war of 1870, Galliéni (1849–1916) earned distinctions in colonial wars in Senegal and Niger, then negotiated a treaty by which France earned a monopoly of all trade in the upper Niger area. He was Governor of the Sudan (1886) and Tonkin (1893–5), then Governor-General of Madagascar, (1896–1905). As a member of the High Command in 1908, and Military Governor of Paris in 1914, he played a decisive part in the battle of the Marne, and was Minister of War from 1915 to 1916. He was posthumously elevated to the rank of Marshal of France in 1921.
2 Probably Louis.

Berjereau to Auguste Lumière

Villeurbanne,[1] 31 December 1908

Dear Auguste Lumière,

If I am a veterinary surgeon and Municipal Inspector at Villeurbanne, it is thanks to you. That is why my gratitude goes out to a man I respect and whom I cannot praise too highly. Without you and without your generosity, which allowed my advancement in 1902, I should not have been able to settle in Villeurbanne; I was already aiming at this job, which I could not have obtained unless I exercised my profession in this borough.

It was only right that I should recall your good deeds, and the fond memory I shall cherish all my life of you and your family.

Yours truly,
Berjereau
Veterinary Surgeon and Municipal Inspector

1 Part of Lyon.

Telegram from Chairmen De Metz and De Trafft to Messieurs Lumière

Kiev, 12 January 1909, 4.20

Participants in second Russian Photographic Congress gathered in Kiev branch of the Russian Imperial Technical Society after conference by Professor De Metz on various processes of colour photography congratulate you on your felicitous and ingenious solution to this interesting and difficult problem.

Chairman of the Technical Society: De Metz
Chairman of the Congress: De Trafft

Henriot to Messieurs Lumière

Paris, 10 February 1910

I have been a faithful customer of yours for the last fifteen years or so and now I am indebted to you. Since I speak of years, it was about twenty years ago or so, I think, I had the pleasure of being introduced to you. I am sure you have forgotten, but I have not. It was at a banquet for journalists – the Parisian association or the Republican association, I belong to both – at the Grand Hôtel. One of us announced, 'Sarah Bernhardt!' then 'Lumière!' and the room was lit up. As chance would have it, thanks to Doctor Vigne[1] I am often called upon to provide sketches in praise of your innumerable merits in various publications, and you are kind enough to heap photographic plates on me, plates I know and admire. As soon as you launched your autochromes, I was the first to try them out and (he says modestly!) to succeed.

You send me delicious products: I must send you mine. The finest hen in the world, even Madame Simone, can only lay its own eggs. I am sending two sketches I water-coloured for you as soon as I received your package, for which many thanks. I am as sensitive as your plates to your agreeable methods.

Yours truly

The sketches are going registered.

Henriot

1 Dr Vigne was a collaborator of Auguste's. They spent every afternoon calling on patients together. In 1904, he appointed Auguste editor of a publication, *L'Avenir Médical*, which was designed to inform the general public and the medical profession of the results of research conducted in the laboratories of their clinic. In 1942, he published a hagiographic work called *Vie laborieuse et féconde d'Auguste Lumière* (Durand-Girard), dedicated to Henri Lumière, Auguste's son.

Aide-de-camp Bourré[1] to Auguste Lumière

Paris, 27 February 1910

Dear Sir,

I have been instructed by His Serene Highness the Prince of Monaco to inform you that you are invited to attend the inauguration of the Monaco Oceanographic Museum[2] which will take place on 29 March 1910.

Various scientific committee meetings, lectures and festivities will take place in the Principality on this occasion, lasting four days, until the evening of Friday 1 March. A limited number of rooms, with board, have been reserved by the Board of the Oceanographic Institute from 28 March on, and they will be available to guests, free of charge, on demand. If you should wish to take advantage of this benefit, I should be grateful if you would inform Monsieur Louis Mayer, Manager and Secretary, Oceanographic Institute, 2 rue Sogelbach, Paris, before 15 March. After this date, no requests will be receivable.

Further, you are requested to show this letter of invitation to the Secretariat of the Oceanographic Museum upon arrival in Monaco, in order to receive the various invitations which you will need during your stay.

Yours faithfully,
H. Bourré

1 Aide-de-camp to the Prince of Monaco in 1906 and in 1907, and head of his scientific cabinet. Bourré took part in the prince's oceanographic expeditions from 1906 to 1914, and was a member of the committee for the perfection of the Oceanographic Institute in Monaco from 1923 until his death.
2 The Lumière brothers subsidized research that was sometimes very different from their own. *Le Siècle de Lyon* wrote on 24 January 1896: 'Messrs Lumière, distinguished scientists, who have established at Monplaisir the splendid industrial plant that we all know, received yet another ministerial visit the other day; they have furnished indispensable funding for marine research into coastal, maritime and trench fauna.'

Headmaster of La Martinière[1] to Auguste Lumière

Lyon, 3 May 1910

Dear Sir,

At a time when we are about to send to Brussels our entry to the International Show, I have the pleasure of telling you, on behalf of the Board of La Martinière, how grateful we are for the kind generosity with which you have permitted us to put this entry on a scale and an artistic footing worthy of this great institution which is honoured to count you among its directors. In addition, I should like to express my own personal thanks.

Yours faithfully,
Headmaster of La Martinière
Wierenberger

1 A *lycée*, or grammar school, founded by the City authorities in the nineteenth century, with a specifically technical vocation. The founder was a Major Martin. Both Auguste and

Louis Lumière were pupils. This letter is addressed to Auguste as a director of the establishment.

Rector of the University to Messieurs Lumière

Lyon, 15 February 1912

Dear Sirs,

Professor Guiart[1] tells me that you have been kind enough to donate a cinematographic machine[2] to the Parasite Research Unit.

It is my pleasure to express the University's gratitude for this generous gift, which bears witness to your enlightened interest in higher education. The Board of the Medical Faculty is particularly grateful to you for your open-handedness and has asked me to thank you on its behalf.

Yours faithfully,

The Rector, Chairman of the Board of the University

Mouly

1 Professor of Medical Natural History at the University of Lyon from 1906 to 1940, Professor Guiart (1870–1965) was a founder member of the French Society for History and Medicine and Curator of the Historical Museum of the Faculty at Lyon (1920). After the First World War, he organized anti-malarial hospitals.
2 Clément Maurice had used a Cinematograph to teach students of surgery. This letter marks a new departure, in that it marks an extension of its use to other medical disciplines.

Jean Marie Casimir Ducos du Hauron to Auguste Lumière

3 April 1912

Dear Sir,

How can I express my feelings and those of my family on learning your act of generosity, as I did when I read your letter this morning! This gesture coming from you does not of course surprise us; for there have been others like it from you to us; but let me tell you that we are, once again, very profoundly touched.

In the cruel times we are witnessing, what calm, what peace of mind, you have given us. I cannot find the words to express our gratitude. I can only say, in my name, in the name of all my family, Thank you! Poor dear girls, how grateful they will be for all that you have done for them!

We are most grateful to you.

I do not wish to be forgotten by any of your family.

Alexis Carrel[1] to [Louis] Lumière

New York, 22 October 1912

Dear Monsieur Lumière,

A few days ago, I met a New York photographer called Mr Gentle. He showed me portraits and landscapes made with your autochrome plates which are truly magnificent.

He tells me he alters the development process somewhat. I thought this might be of interest to you, so I asked him to write to you. Please give my regards to your brother and to your family. I very much enjoyed my time with you in Lyon last summer.

Yours truly,
Alexis Carrel

1 Alexis Carrel (1873–1944), surgeon, physiologist, originally from Lyon. In 1898, while working with Auguste, he performed the first arterial stitches. He conducted many experiments involving blood vessels, including grafts and transplants; he also experimented with the production of hen embryo tissue. In 1912, he won the Nobel Prize for Medicine. In 1936, he published *L'Homme, cet inconnu*.

Jules Papon to Monsieur Lumière

Lyon, 19 February 1913

Sir,

I have not had an opportunity of telling you of my gratitude for your kind interest expressed to Monsieur Collet[1] but, busy as I am, I want to convey, at least by these few lines, my thanks to you.

In the midst of all the problems involved in starting up a charity, especially when one founds it alone, it is precious comfort to have the approval of someone as competent and influential as yourself. And I am always willing to respond to such well-meaning sentiments by offering my work for the benefit of your charity whenever it may find a use for it.

If I understood your kind secretary correctly, your well-meaning interest might even extend to giving me material support. I have some very burdensome obligations just at present, not to mention my charitable efforts which go back thirteen years, because I am setting up my first establishment for advanced tubercular patients. I have had to undertake about 20,000 francs of building work at St Genis l'Argentière, most of which is not paid off yet. And I shall not eliminate this debt with what I charge: 2 francs 50 per day.

It would be most desirable for generous liberalities to come to my assistance. But your charity, Sir, is, I believe, already overburdened with works of all kinds and from what I know – I am sure only a small proportion of what is – I am afraid that you will not be able to find room for my poor foundation. I do not dare send you a formal request. I leave it to you to see what may be possible . . . If this possibility existed, I could only be extremely grateful for whatever you would be able to do for me.[2]

Yours faithfully,
Jules Papon

1 Collet was Auguste's personnal business manager. He later became French ambassador to Paraguay.
2 Auguste Lumière was famous for his research into tuberculosis. He did, however, believe, somewhat unfortunately, that this illness was not contagious, and thus sided with those who, like Louis Pasteur, thought that 'the sickness is nothing, the environment is all'.

House of Durillon Bros to Monsieur Lumière

Lyon, 13 July 1916

Monsieur Lumière
Lyon

Dear Sir,

We are completing assembly of a series of your sets of pincers, but since Doctor Nové Josserand's visit is advanced by one day because of the national holiday and it is due to take place this morning, we would be grateful if you could check and authorize this set of pincers (enclosed) because the wounded man who is to have it would like to go home as soon as the doctor's visit is over.

We are sorry to bother you for one set of pincers, but this wounded man is interesting and we would like to be kind to him.

Thank you in advance.

Yours sincerely,

Léon Gaumont to Louis Lumière

Paris, 8 March [1917]

Monsieur Louis Lumière
Managing Director of l'Union Photographique Industrielle
Lyon, Monplaisir
Rhône

Dear Sir,

Perhaps you already know that, as a result of the death of G. Demenÿ, a committee composed, in essence, of his pupils, has been formed to honour his memory. This committee has requested my assistance, which I should gladly have given; but having learnt that, in their praiseworthy determination to sing the praises of the deceased, the members of this committee went so far as to try and claim for him the merit of having invented the Cinematograph, I protested and stated that I could not follow them on that point. While I willingly admit all the work that Demenÿ did to assist the birth of our industry, I cannot join those who wish to attribute to him the important Part that belongs to others, among which, first of all, you and your brother.

I believe that my protests have been heard, but nevertheless I feel it may be useful to establish a sort of official history of the genesis of the Cinematograph, so that its true inventors are not substituted, in the public mind, by this person or that, happening to possess energetic friends, whose good faith is not in doubt, but who may give birth to a legend.

I know that the Société Française de Photographie intends to commission a study on this subject. I believe that Monsieur Pantonnier is in charge. I was thinking that you must certainly have interesting documents at hand, of which the first chapter of your 'Résumé of the Scientific Research of Messieurs Auguste and Louis Lumière' must give only a brief glimpse. My friend, Doctor François Franck, has been good enough to lend me the copy of this work which you had sent to him and I have read it with a great deal of interest. Perhaps you would let me know what you can let us have, and to establish an account of this matter, as you must know it so well.[1]

Yours sincerely,
Gaumont

1 Almost everyone who contributed to the invention of the Cinematograph has been accorded sole paternity by zealous admirers, most of whom were acting in good faith. Everything depends on how cinema is defined, whether it means just the projection of a moving picture in a darkened room before an audience, on a large screen, etc.
We do not possess Louis Lumière's response to Léon Gaumont's request, except perhaps a

right of reply which he gave a few years later and is almost certainly based on it (Académie des Sciences de Paris, dossier Lumière):

Right to reply, given by Auguste and Louis Lumière in 1924: We promised ourselves that we would never intervene in discussions relating to the origins of the Cinematograph, in the belief that contemporary documents alone should determine historical truths. But the controversy which has just taken place has stirred our many friends to protest, and we have been subject to such pressure that we shall break our self-imposed silence.

'We should first like to express our surprise at having been condemned by the Académie de Médecine without first having been heard, even though one of us belongs to this worthy assembly, as a national correspondent. Anyway, what seems to be forgotten is that an idea, a desire that something should be created, is not an invention. The only thing which counts is the invention itself. If it were otherwise, everyone would be taking out patents by the dozen. Our late lamented friend, Marey, whose everlasting work we are the first to admire, insisted, to the end of his days, on trying to bring about the impossible ideal of moving picture film without perforations. This way of thinking was the exact opposite of our own. We affirm that the Lumière Cinematograph was invented, not thanks to Marey, but in opposition to the very principles inside which he enclosed himself. We discussed this with him many times, on his visits to us in Lyon after 1895, to give us the benefit, in his own presence, and in our laboratories, of the successive improvements he brought to bear in vain on his machine, as evidenced by this letter he wrote us on 18 August 1899, after one such visit.

'We should also like to point out that no challenge, no disputation, ever came to light during the entire history of the patents we took out in 1895 in every country in the world. Is it not strange that it is thirty years later that these protests arise? Does truth have a limited life?

'Marey many times recognized our rights in this respect, notably in 1897, at the Congress of Scientific Societies at the Sorbonne, where page 140 of the minutes contains this statement: "Auguste and Louis Lumière were the first to achieve this kind of projection with their Cinematograph." In 1895, in the *Bulletin de la Société Française de Photographie*, page 275, he wrote, "because of its inconvenience, the kinetoscope was soon supplanted by Messieurs Lumière's admirable instrument, universally known as the Cinematograph, which was a perfect incarnation of projected chronophotography." And in 1900, Marey's report on the Centenary Museum at the Universal Exhibition, "This instrument (the Lumière Cinematograph) at last provided the solution people had been looking for, that is, projection of a moving picture on to a screen before a numerous audience, giving a perfect illusion of movement. The success of this invention was enormous and has not slowed down yet." Finally, in the Report of the Committee of Class XII on the Universal Exhibition of 1900, of which Marey was Chairman, "By a series of inventions, improvements, successive alterations, the Lumière brothers have transformed methods and machines. They have created cinema." Are not such quotations decisive? Personally, we consider that they constitute a precise and definitive judgement and they are enough for us.

Yours faithfully.
Auguste and Louis Lumière.'

Louis Lumière to the Académie des Sciences

Lyon, 9 February 1918

Dear Sir,[1]

I have the honour to request that the Fellows of the Académie des Sciences include my candidature to one of the vacancies created by the

decree of 23 January 1918 (Application of Sciences to Industry).
   Yours faithfully,
   L. Lumière

1 Addressed to Paul Painlevé (1863–1933), mathematician, Minister of Education 1915–16, and in the year after the war. He was one of the founders of the political movement, Cartel des Gauches, in 1924. He entered the Académie des Sciences in 1900 and presided over it from 1910 onwards.

Louis Lumière to Brigadier Guignard

Lyon, 22 May 1918

Brigadier Guignard
Director of Aviation Factories
Avenue du Trocadéro
Paris

Brigadier,
   I have the honour of informing you of the following:
   In order to supply the SFA's demand for catalytic heaters,[1] I had to, in 1914, establish a small workshop and settle on some unit costs, in order to be able obtain supplies. Given the small number of orders (1000 or 1500 devices per batch), I easily fixed this unit price, and I have not sought to make any profit on these supplies as they were part of our National Defence.
   But since your services, and those of the Automobile Factories, suddenly ordered 30,000 heaters, I found myself industrializing the process, in order to be able to deliver on time. The result is that the unit cost was substantially lower, and I now discover, on closing my accounts, that it is 4 francs 20 less per unit. Since, as I say, I do not wish to make a profit on this order, I should be grateful if you would let me know how and to whom I can repay the state the sum of 75,600 francs, being an economy of 4 francs 20 per unit on the 18,000 heaters that I delivered last winter.
   Thank you in advance.
   Yours sincerely,

1 An invention of Louis Lumière's which enabled aeroplanes to take off quickly, even in freezing weather.

Brigadier Guignard to Louis Lumière

4 June 1918

re: repayment

Sir,

Thank you for your letter of 22 May. I am grateful to you for your offer to repay the sum of 75,000 francs, being a profit margin which you do not intend to claim on supplies to our National Defence effort.[1]

This gesture does not come as a surprise, but all the same I should like to thank you for your generosity.

I shall do what is necessary in order for you to repay the above-mentioned amount.

Yours faithfully,
Brigadier Guignard
Director, Military Aviation Factories
Guignard

[1] All research for military application conducted by the Lumière brothers was conducted free of charge. Louis Lumière went as far as paying, personally, for a hundred-bed hospital throughout the duration of the 1914–18 war.

Minister of Armament and War Supplies to The officer in charge, CAMA, Lyon

Paris, 11 June 1918

Reply to letter no. 10.460 H of 26 May 1918

The payment Monsieur Lumière intends to make can only be accepted as 'Supplementary Funds'. I enclose a tax form to be forwarded to Monsieur Lumière, by which this manufacturer can pay 50,400 into the Treasury of the Rhône.

You will inform Monsieur Lumière that, after his payment has been made, a decree will be inserted into the Bulletin of Laws, allowing the Ministry of Armament a credit of the corresponding amount and publishing the fact that this sum comes from an act of generosity by Monsieur Lumière.

for the Minister of Armament and War Supplies and on his instruction,
Colonel in charge, Materiel and Automobile Manufacture

Auguste Lumière to Henri Lumière[1]

Lyon, 18 November 1918

[My dear Henri,

Where do we write to you now? Where are you going? Send us a telegram as soon as you can, to give us your new address. I assume yesterday's flying session was successful, but I shall be happier when these demonstrations end. It is not a life. I think of it all day long.

No peace for us while you do that job.]

A little more patience. But I rely absolutely on your complete prudence and on your double vigilance.

[I attended yesterday the Belgian annual fete, with your mother and Andrée,[2] under the chairmanship of Monsieur Mulatier. The Mayor made a fine speech.]

I spent the rest of the day peacefully working at the laboratory.

Your uncle Amand[3] came home on leave yesterday. Apparently, he cannot be discharged yet.

A hug, Henri, and much love.

A. Lumière

1 Henri Lumière, Auguste's son, was a flying ace. His job was to find out whether planes that had been hit, then repaired, were usable. He discovered a way of straightening up planes that were spiralling down, an accident which, until then, had always been fatal. To his dismay, he was never allowed to fight on the front because he was considered too useful behind the lines. Auguste Lumière was terrified that his son might meet with an accident.
2 Andrée Lumière, Marguerite and Auguste's daughter, was still in good health. By the end of the month she would be dead of Spanish 'flu, at the age of 24. She had spent the war working with her father in the X-ray department of the Hôtel-Dieu hospital in Lyon.
3 Amand Gélibert, second husband of Juliette Lumière, whose first husband was a Winckler. Auguste Lumière had put him in charge of his dispensary.

Auguste Lumière to Henri Lumière

Lyon, 20 November 1918

My dear Henri,

Since your departure, we have had no address. Where can we write? When will you get this letter? Are you going back to Dijon? I'll send this letter to the Hôtel de la Cloche[1] just in case. Tell us your plans and where we should write.

Andrée has had another bout of 'flu, more serious than the first bout. Last night, her temperature was 39.2°. I hope that is as far as it will go. The epidemic seemed to pause for a while, but now it is as bad as ever.

It is very cold. An icy wind has been freezing us for two days.

I long to know what you are doing and I hope your telegram is going to give us a new address if you do not go back to Dijon.

Nothing special. A hug, Henri, and much love.

A. Lumière

1 The most famous hotel in Dijon. The basins in its rooms were said to have a third tap, dispensing Burgundy wine.

Auguste Lumière to Henri Lumière

Lyon, 22 November 1918

My dear Henri,

Monsieur de Geninville's telephone call[1] led us to believe you were coming to Lyon. I have sent Monsieur de Geninville the money you asked him for.

I see from your letter received yesterday and dated the 19th that you must have stayed at Dijon, that you are flying on Sunday and can't come.

If you go to Pau on Tuesday, will you pass through Lyon?

I hope that you will be very careful during the demonstration. Life stops when you are doing this job.

Andrée is a little better, but she was 38.5 last night.

Your uncle Louis and René[2] are off to Paris tomorrow. They are attending a board meeting for the company. Aunt Jeanne is going to Toulon for a few days.

I hope you can come and, in the mean time, a hug, Henri, with much love.

A. Lumière

1 Monsieur de Geninville was manager of the Union Photographique Industrielle des Etablissements Lumière et Jougla (in Paris) from its establishment in 1911.
2 René Koehler, married Jeanne Lumière – Aunt Jeanne – on 25 September 1890. After acquiring his science and medical doctorates, he lectured at Lyon then, in 1894, became Professor of Zoology. He specialized in submarine fauna, wrote about echinoderms and illustrated his works with magnificent drawings taken from Lumière photographs. He was one of the most important members of the Oceanographic Museum team in Monaco from its foundation in 1910. From September 1914 on, he was in charge of care for the wounded, with Amand Gélibert, in Louis Lumière's temporary hospital.

Auguste Lumière to Henri Lumière

6 December 1918

My dear Riri,

What hardship that you should be leaving when we need to be near each other so badly. I hope you will not be away for too long. No news of Monsieur Gillet. No doubt we shall have some information today.

Squadron Leader Blaise came to see me today. He telephoned the Colonel who said it would be as well for you not to fly any more and that he was sending you back to Lyon.

I sent you telegrams to tell you that Aunt Rose[1] was in a stable condition but I did not want to frighten you by telling you that Amand and I had observed that the whole of her left lung had been affected and that even the right was involved.

Amand, who left for Grenoble tonight, thought the situation was hopeless, but at nine o'clock, when Nicolas came, all the danger signs had gone. She spent a good night and this morning the situation is much better. So we are quite hopeful.

Write to us soon, my dear Riri, a long letter. Look after yourself well. Do not be careless and at the first sign of ill-health, look after yourself extremely rigorously.

Give your devoted friend Jourdain our regards and thank him on my behalf for giving you such affection at this time, when it is needed more than ever.

A hug, Riri, with much love.

A. Lumière

1 Louis Lumière married Rose Winckler on 2 February 1893. Her sister Marguerite was Auguste Lumière's wife, her brothers Charles and Jules had married France and Juliette Lumière.

Auguste Lumière to Henri Lumière

7 December 1918

My dear Riri,

Your aunt's condition is improving quickly and I reckon we can soon be quite confident.

We did not hear from Monsieur Gillet yesterday, but your uncle Louis wanted to wait until today before telephoning him. He's going to do it this morning. I'll let you know the outcome of that conversation immediately.

You must come back. Life is not liveable apart like this, after that other terrible, eternal separation.[1]

We received your telegram from Bordeaux; we expect another today from Pau. When you call on Monsieur Campian, thank him for sending us his condolences. In fact, I shall write to him today.

Give us as much news as you can. We need it. Tell us about your journey, your arrival in Pau, what you are going to be doing, the welcome you got at the school and from Monsieur Campian. Tell us everything in as much detail as possible.

Nicolas is going to see Aunt Rose because Uncle Amand was not able to come last night as he had hoped.

A hug, Riri, with much love.

A. Lumière

Best regards to your friend Jourdain.

1 Auguste Lumière refers here to the loss of his daughter Andrée the previous month. Like Henri, he remained inconsolable.

Auguste Lumière to Henri Lumière

8 December 1918

My dear Henri,

We have received neither telegram nor letter from you today. The day was made even worse by this lack of news. Send us telegrams for a few days more.

Monsieur Gillet has seen Monsieur L., who can do nothing as the military authorities have removed the powers he had. There is nothing for it but to ask the Colonel, which is what we are going to do without delay.

Aunt Rose has lost her fever in the most remarkable way. She is cured. Such an outcome was beyond hope, particularly at such speed.

I am relying on you absolutely to resist being tempted into an aeroplane. We must have absolute and definite certainty on that subject. And we must also get you to come home as quickly as you can. It is essential. Life here is miserable without you, and all the more so because the children are no longer at home. How I long for a good letter from you.

A hug, Henri, with much love.

A. Lumière

Rodolphe Berthon to Louis Lumière

Paris, 12 January 1919

Dear Sir,

I have had a small instrument made according to the type which you requested in order to study the Integral Photography device invented by Professor Lippmann.[1]

I only had ordinary glass available; its index for photogenic rays is not well established. I had to be satisfied with softening the relevant surface in order to make my observations directly; but I obtained calibrated glass to make up a device for you, the back curve of which is polished and ready for emulsion coating.

My first observations suggest that the light beam cannot exceed 20°. We must therefore place in the centre of the curve of the reflective object a diaphragm at most equal to one third of the radius of the curvature.

In addition, I was curious to trace the curvature of fixed sagittal and tangential foci for variable indices. If one uses glass calibrated at 1.53, the two foci are within the theoretical curvature of the field. At index 2, tangential focus coincides more or less with the curve of the field, but saggital focus sits much further back.

At index 1.7, both foci sit in relation to the curvature of the field. Unfortunately, I cannot make up a device with glass index 1.7 because such glass is too heavily coloured and basic. I shall settle for an index of 1.65, and the result will be approximately the same.

The device I shall be sending you soon will be based on the G' ray of the spectrum. It should enable precise photographic experiments.

The incidence of aberrations in this photographic system will render any application quite tricky. I admit that the device you suggested seems far more interesting from an optical, and probably from an artistic, point of view.

I intend to complete the work this week and I shall bring you both the integral photography device and the 2.5 lens.

Best regards to your brother.

Yours sincerely,

Rodolphe Berthon

1 Integral photography was a process which employed very fine grain film in order to combine the use of multiple lenses, all as small as possible. A special photographic plate is produced in order to reproduce colour and the relief image of a network of micro-lenses obtained by hot-pressing some material with similar powers of refraction to optical glass (hence this correspondence about what the ideal material might be: pure celluloid, celluloid

with an admixture of naphtha to increase its refraction, or bakelite).

The focal length of each lens is very short and it records an image of the object in the surface of the film emulsion. After printing, this gives a multitude of positive images. Turning the network of micro-lenses towards the viewer, who then looks through the film, an image of the object appears, life-size, and in three dimensions.

Lippmann's idea encouraged Berthon, a few years later, to engrave microscopic lenses directly on to the gelatine, celluloid-side, and to record three-dimensional or colour images on to cinematographic film.

Various photographic processes stemmed from Lippmann's ideas: peristereoscopes (Bessières, 1926), Olostereoscope (Lassus Saint-Geniès, 1933), 'Crinkle selection' ('Selecteur gaufré') (Maurice Bonnet, 1941). Lippmann's work was the ancestor of holography and modern day micro-lens technology which is applied mainly in astronomy. (Early research was conducted in connection with Star Wars in the hope of devising perfectly accurate missile-guiding systems in the atmosphere.)

Auguste Lumière to Henri Lumière

Lyon, 1 March 1919

My dear Henri,

We were very pleased to hear your news via Aunt Jeanne who had just spoken to Paris on the telephone. Your good news was reassuring, and we spent the night more easily. In the ten o'clock mail, we found your card and we are delighted to know that you are thinking of us. Since our atrocious catastrophe, you have been the best of children, the most affectionate and consoling. You have softened our horrible loss, you have given us peace and done us much good. You will go on this way, Riri, I know, and our old age will be less miserable.

Nothing new here. Georges[1] tells me that Luc Couel has given a most satisfactory estimate, much less expensive than the person to whom you wanted to go first. The four hubs are less expensive than one, and all the parts charged at pre-war prices. I hope you like it. I am longing for you to come home. In the meantime, look after yourself.

A hug, Riri and much love.

A. Lumière

1 Georges Winckler, son of Juliette and Jules Winckler.

Auguste Lumière to Henri Lumière

Lyon, 2 March 1919

My dear Henri,

We have just received your letter informing us you were not coming home until Thursday. Obviously, we should like you home as soon as possible, specially since the 'flu is all over Paris. If you feel the least bit unwell, come home immediately; but I hope you will be careful and that you will return in good health.

The house is even more lonely when you are not here and I really need you back.

No news. The same old life. I work as hard as I can and time passes painfully, but it does pass.

Renée[1] is a little tired. She vomited several times this morning.

Denise[2] is better.

I am a bit better, too, though my temperature is a touch high this evening.

A hug, Riri, and much love.

A. Lumière

Write every day. Give Marcel[3] a big hug from us.

1 Renée Trarieux-Lumière, born 1918, daughter of Suzanne Lumière and Albert Trarieux, grand-daughter of Louis.
2 Denise Winckler, daughter of France Lumière and Charles Winckler, born in 1918.
3 Marcel Koehler (1892–1958), son of Jeanne Lumière and René Koehler. Student at the Ecole Centrale, then became an engineer.

Auguste Lumière to Henri Lumière

Lyon, 3 March 1919

My dear Riri,

No news from you today. Probably you wrote, but the post is not so good on Sundays. I hope we shall get a letter this evening, so I can sleep tonight, unlike last night which was bad again. We are still a bit worried because of the 'flu. Anyway, I am anxious to have you back.

Nothing to speak of here.

A hug, Henri, and much love.

A. Lumière

Give Marcel a hug from us.

Louis Lumière to Gabriel Lippmann

Dear Sir,

Since having the pleasure of calling on you last Wednesday, I have devoted a considerable amount of thought to the application of your most ingenious idea of integral photography and believe I have perhaps found an acceptable method, as follows:

Prepare sheets of moulded celluloid, in the following manner

image side,
spheric elements of radius Ri

diaphragm sheet D

object side,
spheric elements of radius Ro,
where Ri and Ro are specific quantities

Press the sheets together, flat surface to flat surface, placing a thin sheet of celluloid (D) pierced with holes to act as diaphragms, and ensuring that the distance from tip to tip is Ri+Ro.

Finally, coat the Ri side with very fine-grained emulsion.

Refractive elements:

Celluloid possessing, according to an approximate measurement which I have taken using white light, a refractive index of 1.51, the ratio of curvature of the radii should be, unless I am mistaken:

Ro/Ri = 1/1.96.

In order to the obtain the correct material to make the mouldings, the following solution seems plausible:

Make a hydraulic press in copper, brass or alloy by means of a honeycomb of ball bearings. These bearings can be given a mirrored finish; they should be spherical; and their diameter accurate to within 2 or 3μ. Certain manufacturers guarantee this.

These bearings should then be placed in a rectangular, steel frame (C), whose dimension should be a multiple of 2Ri, in such a way as they fit tightly into the frame without any loose play; and then the copper sheet should be placed above, and fitted equally tightly, without loose play.

A piston pressing down on this frame would produce a copper honeycomb mould corresponding to the image side.

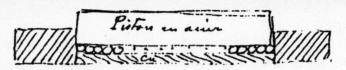

The operation could be repeated with a second copper sheet, in the same frame, with ball bearings with a diameter of 2Ro, fitted with short tubes with a thickness equivalent to Ri − Ro (and a height fractionally larger than Ro) which would fit, as before, into the frame without any kind of looseness. The spacing should be the same for each of the honeycombs and it can be so arranged that the two honeycombs are co-axial if the two forms are superimposed in the frame.

All that is left is to grind out any particles left in the moulds by compression.

Using the same frame, two sheets of transparent celluloid can be placed between the two forms, of such thickness that, when pressed, and taking into account the thickness of a third, diaphragm sheet of celluloid, the distance from tip to tip is Ri + Ro.

A fair range of ball bearings is commercially available, in fractions of English inches, the smallest being 1.59 [millimetres], but unfortunately no measurements have been taken of the refractive indices of celluloid. One could, however, choose to adopt the following diameters which exist: 2.78 and 4.76mm (2.78 and 4.66 would be ideal), though this would mean allowing for a slight margin of error if the axial thickness was given as 2.78 + 4.66. I believe that the effect of this error would be hardly significant. The most regrettable aspect is the weakness of celluloid's refractive index. Perhaps it could be reinforced by an admixture of naphtha a (n = 1.62).

Perhaps you would be kind enough to let me know what you make of all this and if you believe there is any point in attempting this route, tell what the maximum diameter in relation to Ro you think would be right for the diaphragm holes, in order to have sufficient definition without excessive occultation. (Celluloid's low index is extremely unfortunate in this respect.)

Thank you for all your help in this matter,

Yours sincerely,

Gabriel Lippmann to Louis Lumière

Paris, 16 November 1919

Dear Sir,

Your notion of using polished steel ball bearings seems excellent: mechanically speaking, it is the right solution. These are the methods of a proven inventor, capable of great precision.

As you say, it would be preferable to improve the manufacture of the requisite celluloid, from an optical point of view, in order to make it more refractive and more consistent.

You will no doubt manage to produce a kind of celluloid which bears the same relation to ordinary celluloid as optical glass does to ordinary glass.

I am confident of your inventiveness and your dexterity and I am delighted the problem is in such good hands.

I have no information of the choice of diameter for the diaphragms.

Yours sincerely,

G. Lippmann

Louis Lumière to Messieurs Picard and Lacroix

Lyon, 6 December 1919

To the Perpetual Secretaries of the Académie des Sciences
Paris

Dear Sirs,

In response to the request which you were kind enough to send me, it is my pleasure to forward to you today, by post, two copies of a note on my research work, together with a summary of research conducted jointly with my brother and other technicians, a summary which I feel it is appropriate to enclose with this note.

Yours sincerely,

L. Lumière

The Académie des Sciences to Louis Lumière

Paris, 15 December 1919

Dear Sir and honoured friend,

We are pleased to inform you that the Académie des Sciences elected you, at its session of 15 December 1919, to a seat in the Applied Sciences section.

As soon as we have received official notice of the decree confirming this election, we shall invite you to take part in our work.

Yours faithfully,

Louis Lumière to the Académie des Sciences

Lyon, 18 December 1919

Thank you for your letter of 15 December in which you inform me of my election on that day to a seat in the Applied Sciences section.

I am most grateful to you for this letter and for the honour which the Académie des Sciences has chosen to confer on me.

Yours faithfully,

L. Lumière

Employees of the Lumière factories to Messieurs Lumière[1]

December 1919

Upon the occasion of the election of Monsieur Auguste Lumière to the Académie de Médecine and the election of Monsieur Louis Lumière to the Académie des Sciences, the employees of the Lumière factories are pleased to congratulate its managing directors. These honours are the culmination of two fertile careers, rich in fine inventions; but these official rewards cannot do justice to the great human qualities of Messieurs Lumière, and that is what the employees of the factories can do, with much affection.

1 Preface of a book given by the employees of the factory, containing all their signatures.

Louis Lumière to Gabriel Lippmann

Lyon, 5 January 1920

Monsieur G. Lippmann
Fellow of the Institut
Physics Research Laboratory at the Sorbonne
Paris

Dear Monsieur Lippmann,

Please forgive the delay in replying to your kind letter of 1 January, and also for using a typewriter. I am in a terrible rush and this way I save time. I hope you will not hold it against me.

The index which you were good enough to communicate to me concerning the bakelite sample I saw in your laboratory seems interesting, particularly as this substance must be malleable at low temperatures. I should be most grateful if you would put me in touch with your supplier, whose address I took. I went to it (Monsieur Boisnère,[1] 96 avenue Mozart), but I was astonished to discover that the address in question was a piece of wasteland. I asked after the person in question in the houses around but no one knew. Perhaps, I miswrote the address. In any case, I should be grateful if you could put me in touch with Monsieur Boisnère if you can find him.

I have tried having bakelite[2] made up here, but I know that it will take a large number of experiments before we obtain adequate transparency and, above all, colour neutrality. When I do obtain suitable plastic, I shall try the experiment without diaphragms, since the discrepancy is not significant and can be restored at a later stage.

I am most grateful to you for your New Year's wishes and I hope you will accept my own wishes to you and you family.

1 In fact, A. Boissière, 90 avenue Mozart, chemist and manufacturer, who was to supply bakelite for 'integral photographic plates'.
2 A substance invented by the Belgian chemist L.-H. Baekland, born 1863, in 1910 by polymerizing phenol and formaldehyde. It succeeded casein plastics, like galalith, which had been produced since 1897 by polymerizing casein with formaldehyde. Its refractive index is similar to that of optical glass.

A. Boissière to Louis Lumière

Paris, 8 January 1920

Dear Sir,

I have just received a letter from Monsieur Lippmann in which he tells me you called on me at my apartment, 90 Avenue Mozart, and that because of an unfortunate error in the address you were unable to find me. I am most embarrassed that you should have come from so far for nothing as I should have been delighted and honoured to talk with you about bakelite and the details which interest you.

Monsieur Lippmann probably told you that I could mould this substance between sheets of glass or metal, and that one could obtain as fine a moulding as one may want, including phonograph discs. My special process produces a colourless or sometimes slightly yellow result, if there are impurities in the phenol. The temperature required to harden bakelite is 140–160°C.

I did not quite understand from Monsieur Lippmann's enquiries whether you wished to obtain moulded plates or to print smooth plates. I am working on a small machine to make the plates. I should be delighted to send you some samples and I am entirely at your disposal to supply you with any further information you may require, or, if you should return to Paris, to meet you.

Yours faithfully,

A. Boissière

Louis Lumière to A. Boissière

Lyon, 9 January 1920

Monsieur A. Boissière
90 avenue Mozart
Paris

Dear Sir,

Thank you for your letter of 8 January and for the information it contains.

I much regret having mistranscribed your address, because I should very much have liked to discuss with you the matter of the bakelite samples you gave Monsieur Lippmann. I expect to be in Paris towards the end of the month and I shall then suggest that we meet. In the meantime, I should be most grateful if you could send me some samples of bakelite, as transparent as possible, and if you could inform me whether, in that state, this substance can be melted without danger of colouring. Also, if heating to 140°/160° will not increase colour, render it insoluble in alcohol and infusible.

I wish to apply this interesting substance to the process of integral photography invented by Monsieur Lippmann as it would be a consider-able advantage if the substance used had as high an index of refraction as possible. The sample you have given Monsieur Lippmann is already interesting in that respect, but I wonder whether it might not be possible to go still further by introducing an admixture of phenol, which has a more complicated molecular structure. I remember that about fifteen years ago we conducted similar experiments with resorcin, for quite another purpose as it happens. The application we are considering requires either fusibility or a high degree of malleability, because we want to press reasonably large areas with precision.

I look forward to hearing from you.

Yours sincerely,

L. Lumière

A. Boissière to Louis Lumière

Paris, 12 January 1920

Monsieur L. Lumière
262 cours Gambetta
Lyon

Dear Sir,

I have received your letter of 9 January and I wish to reply as promptly as possible. I do not have samples of bakelite in my possession so I cannot send you any, but I shall make some up and have them sent to you as soon as I have.

I cannot yet produce sheets, because my mould is not ready, but I can send you sticks of it, so you can see what it is like. I am afraid it will be a few days, because I am setting up a new laboratory and I have not yet got all my equipment.

The sticks you will receive cannot, in that state, be liquefied; they become malleable when heat treated, although not as malleable as celluloid, but they can be bent and, when cool, that curve remains solidified. This heat treatment can be performed in boiling water, and will not colour the substance.

These sticks have been produced at 150°C. They are neither soluble in alcohol nor fusible.

As to the refractive index that Monsieur Lippmann was good enough to register for me, it is 1.68, but I do not think that the condensation process applied to resorcin is applicable to your experiments because, though the substance produced is transparent, it acquires, on drying, a yellow or dark red tinge, even if very pure chemicals are used.

I believe that one may be able to modify the index of phenol by incorporating various soluble subtonics.

For the purpose you have in mind, I think the best would be to make sufficiently malleable sheets, so that they can be hot-pressed between metal sheets.

I should be delighted to see you towards the end of the month, it being

much easier to talk about these matters than to write about them.
Yours faithfully,
A. Boissière

Louis Lumière to Rodolphe Berthon

Lyon, 13 January 1920

Monsieur Rodolphe Berthon
OPTIS Works
7 rue du Chemin Vert
Paris

Dear Sir,
Thank you very much for the information contained in your kind letter of the 12th and for all your trouble in making the machine I ordered. Since you are willing to try to make one in glass, with an index of 1.65, I should like, if it is not too late, that this be calculated not for a G' ray, but for a D ray, and that the reverse surface be left very finely softened, rather than polished.

I shall always be able to operate with a yellow screen and to sensitize the emulsions accordingly. This method will have, however, the advantage of allowing me to see with the naked eye the quality of the image obtained; also, softening the surface will facilitate spreading emulsion on the reverse surface. I do not think this softening will significantly affect definition.

I look forward to your visit with some impatience and I shall examine with the greatest of interest the f/2.5 lens which you are kind enough to be making for me.
Yours sincerely,

Louis Lumière to A. Boissière

Lyon, 19 January 1920

Monsieur Boissière
90 avenue Mozart

Dear Sir,
Thank you for your kind letter of 12 January. I should be very pleased to receive, as soon as you can, a few specimen sticks of colourless bakelite, such that I can mould it at about 100 degrees as you suggest, in order to determine its malleability and make a few preliminary experiments.

The more malleable it is, the better, so as not to have to apply too much pressure, since I intend to work on reasonably large surfaces and to employ moulds made out of metals that are not extremely hard. Indeed, that is why I wish to obtain as soon as possible the samples for which I am taking the liberty of applying to you.

Thank you in advance.

Yours sincerely,

Rodolphe Berthon to Louis Lumière

Paris, 22 January 1920

Dear Sir,

I am sorry not to have replied to your kind letter sooner, but I have been away for a few days and I had simply, on leaving, instructed that the reverse side of the device for integral photography should not be worked on.

It is very difficult to find high indexed glass at the moment, and the 1.65 glass I have got only has the index for G' rays. Its mean index is 1.63039. At that level, a high number of aberrations remain, but perhaps you will be able to see what the process is worth, anyway. The nearest I have found to minimal aberration glass (I enclose the graph) is 1.66711 flint, for ray D, of which PARRAMANTOIS has only 1 kilogram available.

As to the f/2.5, we have found a shutter that is large enough, but fixing the glass is a tricky business: aluminium tubing is too thin, even if belted with copper, and more importantly, contains two protuberances which hinder centring and correspond roughly to where the slots are. I need a few days more to see whether I can deliver it to you thus and whether it will perform as it should.

I should add that I have started work on another lens, still more luminous, but which can only be applied to formats like the 'Cinemato-graph', for geometric irregularities cannot be entirely eliminated.[1] The angle of anastigmatic correction will be much reduced. Aside from this, it should be possible to provide definition in cinematographic format with 55mm focal length and f/1.8.

This device is not advanced enough that I can envisage commercial manufacture yet.

The half-balls in dense Flint[2] will soon be ready, according to your instructions, and sent off to you, unless you would like a test, first, on denser glass, in which case I can hang on to these half-balls for use in my optical laboratory.

Yours sincerely,
Rodolphe Berthon

1 In January 1920, Louis Lumière took out a patent for photostereosynthesis, or three-dimensional photography. A series of negatives of the same subject, but with different degrees of focus, when superimposed on glass, showed the subject represented as in relief – a kind of photographic sculpture. The camera sits on a rail and shifts one or two centimetres per shot.
2 Flint: leaded, optical glass.

Louis Lumière to Rodolphe Berthon

Lyon, 24 January 1920

Monsieur Rodolphe Berthon
7 rue du Chemin Vert
Paris

Dear Sir,

I have just received your kind letter of 22 January and I am most grateful to you for all your trouble over the dioptics[1] which I have ordered in order to investigate the best conditions for Monsieur Lippmann's integral photography.

I am inclined to accept a device with a mean index of 1.63. I expect that will be good enough, bearing in mind that the substance I intend to employ has a mean index of 1.66 to 1.68.

If I failed to acknowledge receipt of the first machine you sent me, and which I did receive, it is because you had led me to hope that you might come and see me towards the end of last week. I am sorry you were unable to come and I should like to thank you for sending me the machine.

As regards the f/2.5 lens, I am anxious to receive it as soon as possible, without shutter if necessary, if the one you have got is not perfectly centred. I can always use a plate shutter.

The new lens you describe at f/1.8 will certainly be of interest to cinematographers and I should very much like to have one when you start manufacture.

Is there any chance you will come soon?

Yours sincerely,

1 A dioptic is an optical surface separating two uneven refractions.

Rodolphe Berthon to Louis Lumière

Dear Sir,

Thank you for your kind letter of 24 January. I am sorry to say that the tests involving 'Flints' with very high indices were not satisfactory regarding your experiments with Monsieur Lippmann's integral photography.

High index optical glass is supplied in sheets rarely more than two centimetres thick. I therefore had to conduct my tests using sheets stuck one on top of another, which leads to internal reflection that proves damaging to the image as soon as a certain angle is reached.

Would an index of 1.6047 satisfy you?

In that case, I could construct a device the half-ball of which would have a radius of 26.6 millimetres, the reverse dioptic 44.2mm and the thread round this spherical crown, 76 millimetres.

For once, I shall have three sheets thick enough to constitute the entire device. I attach a sketch.

Within a very few days, and this time I am sure of it, I shall have occasion to come to Lyon; I shall take the opportunity to hand over to you the lens; but tests suggest I should deliver it on a normal mount.

I trust these delays are not inconveniencing the most interesting research which you are conducting.

Yours sincerely,
Rodolphe Berthon

Louis Lumière to Rodolphe Berthon

Lyon, 31 January 1920

Monsieur Rodolphe Berthon
Optis Works Ltd.
7 rue du Chemin Vert
Paris

Dear Sir,

I have just received your letter and I am grateful to you for your trouble over my orders.

Would you be kind enough to make up the dioptic for which you sent me a sketch, with refraction index 1.6047, as indicated, without fixing the forward half-ball so I can introduce very thin diaphragms into the system and thus ascertain what is the largest acceptable dimension? Please leave the back surface finely softened, as in the first model you sent me.

I shall be delighted to see you when you come, and look forward to it.

P.S. I shall be in Paris from 9 to 12 February incl.

A. Boissière to Louis Lumière

Paris, 10 February 1920

Monsieur Louis Lumière
262 cours Gambetta
Lyon

Dear Sir,

I am sorry I have not been able to send you the samples of bakelite which you requested in your letter of 12 January past, because I was not yet settled in, but I shall be sending them to you shortly.

Yours sincerely,
A. Boissière

Rodolphe Berthon to Louis Lumière

Paris, 24 February 1920

Dear Sir,

I am sorry to have missed you but you told me you would not be free until quite late and so I attempted to make use of the afternoon to start making up transparent Bakelite.

I am delivering to your Hotel a watch-glass containing a few grams of this product.

Monsieur Tesse and Co., makers of varnishes, 15 rue des Rosiers, St-Ouen, have not yet sent me the samples I requested; I shall probably have them tomorrow and if you are not here, I shall bring them to Lyon.

I expect to have the 1/2.5 on Thursday. As soon as I have conducted stringent tests, I shall be on my way.

I enclose a note on condensation by-products of phenol and formalin; I am sorry it is so short and scrappy, but I do not have the time to pull it together.

I am delivering to your Hotel with the watch-glass, a container with raw commercial methyl acetate, manufactured by Camus-Duchemin Ltd, 29 rue d'Astorg.

I should be delighted if these few bits of information could be of use to you in your difficult studies; in any case, as soon as I have any further information I shall forward it to you.

Yours sincerely,

Rodolphe Berthon

Alexis Carrel to Auguste Lumière

New York, 6 March 1920

My dear friend,

Thank you for your letter of 16 January which filled my laboratory with visions of the Mediterranean.[1] I hope your stay at La Ciotat is helping you get over the exhaustion of the war. Here in New York we are trying to get back to work. Everything is going very slowly. I do not have my new laboratories yet. The war has disorganized things here just as much as in France. Incessant strikes have brought many things to a halt. We have trouble obtaining most of the instruments we found easily before the war. We really are living in a new era and it is anything but better than the old era. Everyone's productivity is 100% lower than before the war.

Yours ever,

Alexis Carrel

1 Alexis Carrel had written to Auguste Lumière in English. As a joke, Auguste Lumière replied in Provençal.

Gabriel Lippmann to Louis Lumière

Paris, 23 March 1920

Dear colleague,

I have spoken to Monsieur Boissière on the telephone. He told me, as he told you, that he has been delayed in trying to set up his laboratory. He told me he had not forgotten about producing sheets of bakelite. He asked if you were in a hurry. I said you were. Anyway, he is seeing to it.

Is making these sheets particularly difficult? He said it was not.

Yours truly,

G. Lippmann

Louis Lumière to Gabriel Lippmann

Lyon, 1 April 1920

Monsieur G. Lippmann
Fellow of the Institut
Paris

My dear and eminent colleague,

Thank you for your letter of 23 March and for talking to Monsieur Boissière on the telephone.

I have determined several appropriate thicknesses for the optical system in question: 1.55 and 2.96 millimetres for the moulds we use ball bearings 4.76 and 7 millimetres in diameter, as commercially available; this will give exactly an index of n = 1.68. I shall write directly to Monsieur Boissière to give him these measurements.

Thank you once more.

Yours sincerely,
Louis Lumière

Louis Lumière to A. Boissière

Lyon, 1 April 1920

Monsieur A. Boissière
90 avenue Mozart
Paris

Dear Sir

Following your conversation with Monsieur Lippmann a few days ago, I am writing to let you know that the required thicknesses for the bakelite sheets which you have been good enough to promise me are 1.55 and 2.96 mm.

I should be obliged if you could send me samples in any form, while I am waiting for these sheets, as soon as you are in a position to produce them, so that I can study the malleability of the product, up to a temperature where discoloration begins.

I should be grateful if, when you send me the samples, you could let me know the best temperature to use.

Yours faithfully,
Louis Lumière

Louis Lumière to *Ciné-Tribune*

Lyon, 30 June 1920

The Editor,

Although I am not given to polemics, I cannot let pass the tendentious articles which your journal has just published under the heading 'Looking back on French cinema' in its issues dated 10 and 24 June 1920, in which I am attacked. These articles contain various untruths which I feel obliged to correct.

In the penultimate paragraph of the first of the articles, the author, Monsieur Francis Mair, writes: 'Demenÿ, now alone in the laboratory, was conducting his own research. In a lecture dated 6 December 1891, at the Conservatoire National des Arts et Métiers, before an audience of 1200 people, he predicted that photographic synthesis of motion would have a great future; he showed that, as far as the present state of things went, the possibility was that it would be the same machines which had broken down movement into its component parts which would come to synthesize it.' This assertion is absolutely untrue. The lecture referred to was published in its entirety by Demenÿ (30 pages) in *Annales du Conservatoire des Arts et Métiers*, 2nd series, volume IV, and there is no such statement. The only reference to synthesizing movement is as follows: 'Finally, we have just recently succeeded in photographing the motions of speech and physiognomy. By building a special zootrope and reconstituting the illusion of this motion, we were able to read the lips of a speaking photograph.' And that is all!

This is very different from what Monsieur Francis Mair affirms. The reversibility of his device for analysing motion was so far from Demenÿ's mind that in his patent dated 10 October 1893, in other words almost two years later, it was materially impossible because the optical field was obscured by the mechanism which drove the film. He does not, in fact, mention reversibility. In this patent, as in those of Friese-Greene[1] and Evans,[2] of 21 June 1889; of Evans, of 8 March 1890; of Varley, of 26 March 1890; of Bouly,[3] of 12 February 1892, which preceded it and which led to similar results to those obtained by Demenÿ, the images are not equidistant, nor are they perfectly sequential; the films are not perforated; and none of the elements in the device are sprocketed.

Only in an additional certificate, taken out by Demenÿ on 25 May 1895, does he mention reversibility, does he clear the mechanism out of the way of the optical field and *make use of perforated film and sprocketed cylinders. But this date is two months subsequent* to the lecture I gave at the

Society for the Advancement of National Industry (22 March 1895) *during which I projected, before an audience of several hundred people, a long series of cinematographic images (more than 800), using a device which my brother and I had patented on 13 February 1895* and which provided a practical solution to the problem.

I recognize that Demenÿ possessed a real knowledge of matters physiological, and a consummate mastery of physical education, but he unfortunately travestied the truth, as it is easy to prove.

Open his book, *Les Bases Scientifiques de l'Education Physique* (publ. F.Alcan, 1911), and turn to page 316. You will see a figure captioned, 'Fig. 195 – Demenÿ's chronophotographic device (1893).' *This is untrue.* This figure does not relate to his patent of 1893, but to the additional certificate he took out on *25 May 1895*.

The difference is crucial. His device of 25 May 1895 is reversible, and provides sequential images, but it is subsequent to mine; his device of 1893 is not reversible and does not provide equidistant primary images.

Demenÿ plays semantic games when he writes in his pamphlet, *Les Origines du Cinématographe*, on page 26: 'In my patent of 10 October 1893, I introduced a major new improvement. This was to insert the eccentric part in the passage of the film between a magazine, as large as I liked, to a spool. In order to obtain evenly spaced images, I had only to use a roller or a sprocketed cylinder similar to that already in use in the telegraph system. This device worked very well and immediately gave me definitive results. Thus I impressed, on 6 centimetres of film, Pasteur's funeral.'

Pasteur died on 28 September 1895!

What are we to make of these definitive results obtained immediately at the beginning of October 1895, if this date is compared with the date of his patent, 1893, as he tries to associate the two?

The truth is that if, as he says, he had only to use a sprocketed cylinder, *he did not do so until his additional certificate of 25 May 1895.*

He is careful, on the following page of the same pamphlet, not to put a date in the caption of an illustration entitled 'Reversible device or Demenÿ Cinematograph', and he is careful, also, to place beside this figure a picture of his 1893 device captioned *with the date* (non-reversible device).

There are other careful contradictions in this pamphlet which I shall not point out.

In a second article by Francis Mair, which appeared in *Ciné-Tribune* dated 24 June 1920, the following statement appears:

'Meanwhile, other inventors were looking into the best way of obtaining projections of moving pictures, among them Monsieur Louis Lumière, who was aware of Demenÿ's work and believed that the solution was to be found in that direction.'

This gratuitous and unflattering statement oversteps the mark. Why should I have thus 'believed that the solution was to be found in that direction'? Was it to steal it from him? Anyone who knows me will testify that I cannot be accused of such a thought.

The truth is different.

It is only as a result of pressure from Demenÿ, as we shall see, that I called on him. Indeed, I only met him once in my life.

After having been in correspondence with him concerning supplies of special positive plates which he was requesting for his Phonoscope, in October 1893, he wrote to us on 5 October 1894, the following letter:

To Messieurs Lumière Sons,

I have already had occasion to enter into correspondence with you on the subject of manufacturing perforated glass discs for use as zootrope images for luminous projection. I am also aware of your interest in all forms of popularization of scientific advances in photography. I have built simplified devices, the use of which is simple and straightforward enough to be placed in the hands of an amateur, or, in other words, to leave the laboratory. There are two such devices:

A device to produce photographic series of one to twenty images a second, one image at a time, successive series or uninterrupted, 1/10 to 1/1000 second exposure per frame, any size. I have, however, adopted two formats, 4 x 6c and 9 x 6c.

The second device I call a phonoscope because, originally, I used it to examine the movements of speech. It is the synthetic apparatus, inseparable from the first. It has several applications: to view very fine positive prints on glass, or to enlarge by projection images of motion. This last being of great interest from the point of view of capturing living portraits, which is my aim.

I am writing to ask whether you are not coming to Paris soon and, if so, whether you would call on me at my house, where I have set up a laboratory and where I could show you the models and discuss what could be made of them.

I have had two backers to assist me in my experiments, but the business is large enough to be conducted on a large scale and I am just about to expand our little research company. I should be delighted if you would join us, and in order to inform you about the terms of our association I am sending you draft statutes, as well as a description of the amateur device.

I should be pleased to have your favourable response to this idea and I look forward to meeting you.

Georges Demenÿ

It is worth noting that at the time of this letter, 5 October 1894, the devices were not reversible, because there were two of them, *'the second . . . the synthetic apparatus inseparable from the first '* and that, *it synthesized by using positive images on glass.*

Our duty as directors of a company manufacturing glass plates was to investigate a business which might constitute an outlet for our glass plates. We told Demenÿ that one of us would call on him on a subsequent trip to Paris.

On 1 November, we received another letter from him, as follows:

Messieurs Lumière,

I note from your letter 9 October that you show some interest in the popularization of photographic research into movement.

As we are very likely to meet next week, to examine the best way of progressing to spread public awareness of our research, I should be pleased, if you were thinking of coming to Paris, if you could arrange your trip to coincide with this period. You would be of considerable assistance to us by your competence and your experience.

Yours sincerely,

G. Demenÿ

Since I was going to Paris, I called on him. We did not discuss technical matters. He told me about the difficulties he was having with his backers and insisted that we ought to be taking an interest in his business. The device in question was a phonoscope on glass plates. I did not see any device while there. It is very easy for me to affirm this today, since I am still at the same point: I have never seen any Demenÿ device.

I informed him that it was impossible for us to subscribe to shares in his company, and that we might be able to look into the matter once he was free of obligation to his backers.

I also informed him that I had already been looking into the matter of projecting long series of cinematographic images for some while.

We had no further oral communication.

On 28 December 1894, I received this letter from him:

Dear Sir,

I have seen Monsieur Lavanchy Clarke,[4] one of the partners about whom I informed you. He is on his way south and intends to ask you to see him on his way Sunday or Monday.

I should be very grateful if you would agree to spare a moment to discuss our business with him, as I am sure you will find a practical solution to apply the work I have undertaken. The weather is not good enough to take pictures; I shall send you some in a few days.

Yours,

Georges Demenÿ

Then, 19 March 1895:

Dear Sir,

I gather that you are coming to Paris to give a lecture on photography. I should be very grateful if you could spare me a few minutes to continue our previous discussion.

Yours sincerely,

Demenÿ

Perhaps you would let me know by telegram as letters are no better here than in the provinces.

Finally, 27 March 1895, this last letter:

Dear Sir,

When you were in Paris recently, I sent word to your hotel (Rougemont) to ask you to see me. I do not know whether you received this and I very much regret not having heard of your lecture in time, especially as I now know that you have solved questions which I have been particularly investigating.

I am writing to ask whether you are still willing to conduct research jointly with me, and to exchange your results with mine, which are very practical.

I look forward to hearing from you.

Demenÿ

Does it not follow from all this that *it was Demenÿ who was the supplicant?*

And is it not true that he was still working on his phonoscope when I showed for the first time (22 March 1895) a projection of moving pictures, using an entirely original device which provided a complete and practical solution to the problem?

You will agree, further, that this device did not suddenly spring into my hands, but was the fruit of months of research and work. As I have said elsewhere, I started working on this question when Edison's kinetoscope appeared.

I am sorry to have been induced to write this refutation because I believe that it would have been wiser to leave poor Demenÿ's ashes in peace. But no one, I think, will blame me for wanting to defend the truth of this story which Monsieur Francis Mair, impelled, no doubt, by friendship with Demenÿ, has unquestionably distorted in the articles which have just been published in *Ciné-Tribune*.

I rely on your spirit of fairness to publish this letter.

Yours sincerely,

Louis Lumière

1 William Edward Green, known as Friese Greene, met Rudge, the mechanic, in London. Rudge was obsessed with large-screen projection of magic lantern images. In 1884, he took out a patent for the 'perfection of displays of dissolving pictures and all sorts of other pictures and to give the illusion of life by means of magic lanterns' (Biofantoscope). He manufactured a magic lantern which showed a man removing his head like one removes a hat, and then replacing it. He was elected to the Royal Photographic Society and took credit for Rudge's inventions, which ended their collaboration. Then, with Evans, he became interested in a method of rendering movement by a series of stills; finally, with Varley, he tried to combine his various devices to allow projection of a quick succession of photographs with a phonograph, to match sound and image, but his attempts did not meet with success because he never solved the question of projection (see Ray Allison, *Friese Greene, Close-up of an Inventor*, London 1948).
2 Mortimer Evans, an engineer from London, worked with Friese Greene to achieve a 'machine destined to take a series of stills', patented on 21 June 1889 and perfected by Evans in March 1890. This device allowed pictures to be taken on film, but not their projection.
3 Léon Bouly (1872–1932) developed, before the Lumière brothers, a machine that was less effective than theirs but was also called 'Cinematograph'; its patent describes a machine to break down and reconstitute movement; it was taken out in 1892.
4 At this stage, Lavanchy Clarke was still involved in the Phonoscope Company founded by Demenÿ, Stollwerk and himself.

Emile Picard[1] to Louis Lumière

Paris, 29 November 1920

My dear Colleague,

I want to thank you immediately for your generous donation to the

Society of Friends of Science and also for all you have done for our charity in the city of Lyon.

Yours sincerely,

Emile Picard

1 French mathematician (1856–1941), specialized in uniform and multiform analytic functions; and in functions with several variables. He also made a contribution to early algebraic geometry by his research into the application of simple integration to the study of surfaces (1885). He entered the Académie des Sciences in 1889 and the Académie Française in 1924.

Auguste Lumière to Henri Lumière

La Ciotat, 11 May 1922

My dear Henri,

We had an excellent trip. La Rolland[1] worked like clockwork. Not the slightest incident. We reached La Ciotat at five thirty, after driving down the right bank of the Rhône, which is a much better road and more picturesque. Sadly, it rained much of the day. It rained at La Ciotat in the evening too, but now the weather seems to be getting better.

I went fishing this morning and caught a few. I enclose a letter from the editor of the *Revue Scientifique*. Will you discuss it with Louis and decide what to do. We must not alienate this important magazine. Get Collet to write a good letter – explain times are hard, exports are ruined, that we must reduce our overheads until the economy improves and so on.

I hope you are all well and nothing untoward has happened since I have been away.

Send me some news.

A. Lumière

1 The name Auguste Lumière gave his car. He had it built broader than usual and, in particular, taller than usual so that ladies could enter it without removing their hats. He kept this vehicle for many years, which became with time rather old-fashioned; to the point that the people of Lyon would recognize it from a great distance and know that there went Monsieur Auguste.

Auguste Lumière to Henri Lumière

La Ciotat, Wednesday 24 [May] 1922

My dear Henri,

Thank you for your nice letter which arrived this morning. It is very good of you to send us such interesting news. Albert,[1] Louise and Nano[2] have arrived in the middle of a first-rate heatwave. I find it is only bearable out at sea. This morning, while it was stifling on land, I was almost cold out at La Cassadaigne, and then when I got back, what a contrast! The fishing is not so good now the weather has turned fine. But I have never failed to bring home a decent fry-up, forty or fifty fish with at least five or six big ones. But I go out at 7 at the latest. They bite most easily in the early hours.

It is so hot now one can hardly go out in the middle of the day.

I will happily stay a few days here but not much more. I would like you to arrange for someone to come and collect us quite soon because it is really at Lyon – in the laboratory – that I feel best.

It is too hot for us go into Marseille for the time being. As regards the autochromes, I don't think there is much to be done because we can't change the frame and cut out the bottom row, the exhibition would be a little on the meagre side. I think the greyishness is due to a lack of tone in the printing which is not as vigorous as it used to be. Now that Louis has put things in order again, we shall probably be able to get results as good as the originals. Then we can change the greyest prints.

If we go back, I'll see to the lighting.

La Micelle[3] comes out to sea every day. She was terrified at first, she had to be carried on board. But now she jumps nonchalantly from one boat to another or on to land; she has found her sea-paws.

We are waiting for the worst of the heat to die down so we can go out for a drive.

I look forward to hearing from you all. A hug, Riri, and to Louis, Rose, Yvonne[4] and all the family.

Auguste

1 Albert Trarieux married Suzanne Lumière, Louis' daughter. After being sub-prefect in Sens (near Paris) and principal private secretary to the Minister of Education, he became, from 1921 to 1925, secretary-general of Gaumont in Paris. In 1925, he joined the Lumière firm, and from 1940 to 1956 he was managing director, his cousin Henri Lumière being chairman. He was also, for many years, chairman of the photographic industries employers' federation (Syndicat Général des Industries Photographiques).
2 Madame Mathieu, a distant cousin of the Lumière brothers. She and her husband were

friends of Auguste and Marguerite Lumière.
3 Auguste Lumière's dog, named after particles in collodion solution.
4 Yvonne Lumière (1907–1993), Rose and Louis Lumière's daughter, married Jean Lefrancq.

Henri Lumière to Will Day Ltd

Lyon, 8 September 1922

Will Day Ltd
London

Dear Sirs,

We have just received your letter of 29 August together with an edition of *Illustrated London News* forwarded to us by your head office.

We are sending you one of the first cinematographic devices used in performances all over the world in 1896.

This machine is numbered no. 35. As you already know, such machines shot the film, made the prints and projected them.

This is the only such device which functioned as early as 1895, and all the performances given in all the capital cities in the world were given using this type of machine. It is fair to say that the inventor of cinematographic performances, as they are known today, was Louis Lumière, because such performances, as shows for the public, began on 25 December 1895 at the Grand Café, boulevard de la Madeleine in Paris,[1] where the first fee-paying public performance was given.

There had been several private performances previously, before various scientific societies. The first of these was given by Louis Lumière, on 22 March 1895, at the Society for Advancement in Paris, at the request of Monsieur Mascart, Chairman of the Académie des Sciences.

You say in your article that the first performance was in Marseille. This is wrong. It took place in Paris, and then in Lyon, on 25 January 1896.

Please do not hesitate to contact us if there is any further information you require.

Yours faithfully,
H. Lumière
Union Photographique et Industrielle
Lumière & Jougla Factories United[2]

1 Two mistakes: it was 28 December 1895, not the 25th, and boulevard des Capucines, not boulevard de la Madeleine.
2 In 1920–1, the Planchon Cellulose Company had an accumulated deficit of 2.2 million francs; so synthetic fibre patents in the firm's possession were sold off and a new company,

Lumière & Jougla, was formed, to sell films and film stock. In 1928, Jougla vanished and the company retrieved its original name.

Auguste Lumière to La Martinière

Lyon, 2 November 1923

My dear Chairman,

I am deeply grateful to you for your good wishes and kind congratulations which you have been good enough to pass on to me on behalf of the Governors of La Martinière.

I sincerely thank them and you because I do not forget that if I have been able to acquire some renown it is mainly because of the invaluable teachings of my masters at La Martinière.

I am deeply grateful to the School.

Yours sincerely,

Auguste Lumière

The House of Lumière to René Petit

Lyon, 15 September 1924

Monsieur René Petit
Grand Hotel
Place Stanislas
Nancy (M&M)

Dear Sir,

Our Paris headquarters has forwarded to us your letter of 6 September together with the autochrome plate which you sent there. This plate is slightly under-exposed, but the main trouble – black, comma-shaped spots, mainly on the dress – is due to a manufacturing flaw. Such flaws, as we are careful to forewarn our customers on page 39 of the enclosed instructions for use, are invisible at quality control since they appear during development, and the only remedy is to touch it up.

You mention scratches on the gelatine surface, but these are not a problem because they are invisible when held up to the light and they will, in any case, be softened by varnishing the plate. These scratches are caused during manufacture; they are more or less always present; and they are all the more visible in this instance because, as the picture is underexposed, it has been overdeveloped.

204

We are going to retouch your plate and return it to you. We shall be delighted to touch up any other plates showing similar defects, and to replace any plates which you send us and which prove impossible to retouch. Such incidents being comparatively rare, there is every chance that your remaining boxes contain no defective plates.

In order to print autochromes on to paper, the only method to give decent results is three-colour typography; other processes all present a variety of drawbacks or problems of varying degrees of seriousness.

Yours sincerely,
Lumière

The House of Lumière to René Petit

Lyon, 25 September 1924

M.P.
The Manager
Grand Hotel
Place Stanislas
Nancy (M&M)

Sir,

We have received your letter and we are returning your plate without having been able to retouch the black lines which are the cause of your complaint because they are too numerous and too close together. These lines arise out of spots on the glass.

We recommend, see page 5 of the enclosed instructions for use, that the plates should wiped on the glass side; this recommendation has not been observed; hence the spots.

Yours sincerely,
Lumière

Auguste Lumière to La Martinière

Lyon, 24 October 1925

My dear Chairman,

During recent years, my health has not often allowed me to attend La Martinière Governors' meetings and I am sorry to say that this situation has not improved over recent months.

In the circumstances, I am aware that I am not fulfilling as I would wish the function to which I have been appointed and I should be most grateful to you if you would forward my resignation as a Governor.

I am particularly sorry to be obliged to take this decision because I have always felt exceptionally thankful to La Martinière for providing me with the essential principles which I have followed in life, and a special fondness for my colleagues, to whom I send, as to you, my sympathy and my regrets.

Yours sincerely,

Auguste Lumière

Marshal Foch to Louis Lumière[1]

1 November 1925

My dear comrade,

I am writing to beg you not to overlook Monsieur Emile Picard's appeal. He is Chairman of the Society for Support and Friends of Science, which needs your help badly in these difficult times.

1 The tone of this letter and the fact that Louis Lumière used it to scrawl a rough draft of his curriculum vitae prior to entering the Académie des Sciences suggests a degree of familiarity in relations between the two men.

Auguste Lumière to an unknown correspondent

1925

Dear Sir,

Coming after the enlightened views and advice of the leading authorities you have consulted, the opinions of a humble researcher of no particular rank cannot weigh very much; following your wishes, however, I shall attempt to give you my impressions of the phenomena which you have described to me, but naturally only within the specific limits of my competence, and only so far as the symptoms you indicate are connected with what it has been given me to observe in my now long career as a biologist.

Alas! We all grow older and among the symptoms which you possess, a number, and perhaps the majority, belong to the predestined development of any normal living thing.

If I compare my physical powers, and even certain of my intellectual faculties, with what they were twenty or thirty years ago, I am forced to notice, for example, a gradual weakening of my sense of sight which was once powerful if not perfect, without any tendency to refraction; but now the faculty of adaptation has grown considerably weaker, defects have appeared for which my faculty of adaptation no longer compensates.

There is no specific reason for physical diminishing or intellectual exhaustion which is really physiological, and must be put down to age. I feel this weakening myself; no one escapes it.

If I may say so, there is no reason to allow oneself to be haunted by the prospect of late after-effects of syphilitic infection. When treatment has been given early and with sufficient determination, there is every chance for genuine cure.

As regards arsenic intoxication, all sorts of accidents are possible:
– disorders resulting from humoral disruption which translate as an immediate shock after the injections, or later symptoms, around the seventh day, such as eruptions, athralgia, fever and so on. But these disorders are temporary and usually vanish without trace after a few days.

– Lesions due to the fact that by-products of arsenic tend to select the protoplasmic elements of certain nerve cells. This happens in repeated or protracted arsenic treatment. The best known examples of this are paralyses or neurites, but they can also take other forms and have repercussions notably on the functioning of nerve cells, including modifications of cephalo-rachidic fluid consequent on the modification of these functions. As these are lesions, cure can take some time: intoxicated cells must be replaced by new cells and nerve tissue is slow to regenerate. Patience is required.

Before going into the purposes of cell regulation, let me give you an example from my own personal history.

More than three years ago, around 15 September 1922, I caught a bad sore throat which did not even require me to give up my activities for a single hour. Unfortunately, I had chanced upon a germ which secreted toxic substances that spread throughout my organism and selected a particular group of cells in my neck marrow, altering these elements to such an extent that within two weeks I had woken up, on 1 October, with a stabbing pain at the left mastoid of my cervical plexus. I thought at first it was periphlegic neuritis and I asked one of my friends, a professor of clinical surgery, to give my nerve an immediate injection of novocaine so that I should be rid of these extremely painful phenomena. Since the treatment was a complete failure, I knew that the problem was a central one. Indeed, the pain spread to my face, then my left shoulder, then my left arm and so on. Two weeks later, it spread symmetrically to the right side, in the region of the middle nerve. So there was an inflammation on the arachinoid, around the sixth and seventh cervical.

A lesion took root; after a month and a half of horrendous pain in bed, with my doctor friends seriously worried, my condition gradually improved and I have been able to resume my former life, so that I am still in pain, particularly in the evenings, and this has been going on for thirty-seven months without a single day's rest.

That is typical of cellular lesions by intoxication. It is extremely persistent.

Metallic and metalloid elements can thus lead to various nervous alterations, expressed in different ways in relation to the areas under attack. I have not given up hope of a cure. Indeed, I believe I am improving, but slowly, and in stages.

Do not lose heart, therefore; if, as you believe, you have suffered some kind of intoxication, it will take a very long time before you are completely restored.

I hope it is not too long all the same.

Yours faithfully,

Raoul Grimoin-Sanson[1] to Louis Lumière

Paris, 26 February 1926

Dear Louis Lumière,

Monsieur Gabelle has requested that I should repeat last year's exhibition at the Conservatoire National des Arts et Métiers: a retrospective exhibition on the Cinematograph. I am writing to ask whether you would lend, or better still give me, old instruments which you could spare for the Conservatoire National des Arts et Métiers.

May I also take the liberty of asking for a fine photograph of Messieurs Auguste and Louis Lumière (if possible 50x60, or smaller that I could enlarge).

Many thanks.

Yours sincerely,

Raoul Grimoin-Sanson

1 Originally a conjurer, Raoul Grimoin-Sanson then became a photographer in Paris. On 13 November 1896, he took out a patent for improvements to panoramas 'by complementary projections of various cinematographic machines'. He called the it cineorama. His cinecosmorama, patented in 1897, permitted performances based on the cineorama. Films shot from hot air balloons were shown to an audience seated in a mock hot-air balloon. This

idea caught the interest of the organizers of the Universal Exhibition of 1900 and Grimoin-Sanson was able to establish a limited company to develop his invention. He used a hundred projectors, insufficiently insulated and each illuminated by an arc-light, so that the heat was unbearable. At the last scheduled performance, the worker in charge of rewinding the films was seriously indisposed and the police department banned the cineorama. R. Grimoin-Sanson also developed a phototachygraph, which was one of the early competitors of the Cinematograph.

Louis Lumière to Raoul Grimoin-Sanson

Paris, 22 February 1926

Raoul Grimoin-Sanson
40 rue François 1er
Paris

Dear Sir,

I am sorry to have been so slow to respond to your letter of 16 February, which followed me to Lyon and back, where I have just spent forty-eight hours.

At a board meeting of the Conservatoire National des Arts et Métiers, I discussed the matter about which you write with Monsieur Gabelle and I am pleased to say that I shall willingly make available to the Conservatoire whatever machines appear in the Cinematograph retrospective exhibition when the time comes.

Perhaps you would let me know when you want them sent. But since the question of setting up a Museum of Photography is not yet settled, I cannot yet donate these machines to the Conservatoire, even though, in my opinion, that is where all the collections relating to the history of photography and the history of the Cinematograph should be assembled.

I am writing to Lyon to have a 50x60 photograph of my brother and me made up and I shall have it sent to you when the time comes.

Yours sincerely,
Louis Lumière

Maldiney[1] to Auguste Lumière

Besançon, 14 June 1926

Dear Sir,

I have just received your kind letter and for which I thank you warmly.

I should have liked to have sent to your brother Monsieur Louis

Lumière, as well as to you, a copy of *Franche Comté et Monts Jura* and I should be grateful if you would let me have his address. It is unfortunate that the printer cut some of the article I sent him and that he published it without showing me the proofs, but it is too late to do anything about that.

I am still hoping to come to Lyon to return the pictures which you were kind enough to lend me and which we displayed in Besançon. I have had all sorts of setbacks, including a bad cut on one hand from an old photograph that was in the bottom of an old crateful of debris from the laboratory. Then, picking up a log, I gashed myself without being able to clean the wound immediately, so that I caught tetanus, from which I am not yet fully recovered, despite an anti-tetanus shot delivered two days later by an intern at the hospital. I still have sudden paralysis of the jaw and neuralgia. The cut was in late January. Now the exams have been brought forward, both in the Faculty and in the School of Medicine, so I shall not be free until 20 July. If, by any chance, I can get to Lyon, I shall let you know so as to have the pleasure of talking to you. Otherwise, I shall send the photos so as not to keep you from having them for too long.

Thank you very much for the picture of you, which you were good enough to give me. If possible, I should also like to keep the one of your father and the one of Monsieur Louis Lumière, which will be of use when I can, as I have said I would, have a commemorative plaque installed on the house you were born in, place Victor Hugo (formerly Place Saint Quentin). As I said at the Competitive Society and at the Congress of Scientific Societies of Franche-Comté, if we were in America, the plaque would have been up ages ago. And strangers visiting Besançon would be able to see that the Place Victor Hugo contains both the house Victor Hugo was born in and the house the inventors of the Cinematograph, and numerous other scientific discoveries, were born in, only a few metres apart.

I enclose a postcard and a photograph of my own, taken of Place Victor Hugo, which has been having roadworks for weeks now (they are putting in sewers). Victor Hugo's house is on the left (first house); the commemorative shield sits in between the two windows. Your house is in the middle of the picture, at the corner of the main street which you can just see: there is a grocer's on the ground floor.

I intend to publish postcards with this information, but using a better photograph. They are building a Rue Lumière in the middle of Saint-Claude, behind the Viotte railway station. It was decided not to change any of the street names in the town centre. Forgive my giving you all these details, but I believe they may be of interest as family memories.

I have just finished the free public lectures in photography I have been giving at the University of Besançon for the last fifteen years with a lesson on colour photography according to the Lumière process. There are many foreign students at the Faculty and they are delighted with the pictures I show them. They all say they want to try making some of their own, during their holidays in Franche Comté.

Yours sincerely,
Maldiney
Faculty of Science at Besançon

1 A friend of Antoine Lumière's, professor at the University of Besançon, Maldiney arranged to have a commemorative plaque put on the house where the Lumière brothers were born in Besançon.

Albert Calmette[1] to Auguste Lumière

Paris, 29 August 1926

Dear Sir and Friend,

I was expecting to see you one of these days because Gélibert told me you would come, but no doubt you are very busy so I shall lose no time in thanking you as warmly as I can for the splendid photographs you sent us. They are truly like paintings, one can look at them without tiring. I know that, later, our children will be proud to have them.

My wife joins me in expressing our gratitude to you. Please pass on our compliments to Monsieur Bellingard,[2] who is an eminent artist.

I hope that when you next come to Paris you will give us the pleasure of coming to our house.

Please place my respectful homage at the feet of Madame Auguste Lumière.

Yours truly,
Calmette

1 Albert Calmette (1863–1933), doctor and bacteriologist, founded the Bacteriological Institute of Saigon in 1891 and the Pasteur Institute of Lille in 1896. He discovered serum therapy against poison and against infections and developed, with Guérin, preventive vaccination against tuberculosis (BCG). He entered the Académie des Sciences in 1926. His brother was the famous journalist, Gaston Calmette, and his son would marry Hélène Gélibert, Auguste and Louis Lumière's niece.
2 A close friend of the Lumière brothers whom he met through Gabriel Doublier. They gave him the nickname 'Papus'. He was a talented portrait photographer and worked a great deal for the family.

Raoul Grimoin-Sanson to Louis Lumière

Oissel, 25 September 1926

Monsieur Louis Lumière
Monplaisir, Lyon

Dear Sir,

I am just finishing arranging the retrospective exhibition about cinema at the Museum of the Conservatoire National des Arts et Métiers and I should like to take the liberty of reminding you that I should be grateful if I could display your very first device, the one you lent in 1924.

We should also be most grateful if you could let us have a 50x60 enlargement (if possible) of the fine photograph representing the inventors of cinema, Messieurs Auguste and Louis Lumière. A few posters – the two first in particular – would look very good in the exhibition.

Thank you in advance.

Yours sincerely,

Raoul Grimoin-Sanson

(pupil of Jules Marey)

G. Tradier[1] to Doctors Lumière and Gélibert

Symphorien d'Ozon, 29 December 1926

Dear Doctors,

I should feel guilty of failing in my obligatory duties if I did not take advantage of a tradition which gives me an opportunity to express my heartfelt good wishes to my two good and kind doctors who are restoring me to health.

I have a wish of my own, too. I should like to hear you say that I can go back to school, and when you grant this permission, which I long for, I shall work twice as hard, hoping I can bring my prizes to you; that will be my way of showing my gratitude: I can do no more. And if I am lucky enough to become what I should like to be, you shall possess, unless God, no better friend.

G. Tradier

1 Probably a young patient of Auguste Lumière and Amand Gélibert in their dispensary, Rue Villon in Lyon.

Louis Lumière to Lacroix

Saint-Raphaël, 18 May 1927

My dear colleague,

Thank you again for delaying your talk on your great trip to Japan until after my return. I am due back in Paris on 29 May, so I shall be able to attend the 20 May session.

If you should have any requests relating to the device you will be inaugurating, perhaps you could let me know by return of post, so that I can transmit them to Monsieur Gaumont, whom I am expecting to see next Sunday (22nd) at Sainte Maxime.

I suppose Monsieur Caurjon has arranged with the engineer in charge all that is needed to project your 45x107 pictures and that the machine has been fitted with a window of the appropriate size, and a short enough lens so that the projection approximately covers the screen.

May I also inform Monsieur Gaumont of your interesting talk so that he can attend?

Would you be kind enough to give me a deadline which allows enough time to make any extra arrangements so that the technical aspect is up to the standard of your much awaited talk.

Please remember me to Madame Lacroix.

Yours sincerely,

Louis Lumière

I expect it would be quite easy to find a projectionist to show the slides if you so wished.

Louis Lumière to the Académie des Sciences

Neuilly sur Seine, 26 December 1927

The Perpetual Secretaries of the Académie de Sciences
Institut de France
23 quai Conti
Paris

My dear colleagues,

I am pleased to inform you that the note which you requested in your letter of 24 December was not handwritten but typed and that I sent it to the printers, Gauthier-Villard, at the same time as the proof which I had been sent.

Yours sincerely,
Louis Lumière

Auguste Lumière to Trillat

11 August 1928

My dear Monsieur Trillat,

Thank you for your brochures on the work of your laboratory which seems most active, for which I congratulate you.

Your hypothesis is worth further reflection as it fits the known facts; I propose to think about it and examine the possibility of conducting experiments along those lines.

Having set up, in my laboratory at the clinic, apparatus designed to treat certain patients by ion germination, some of the grains were profoundly transformed and I too asked myself whether there might not be in that fact an element of mutation. I have so many patients, I cannot do any testing, though it would be fascinating. I shall try to make time, though there is such satisfaction to be gained from treating patients conventional treatment has abandoned that I continue to be attracted to the possibility of alleviating their pain.

Yours sincerely,
Auguste Lumière

Vendôme Clinic to Auguste Lumière

Lyon, 22 November 1928

Dear Sir,

I speak on behalf of every one of the sisters here when I thank you for your continued generosity towards us.

We are most grateful. Please accept our profound gratitude for this new gesture of paternal kindness to the Nurses of the Vendôme Clinic.

Our fervent prayers for the continuation of your good health are the truest way we thank you. For the time being, all the staff is well!

Yours sincerely,
Sister Raphaël
Director

The Académie des Sciences to Auguste Lumière

Paris, 26 November 1928

Dear Sir,

We are pleased to inform you that, at its session of 26 November 1928, the Académie des Sciences has elected you to the post of Correspondent in the medical and surgical section, in lieu of the late Monsieur Felix Lagrange.

Yours sincerely,

Auguste Lumière to the Académie des Sciences

Lyon, 30 November 1928

The Chairman
The Académie des Sciences

Dear Chairman,

I am writing to thank you and your colleagues for the considerable honour the Académie des Sciences has done me in nominating me Correspondent in the medical and surgical section.

I am deeply grateful for this honour.

Yours sincerely,
Auguste Lumière

Auguste Lumière to the Académie des Sciences

Lyon, 30 November 1928

The Perpetual Secretaries
Académie des Sciences
Paris

Dear Sirs,

I am pleased to enclose the form you have asked me to complete and to express my gratitude for the official notice you have given me of my election as Correspondent in the medical and surgical section.

I am most honoured by this appointment and I thank you for the congratulations which you have been kind enough to offer me.

Yours sincerely,
Auguste Lumière

Louis Lumière to Auguste Lumière

Houlgate, 16 August 1929

My dear old boy,

I am very sorry to hear about Papus' big accident. Will he be all right? I hope so and I hope you will send him my best wishes for his recovery. If, as I hope, he gets well, it will be down to you because if you had not had him operated on so fast he would have been gone.

What a day you must have had, my old boy! Hardly a holiday.

You should rest. All this work will play you a nasty trick one of these days. Believe me.

I think you're going to spend a few days at La Ciotat. Enjoy the sun and stay as long as you can. Then I hope you will come and spend a few days here.

Yesterday was lovely and I made use of it to spend some time on the Casino course, taking the oxygen and warming myself by the rays of the great furnace.

I have been getting better for the last two days, though I still have nervous pains. Last night, they kept me awake.

The weather is turning, which is a great shame . . .

Albert is much better. He went out yesterday. He and Suzanne are coming down by train this evening.

Please send me your news, and Papus' and the Boulades'.[1] I should like to write a letter of condolence to the poor woman.

The children here are better than ever, sun-tanned and hardened from long days on the beach.

A big hug to Marguerite, Henri, Odette and Aunt Marie.[2] The most affectionate of accolades to you, old boy.

Louis

1 Antonin and Léon Boulade were, like the Lumière brothers, former pupils of La Martinière. They built the arc-light for the first cinematographs. Antonin died in a motor accident (buried 9 August 1929); his wife, at the time of writing, was still in hospital, in a serious condition.
2 Probably Marie Lumière, Antoine's sister, and Isabelle Petitrenaud's mother.

Auguste Lumière to Henri Lumière

La Ciotat, Thursday 192[ ]

My dear Henri,

Yesterday, the squadron was in the bay. Herriot[1] was on the *Provence*. With the children, we went down to have a look at the nineteen men-of-war in the harbour in front of the house. We thought we might be able to greet the President and sure enough when he saw me he shouted, 'Ah! Auguste!' He took a boat out to a torpedo ship with the Admiral and the Minister for the Navy and they boarded the *Saint Georges*. Charles made some verascopes[2] which I am sending you. Can you have them printed, verascope on glass and enlargements on paper, as carefully as possible, and then send them back to us soonest. You can keep the negatives.

Nothing else here, except that I would like to be home. I have not yet received the publications you will have sent me on Monday.

I am longing to be with you.

A. Lumière

1 Writer and politician. At the time of the Dreyfus Affair, Edouard Herriot joined the Radical Party and led it from 1919 to 1957. He was Mayor of Lyon from 1905 onwards, Senator from 1912 to 1919, Minister of Public Works from 1916 to 1917, and Member of Parliament from 1919 to 1940, Minister of Foreign Affairs from 1924 to 1925, Minister of Education from 1926 to 1928. He was Prime Minister in 1932, then Minister of State from 1934 to 1936 and Speaker of Parliament from 1936 to 1940. He called for unity around Marshal Pétain in 1940, then distanced himself from the Vichy government. He was deported to Germany in 1944. Speaker of Parliament again from 1947 to 1954, he entered the Académie Française in 1946. He published several works including, *Madame Récamier et ses amis* (1904), *La Vie de Beethoven* (1929), *Lyon n'est plus* (1939–40) and *Jadis* (1948–52). He sat with Auguste Lumière on the board of the Civilian Hospitals of Lyon.
2 Verascopes invented by Jules Richard of Paris, mentioned in *La Nature* for the first time in 1894. A frame-holder containing 6 47 x 107mm plates enabled twelve pictures to be shot. The lenses were fixed diaphragm, aspheric, f/6.3, 55mm and the shutter vertical-plane, single speed and connected. It was the first small stereoscope and it was a great success.

Louis Lumière to Georges Méliès[1]

Bandol, 4 September 1931

My dear Monsieur Méliès,

Your kind letter has found me at Bandol and I am writing to say that I shall willingly sponsor you. I do not know, however, whether I shall be able to attend the party because, according to the Federation, it is due to be held on 7 October. That is exactly the time when I should be going to Rome where I have promised to attend, this year, the Session of the International Institute for Educational Cinema. You mentioned 15 October (has the date changed?) If that was the day, then perhaps I should be back in Paris, though it would be touch-and-go. In any case, if I get back on time, I should be delighted to be with you.

Yours sincerely,
Louis Lumière

I forgot to bring my Cinema Directory and I don't have your address. Perhaps you could let me have it.

1 Georges Méliès (1861–1938) was the son of a wealthy businessman. He started out as a drawing-room conjurer before buying the Théâtre Robert-Houdin in 1888, where he put on magic and fairytale shows. He attended one of the first performances of the Lumière Cinematograph at the Grand Café and offered Antoine Lumière 10,000 gold francs for the machine. Lumière senior refused. But Méliès had understood the enormous potential behind the device. He procured a similar one, started up a production company and began making films, the first of which were copies of Lumière films. In 1897, he built the first French studios at Montreuil where, for the next sixteen years, more than 500 films were shot, many of them reflecting his taste for magic tricks. He was not interested in representing reality, not even theatrical reality, but in creating original works that could not exist anywhere else but on film. He used theatrical effects, but also invented uniquely cinematographic special effects like stopping the frame. Méliès was not, however, a businessman. Cinema changed very rapidly and his last productions were out of touch with public taste, and therefore financial failures. He did not survive the war but went into liquidation and was all but forgotten. In 1931, at a banquet attended by three hundred people, Louis Lumière handed over to him the Légion d'Honneur.

Auguste Lumière to Doctor E.

Lyon, 21 September 1931

Doctor E
5 chemin de . . .[1]
Vaissieux by Caluire
Lyon

My dear Doctor,

I have just read in *La Vie Lyonnaise* your kind article about the second edition of my book and I wish to let you know immediately how grateful I am.

You cannot know how pleased I was to read your column and here is why. More even than when my work first appeared, I have the impression that the word is out that my work should be met with silence. The most important medical journal in France, *La Presse Médicale*, did not report my first work, but a number of publications did analyse it and also several daily newspapers which, I know, have now been pressured into not mentioning this new book.

There are no arguments against my criticisms, so the only way to neutralize them is not to discuss them. And yet, there is no more serious problem. It is even more serious than universal peace, because wars, however bloodthirsty, take fewer lives over the millennia than tuberculosis has.

Thank you, Doctor.

Yours sincerely,

Auguste Lumière

1 Name and address deliberately suppressed.

Louis Lumière to Georges Méliès

My dear Monsieur Méliès,

Thank you for your kind letter which I have found at Bandol after a few days' absence. The banquet for you and Monsieur Delac is appointed for 22 October and I shall be very pleased to attend, since I shall definitely be back in Paris by then.

Yours sincerely,

Louis Lumière

Albert Trarieux to Auguste Lumière

23 October 1931

My dear Uncle Gut,

Thank you for your affectionate letter and for your kind thoughts, which don't surprise me, coming as they do from you. I do not need to remind you that what we wanted with all our heart was that you should both receive simultaneously that honour which you both deserve.

Unfortunately I believe, as you do, that promotions to the rank of grand officer[1] are so rare that it will be very difficult to get two in one. But what must not happen – and this is also Desbordes' feeling[2] – is that, out of touching, fraternal abnegation, you should give up your own hopes. You know that Papa would be as happy as for himself; to tell you the truth, I told him of your wish to withdraw; he will certainly tell you himself what he told me, which is that, on the contrary, you should not reject any favourable advances.

In any case, you are no hindrance to one another. If one of your names came out sooner than the other, it would only be easier to right the balance, which would seem natural.

What is desirable is that ministerial attention should be drawn to your respective merits on different sides, even separately. Indeed, that may be the only way to get both of you accepted at the same time.

If Vigne can obtain support which would, I expect, be effective in influencing the Ministry of Health, please do not stand in the way. We can perfectly easily act on Education, on which cinema depends, on behalf of Papa, at the same time. Perhaps two ministers, each backing a candidate of your merits, can move their colleagues to give them satisfaction jointly.

What would be helpful is if Henri could let me know what is happening on your side because, to the extent that one has any influence at all, one may be able to help without in any sense harming Papa's chances.

The main thing is that both of you are mentioned and that people act on both your behalfs. You damn well deserve it.

A hug, dear Uncle Gut, with much affection.

Albert Trarieux

I enclose a cheque for the loan coupons and bonds due for repayment.

1 Translator's note: Grand Officer of the Légion d'Honneur, a very high rank, much rarer than, say, an English peerage.
2 André Desbordes, friend of Albert Trarieux, a tax controller.

Gabrielle Camille Flammarion to Auguste Lumière

Juvisy, 17 September 1932

Illustrious maestro,

What a joy to receive the autochrome plates which you were kind enough to send us and for which I thank you with all my heart. Alas! The eclipse of the moon once more was obscured by clouds. We saw almost nothing.

Astronomy is a school for patience. We are never discouraged and we trust next time will be better.

Yours sincerely,

Gabrielle Camille Flammarion

Louis Lumière to Alphonse Seyewetz

Juan-les-Pins, 26 September 1933

My dear Seyewetz,

Thank you for your kind letter and congratulations on such an interesting trip in such a short time. Our friend Grignard[1] did indeed write to me some time ago to ask whether I would agree to join the Académie de Lyon[2] as correspondent fellow, at the same time as Auguste was appointed resident fellow. I said that I should be flattered and that I should willingly accept. But I had not foreseen the price you would have to pay, namely that you would have to prepare a document about me! I apologize most sincerely, and since you ask whether I have anything to add, I enclose some brochures about various matters I have looked into since the note which you have was drawn up.

I should also like you to mention the research which led me to make radio loudspeakers,[3] based on applying to the phonograph certain pleated diffuser diaphragms of which a summary description appears in my note of 1918. These diffuser loudspeakers were, I believe, the first of their kind and they have found many applications since, either in pleated or in open-book form (which I called 'Biblos'). More than two hundred thousand of them were built in France, in England, in Germany and in America.

If you have at your disposal a copy of *La Nature*, you might look up one or more articles by P. Hemmardinquer[4] which have appeared in the last year about phonographs with loud speakers which seem to be coming back. He mentions my various devices in these articles, and used photos he asked to have made as illustrations. Unfortunately, I do not have any copies of the relevant issues of *La Nature*; there are two of them, if memory serves.

Thank you in advance for doing this insipid job.

Louis

I shall not stop at Lyon on my way back. The trains are not convenient, but I shall come specially in a little while.

1 Victor Grignard (1871–1935), chemist, Professor at the Faculty of Science in Lyon. Friend of the Lumière brothers. Nobel Prize winner, 1912, for the discovery of organic magnesates.
2 Academy of Sciences, Belles Lettres and Arts, founded in Lyon in the eighteenth century, played and still plays an important part in the development of research in that city. It gathers together scientists, artists and writers whose learned works, usually not familiar to the general public, constitute a first-class cultural and scientific deposit. This academy, like many others, includes non-resident or correspondent fellows as well as resident fellows.
3 Louis Lumière invented the loudspeaker in circumstances which are worth relating because they provide evidence of his intuitiveness and observation, as opposed to, say, Edison, who

was much more of an analyst and conducted five thousand unsuccessful experiments before discovering the light bulb. One summer's day, at the Parc de la Tête d'Or in Lyon, Louis Lumière was at a Café with some friends; as it was excessively hot, the waiter brought a 'Japanese fan'. Fidgeting, Louis Lumière found that if he held the fan taut, and hit the centre of the cone thus formed, the sound was amplified. He confirmed his experiment by tests on a violin. The loud-speaker was invented. This letter shows that he continued to work on applications for an invention dated 1897.

4 Charles Hemmardinquer (1868–1944), received free training in the physical sciences from Jean-Gustave Bourbouze and succeeded him at the Sorbonne in 1894. In 1895, he founded a Society for the Free Teaching of Science which included such figures as Lippmann. In 1909, he established a Technical School of Science which recruited principally the sons of businessmen.

Dr R. Janeteau[1] to Auguste Lumière

Blagnac, 19 July 1934

Maestro and friend,

You are not losing your grip, nor forgetting your friends, particularly since you know how to remind them of your existence by sending them a little treat from time to time, for it is gifts which keep friendships going.

I should like to return the compliment, but I do not have the time, as my clients take up all my time and my health is not good.

I have been in two wars, Madagascar and the Great, I have chronic nephritis and it does not let me forget it. I am talking too much about myself and not enough about you.

I often say to my dear companion-for-life, I'd so like before I die to see the only sincere friend I ever had, Monsieur Lumière Auguste, because I had lots of them, friends, but they were friends to devour me. They had almost four million off me. But I know them, it was my fault, I've an easy purse.

Forgive my blather, but I enjoy pouring out my feelings to a genuinely sincere soul.

Many thanks, Maestro, dear friend.

Give my regards to your family.

Janeteau

1 Trained as veterinary surgeon, friend of Auguste's, later chief accountant at the Lumière offices.

Paul Nadar[1] to Auguste Lumière

Elysée, 6 November 1934

My dear Lumière,

I was on very friendly terms with your father, who called me *tu*, which will not surprise you; I also knew your mother[2] when I was in Lyon and I remember her with great respect and admiration; I see your brother Louis from time to time, though not often enough, as I believe he is always very busy and I cannot leave my work.

As to you, my fond memories go back a long way, to the days when I had founded Paris Photographe, and you and Louis were such useful collaborators; and if opportunities for the pleasure of seeing you unfortunately never arose, I nevertheless remained in sympathy with you, since the atrocious misfortune[3] which befell you at a time when I was in constant and close contact with your family – during the Turin Exhibition – and I was so sincerely taken with the graciousness, kindness, straightforwardness and harmony of everyone around you that I have never forgotten it.

Anyway, while you were becoming an admirable scientist and dedicating yourself to the mysteries of humankind and ameliorating its lot, I was content to carry on trying to make the best portraits I could, never faltering in the belief that my duty consists in providing the people who come to me not just with a photo, but a sincere image steeped in the particular characteristics of the personality concerned. That is how, speaking without pride, I have been able to maintain my rank among portrait photographers and I am satisfied with my profession because I believe that there is nothing more precious in the world than the image of those who are dear to us. I have thus been privileged faithfully to please, earning my keep quite naturally, without ulterior motive.

But now arthritis of the hip (dry arthritis, known as Paulet's syndrome) has crept on me unawares and I am in some pain from its misdeeds. It is becoming really quite awkward and spreading to my right kneecap and, of late, to my right arm. I am great friends with J-L Faure and with Pauchet, who, two and a half years ago, operated on me for water on the joints – the scars are still painful; some time ago, he said to me, 'Why don't you write to Lumière? He has being doing tremendous work, perhaps he has got something he could send you.'

So there we are, dear Lumière. It is not a nice business. I shall be seventy-nine next February. I need hardly add I had injections, electric shocks, X-rays when the problem started, some twelve years ago. I could let you have them: they show that my femur has been affected.

I am sorry, my dear Lumière, to be boring you thus with my torments, but I am sure you will understand. I have worked all my life, but I have never been a man of money and I need to work to make a living. Luckily, I am assisted by my darling daughter, my only child.

It is fortunate she is a gifted draughtswoman and painter, but she is also gifted with tenderness so great it alarms me sometimes, which I am sure you will comprehend as she has never left us, her mother and me.

If ever you come to Paris, my dear friend, I should be very happy to see you and in the meantime, I hope you will forgive this overlong confession, which was, in part, a duty, since Pauchet advised it.

Please send my fondest regards to your family.

P. Nadar

1 Son of the great pioneering photographer, Felix Tournachon, known as Nadar and himself a photographer.
2 Jeanne-Joséphine Costille (1841–1913), Madame Antoine Lumière.
3 Perhaps Paul Nadar refers here to the deaths of Auguste's sisters, France and Juliette in 1924, and Jeanne in 1926; unless he means the death in 1918 of Andrée, Auguste's daughter, from which Auguste never recovered.

Gustave Charpentier[1] to Monsieur Lumière
30 December 1934

My dear great friend,
    Kind regards and fondest wishes to a Glorious Frenchman whom I love and respect.
    Gustave Charpentier

1 Gustave Charpentier (1860–1956), a pupil of Massenet, Grand Prix de Rome, 1887. He composed 'The Coronation of a Muse' in order to introduce instrumental and choral music into popular fêtes. Louis Lumière was a fan of his greatest success, 'Louise'. It showed a taste for realism in opera and for popular colours and poetry.

Auguste Lumière to the Académie des Sciences

Lyon, 22 March 1935

The President
Académie des Sciences
Paris

Dear President,

I should be most grateful if you would count me among the candidates for the vacancy for a non-resident fellow left by Monsieur Flahaut's death.

I am most grateful to you in this matter.

Auguste Lumière
Correspondent of the Académie des Sciences et de Médecine

Louis Lumière to Desfeuilles

Monsieur Desfeuilles
124 rue de Verneuil
Paris 7

Dear Sir,

Thank you for your letter of 3 May in which you inform me that you have been asked by Monsieur André Grisoni, Member of Parliament and Mayor of Courbevoie, to organize a formal session at the Opera to commemorate the fortieth anniversary of Cinema, and inquiring whether I accept the principle of the event.

I am most grateful for this honour and I should be glad if you would thank the organizers and people responsible on my behalf.

I willingly accept your proposal.

Yours sincerely,

Louis Lumière of the Institut

Dr L. de Feo to Auguste Lumière

Rome, 29 May 1935

Dear Sir,

As you probably know already, I have had the pleasure of giving H.E. Monsieur Mussolini copies of your magnificent opus which the Duce received with much interest.

I am delighted to have been able to be of service to you on this occasion.

Please do not hesitate to let me know if I can be of further assistance.
Yours faithfully,
Dr. L de Feo, Director

Alphonse Seyewetz to Louis Aubert

Lyon, 17 June 1935

Monsieur Louis Aubert
Member of Parliament for the Vendée
21 rue de Constantine,
Paris 7

Dear Sir,

I am surprised and somewhat pained to discover that your proposal that the fortieth anniversary of Cinema should be commemorated by the issuing of a stamp with the effigies of Messieurs Auguste and Louis Lumière has not been retained by the member proposing the bill. The draft suggests that the stamp should bear only the effigy of Monsieur Louis Lumière, inventor of the Cinematograph.

The Member justifies this proposal by a letter in which Monsieur Auguste Lumière himself states, with impeccable loyalty, that his brother Louis had invented the Cinematograph in one night. What he meant by this was that his brother had invented the first machine to be of practical use, but that he had himself built a machine designed to project moving pictures on to a screen, and that he had abandoned his project because his brother's solution was superior.

There is no question that the exchange of ideas between the Lumière brothers who, at that time, worked jointly on all their projects, contributed to the invention of the machine. This was so widely accepted by all those who took part in the birth of the invention that among all the rivals who claimed prior invention of the Cinematograph, the name of the Lumière brothers has always been quoted jointly.

In fact, when the city council of Paris had a plaque put on the Grand Café to commemorate the first public projection of moving picture, it never occurred to anyone that the brothers' names should be separated. The plaque reads: invented by the Lumière brothers.

Monsieur Auguste Lumière's collaborators would consider the creation of a commemorative stamp to be an injustice if the effigy of both brothers was not on it and, in their opinion, the two names should never have been separated in the commemoration of this invention, whatever over-modest

226

claims Monsieur Auguste Lumière may make.

I should therefore be most grateful to you, on behalf of all Monsieur Auguste Lumière's former collaborators, if you would attempt to have the draft bill for the creation of an anniversary stamp amended so that it should reflect the terms of the original proposal which were fair.

It may, however, be possible to signal Monsieur Louis Lumière's preponderant part in the invention by placing his representation in the foreground.

Yours sincerely.

Louis Aubert to Alphonse Seyewetz

Paris, 18 June 1935

Dear Sir,

Thank you for your letter of the 17th. I am in agreement with you and I shall do my best when the time comes to ensure that the stamp represents 'the brothers Lumière'.

Yours,
Aubert

G. Méker to Alphonse Seyewetz

Asnières, 25 June 1935

Monsieur A. Seyewetz
Assistant Principal, School of Chemistry
Lyon

Dear Sir,

I saw Monsieur Louis Lumière yesterday and he told me his sentiments about the incidents provoked by documents which are clearly not of his doing.[1]

I foresaw these problems before undertaking to organize Louis Lumière's scientific jubilee. Various conversations with various people however persuaded me that what we were doing was right. The Lumière Gala Committee which is separate from us, is concerned only with Cinema; they have perhaps gone slightly further than they intended, at least in the Pomaret report.

Chatting aimlessly with Monsieur Louis Lumière yesterday, a thought occurred and I put it to him. Why don't Auguste Lumière's friends and collaborators plan a scientific jubilee for Auguste Lumière, to take place in Lyon or in Paris in a few months' time, spring 1936 perhaps? The extent of his research quite warrants such a gesture. I know he will oppose it, as his brother was opposed to us, a year ago, when we started out. But now he is agreeable and there is no reason why Monsieur Auguste Lumière should not give in to pressure from his friends. When I was privileged to meet him at his brother's house a few weeks ago, he was opposed to the ceremony which the Lyon press wants to organize on behalf of both brothers, but he has now accepted it.

A fine ceremony for the Auguste Lumière Jubilee a few months after the Louis Lumière Jubilee would be an excellent reason for insisting on the presence of both on the stamp which will not appear, I am told, until 1936 or 1937. Those who are against this now will not be then.

Do you not think, sir, that I am right and that this is the way to avoid a certain, probably justified, resentment and regret.

I do not think it would be impossible to find in Lyon an organization capable of arranging such an excellent project; there will be some people against you, in the medical profession, as we have some people against us; but anything one does makes enemies, and indeed one is lucky if they declare their hostility out in the open.

I look forward to hearing from you.

G. Méker

1 Historical quarrels are sometimes the doing of scholars, critics and historians, rather than the scientists themselves. Once again, certain more or less malicious misinterpretations were attempting to give Louis sole credit for an invention developed and perfected by both brothers. It is worth remembering that these two men, when they both lived at Lyon, met every night to compare notes, experiments and thoughts. Their mutual trust and friendship was flawless.

Alphonse Seyewetz to G. Méker

Lyon, 29 June 1935

Monsieur G. Méker
11 avenue Casimir
Asnières

Dear Sir,

I have shown Monsieur Auguste Lumière your letter. He feels no resentment at not being associated with the festivities being arranged in Paris for the fortieth anniversary of Cinema and is, on the contrary, delighted that an event is in preparation in Paris to celebrate his brother Louis' scientific jubilee.

The only matter which affected him was the matter of the stamp, which was originally to have been the twin portraits of the Lumière brothers, and then, as a result of a report to the Chamber, to bear only the effigy of Louis Lumière.

Monsieur Auguste Lumière's collaborators and friends were unpleasantly surprised to discover this policy, which was contrary to the original project of commemorating both the brothers. Monsieur Auguste Lumière hopes that no special events will be organized in Lyon on his behalf for the moment, as his considerable medical research, which will one day be admired round the world, has so far been acknowledged by only a small part of the medical establishment. His ideas are gradually winning people over and the number of his official supporters is always on the increase.

Monsieur Auguste Lumière believes that in one or two years his research will have earned its place and that official scientists will abandon the ostracism with which they currently meet his work. At that time Monsieur Auguste Lumière will receive whatever honours he is offered in respect of his formidable medical achievements with pleasure.

Yours sincerely,
A. Seyewetz

Max Skladanowsky to Louis Lumière

Baden-Baden, 1 July 1935

Monsieur Louis Lumière
Fellow of the Institut
156 boulevard Bineau
Neuilly-sur-Seine

My dear Monsieur Lumière,

Your very kind letter found me at Heidelberg where, after the end of the International Film Congress, I was pursuing my tour; I am showing the first German films which I made in 1895 and 1896. Having already been invited to your historic event at the Grand Café in Paris on 28 December 1895, I much regret having missed you in Berlin, for a meeting with my great contemporary, who solved once and for all a problem with which independent workers had been wrestling in four countries, would be a climax and a joy as my life reaches its evening.

I say this because I wish to inform you that I shall go to Venice in August to attend the establishment of an International Film Chamber during the Art and Film Weeks and I am writing to ask – I who am the first person to have attempted our art in Germany – whether I may hope for the true privilege of greeting the famous inventor of the Cinematograph while I am there.

With best wishes for your good health and for the rest of this year.
Yours sincerely,
Max Skladanowsky

Alphonse Seyewetz to Louis Aubert

Lyon, 3 July 1935

Monsieur Louis Aubert
Member for the Vendée
21 rue de Constantine
Paris 7è

Dear Sir,

I am writing because, despite the steps which you were kind enough to take to ensure that in Monsieur Pomaret's report concerning a Lumière stamp, this stamp should be issued with the twin portrait of Auguste and Louis Lumière and not with Louis Lumière's features alone, the Official Proceedings have published a law relating only to Monsieur Louis and not to both Lumière brothers.

We do not understand, here, why there is such interest in eliminating Monsieur Auguste Lumière from the event, with which, as I wrote to you in my last letter, he has every reason to expect to be associated.

Please do what you can to see what can be done to amend this law, even though the vote has gone through.
Yours faithfully,
A. Seyewetz

Louis Aubert to Alphonse Seyewetz

Paris, 9 July 1935

Dear Sir,

It is not possible to amend this law, but you can be sure that when the time comes, the stamp will bear the image of both brothers.
Yours,
Aubert

G. Méker to Alphonse Seyewetz

Monsieur A. Seyewetz
Vice-Principal, School of Chemistry
Lyon

Dear Sir,

I received your letter of 29 June some time ago, but I have been away and thus unable to reply.

I am very pleased to know that these matters, which from a distance can seem somewhat tricky, are now arranged.

I am as certain as you are that Monsieur Auguste Lumière will soon receive just recognition, and is he not in any case already recognized by those of independent judgement?

Monsieur Auguste Lumière was kind enough to send me his recent publications and I shall not fail to read them from beginning to end.

I look forward to seeing you at the Jubilee ceremony on 6 November.

Yours faithfully,
G. Méker

G. Méker to A. Seyewetz

[August 1935]

Dear Sir,

Upon receiving your letter of the 20th of this month I once again tried to persuade Monsieur Auguste Lumière to come back upon his decision not to attend his brother's Jubilee, and gave him the reasons you mentioned to explain why he was excluded from the events organized by The French Renaissance which, in the minds of everyone from Lyon, should really have applied to both brothers.

These explanations did not change his mind. Monsieur Auguste says, rightly: you say that this celebration is not designed to commemorate the Cinematograph – well, no one will believe that, because the main purpose of Louis Lumière's jubilee must be to commemorate the invention of the Cinematograph, which is forty years old this year. In Rome, Paris, Brussels, Amsterdam, only Louis Lumière, the inventor of the Cinematograph, has been singled out as the focus of celebration and his well-deserved fame is certainly the main reason why The French Renaissance has decided to organize this Jubilee.

There was no reason why the Jubilee could not have been in honour of both brothers, who published all their work jointly over a thirty-year period. The Cinematograph was developed during this period of close collaboration. Monsieur Auguste cannot renounce his share in this invention without seeming to have unjustifiably allowed his name, over the years, to be associated with a discovery which was none of his doing.

I am sorry not to have succeeded in the mission which you asked me to perform.

Yours faithfully,

Alphonse Seyewetz to G. Méker

[August 1935]

Monsieur Méker
Secretary-General
The French Renaissance

Dear Sir,

Thank you for sending me the information concerning Louis Lumière's jubilee, together with your letter.

May I once again say how sorry I am, and how sorry everyone who knows the Lumière brothers and everyone who has lived near them is, that Auguste should have been excluded from this event which was originally planned to have honoured both the Lumière brothers.

I am taking the liberty of writing to you because all around me people are complaining that I have agreed to take part in this event.

Auguste and Louis worked together intimately for amost half a century. All their research was shared and Auguste has always implied to me that, if his brother was solely responsible for constructing the definitive Cinematograph, the two of them had exchanged ideas which to some degree helped to bring about moving picture photography.

But even if they did not work together on this particular point, they should still be celebrated jointly because their partnership was official. The patent was taken out in the names of Auguste and Louis and for thirty years Cinema was considered an invention of both brothers. The commemorative plaque on the Grand Café, erected in 1928 by the city council of Paris, clearly reads Auguste and Louis Lumière, inventors of the Cinematograph, as does the plaque in Lyon, rue de la République, to commemorate the site of the first moving picture theatre, and the plaque on the house where they were born, in Besançon.

I cannot help deploring, as do all the friends of the Lumière brothers in Lyon, this recent turn of events, which came close to provoking a misunderstanding between the two brothers. That would have been awful. Only Auguste's deep fondness for his brother avoided that outcome.

Monsieur Auguste will reply to you in person about his attendance at his brother's Jubilee.

Yours faithfully,

Lucien Bamer to Auguste Lumière

Ottawa, 23 September 1935

Dear Sir, My Dear Master,

I do not how to thank you for granting my request and above all for answering so fully. It proves that French genius admits kindness towards less favoured people. My heart is moved. Thank you.

Your kind letter appears in my album with Pasteur, Berthelot,[1] Roux,[2] Fournier, Bretchnikoff, Lippmann, Branly,[3] Richet,[4] Apple, Poincaré, Maurice de Broglie – to name but a few of your illustrious colleagues – for I have been privileged to spend the last forty years collecting nearly five hundred letters, notes, jottings, poems, sketches and musical fragments by the artistic, literary and scientific heroes of our dear France. This collection is not just famous but also unique in Canada.

Your interesting volumes, *The Rebirth of Humoral Medicine, Tuberculosis, Contagion and Heredity*, as well as various pamphlets, including a curious and amusing fantasy 'Le Mechef Omineux d'un Palot'[5] have reached me in perfect condition. I am not qualified to speak for science, my work at the Ministry is translating and drawing up laws governing Canadian shipping, but I shall certainly let our young doctors know your works now they are increasingly turning to France, to Europe, where many of them now go for their studies, having previously been under the sway of Yankee quacks.

Yours faithfully
Lucien Bamer
Director of French Works at the Ministry of the Sea

1 Marcellin Berthelot (1827–1907), chemist and politician. He was Minister of Education, 1886–7, and of Foreign Affairs, 1895–6, and elected to the Académie Française in 1900. Like Louis Lumière, the fiftieth anniversary of his scientific work, in 1901, was celebrated with a grand ceremony at the Sorbonne.
2 Emile Roux (1853–1933), French bacteriologist who collaborated with Pasteur on his

work on hen cholera, rabies and vaccination against infection. He conducted research of his own into toxins and developed the first anti-diphtheria serum (1894). He started a course in microbiology at the Pasteur Institute, and ran that institution after E. Duclaux (1904).
3 Edouard Branly (1844–1940), mainly known as the inventor of wireless reception (1890).
4 Professor Richet developed, with Portier, the concept of anaphylaxia. He also observed irregularities in lactic fermentation.
5 Auguste Lumière shared with Louis a taste for language. This work is a five-page piece of nonsense entirely composed of strange words that really exist in the dictionary. It begins: Dans ces ermes uligineuses, échappant à l'autopsie grâce à quelques suriers et pinastres sabulaires . . .

Grand Chancellor of the Légion d'Honneur to Auguste Lumière

Paris, 8 October 1935

Monsieur Auguste Lumière
Grand Officer of the National Order of the Légion d'Honneur

Sir,

By decree of 30 July 1935, Monsieur Lumière Louis Jean, fellow of the Institut, inventor of Cinema, has been raised to the rank of Grand Officer of the national order of the Légion d'Honneur.

Please find the enclosed minutes. I hereby grant you the authority to invest him.

If you should be unable to perform this task, please return the document to me so that I can instruct another member of the Order with the task of this investiture.

Yours faithfully,

G. Méker to an unknown correspondent

Asnières, 10 October 1935

Dear Sir,

We have the pleasure of enclosing a list of names being the people who have agreed to sponsor the celebration of Louis Lumière's Jubilee.

The Formal Session will take place Wednesday, 6 November at 9p.m. in the Grand Lecture Hall at the Sorbonne. The President of the Republic will attend.

Monsieur Louis Lumière will be addressed by various personalities and will receive a medal bearing his own likeness.

Please find enlosed two invitations for the official tiers and two for the upper tiers. Please do not hesitate to contact us if there is any further information you should require.

Secretary-General

Méker

The Hospice of the Ladies of Calvary to Auguste Lumière

Lyon, 3 November 1935

Dear Sir,

On behalf of our poor patients whom you do so much to relieve by your care and your generosity, I write to thank you.

We can only pray that God should leave a man such as you on this earth, who wishes only to relieve the sufferings of humanity; may our prayers be granted.

Yours

Mother Superior of Calvary

Alphonse Seyewetz to Louis Lumière

[5 November 1935]

My dear Louis,

I thought I should be able to attend your Jubilee tomorrow and thus tell you affectionately and in person how much I admire your magificent work, of which the Cinematograph and the autochrome plate would alone justify the grand occasion arranged on your behalf.

I am proud, my dear Louis, to have worked alongside you for so long and to have had the rare privilege of observing from the inside a course of research which has earned you, today, your nation's thanks.

The 6 November happens to be a day I cannot get away. I shall not, therefore, be able to congratulate you in person and I apologize. In any case, my presence would have passed unnoticed among all the glorious personalities who will gather together in learned assembly to crown you with laurels.

Many congratulations.

Alphonse Seyewetz to G. Méker

Monsieur Méker
Secretary-General of The French Renaissance
11 avenue Casimir
Asnières

Dear Sir,

Monsieur Auguste Lumière has asked me to forward to you the enclosed article entitled 'A History of Cinema' which appeared in *Le Petit Dauphinois*, together with the portrait of Monsieur Auguste Lumière which accompanied it and which is captioned with an indication that the portrait was taken in his laboratory shortly before his death.

No doubt it is the absence of Monsieur Auguste's name beside that of his brother Louis, when they had always previously been together, which caused the journalist to make a mistake. Which is what Monsieur Auguste thought would happen. Fortunately, he is not superstitious and does not believe that this premature announcement anticipates the real thing.

I also enclose a cutting from a Lyon newspaper which gives its judgement on the absence of Monsieur Auguste Lumière's name in the commemoration of the invention of Cinema.

Yours faithfully,

G. Méker to Alphonse Seyewetx

Asnières, 18 December 1935

Monsieur Seyewetz
153 boulevard Pinel
Bron

Dear Sir,

I received your letter of 11 December. I apologize for being so slow to reply and for not replying to your letter of 25 October.

As regards the latter, I had in fact prepared a reply, but I sensed that there was tension between the two brothers and so I did not know whether to send it as I was not sure it would bring about the appeasement I sought, and I have not had any time of my own since, as I had to abandon much of my own business since October and I have had to catch up on it.

You wrote to me that the Jubilee was the fortieth anniversary of Cinema and that we were following on from celebrations abroad. You were wrong and you were induced to be wrong by the film industry which tried, first, to wreck our project, and then, when they saw we were making progress, took the credit.

Read what Monsieur Armbruster[1] and I have been writing since June 1934, and read the speeches at the Sorbonne and read also what Monsieur Fabry[2] said.

In June 1934 we announced our decision, and you were made aware of it at that time. We said that it should be a Scientific Jubilee, but that it would be logical to have it coincide with the fortieth anniversary of Cinema.

As regards the press cuttings which you have been kind enough to send me, they prove, if proof is necessary, that journalists do not know what they write about and as you are a scientist I cannot believe that you approve of this method.

Would you let me know which newspaper published the article signed 'Firebrand' and I shall ask it to rectify its mistakes.

With respect to *Le Petit Dauphinois*, it is most unfortunate that it has been so ill-informed and I assume that you have requested that it correct its error.

Monsieur Auguste's absence from the Sorbonne was commented upon here and if some people also thought that he was deceased, everyone else deeply regretted his not being there, which was much to his disadvantage. I thought of this once more when I saw that he was standing for Monsieur Flahaut's seat.[3]

I have heard it said that Monsieur Auguste Lumière was not pleased with the letter I sent him. I showed it to several people who know both brothers and we are most surprised; my tone was most deferential and I cannot understand that he should have interpreted it otherwise and not replied.

You may rest assured, my dear Sir, that there is no one hostile to Monsieur A. Lumière, at least not in the Group which was responsible for L. Lumière's Jubilee. I may say that on 2 November, Monsieur Gaumont wanted to take the train to Lyon and bring Monsieur Auguste back with him. It was the tone of this correspondence which prevented him from doing so.

A final word. The film industry promised to help us. It did so neither morally nor financially. Indeed, it often hindered, as it never kept the promises it made.

Yours faithfully,

---

1 Léonce Armbruster, chairman of The French Renaissance, made a speech (Jubilé Louis Lumière) in which he clearly stated that 'the names of Auguste and Louis Lumière remain inseparable'. An interview given by Louis Lumière in *Le Progrès*, 13 July 1934, is somewhat different: 'The truth is that the Chairman of The French Renaissance, Monsieur Armbruster,

came to me recently to tell me about his organization's intention of arranging in my honour a ceremony similar to that which had been arranged for Professor d'Arsonval last year. I first refused and then, upon his insistence, agreed, asking him to include my beloved older brother Auguste, who was for so long the inseparable companion of my life and my work. But that was not what he wanted. They wanted to celebrate the invention of cinema and the invention of colour photography. Thus, to my regret, my brother's vast programme of biological research and our old, fertile and fond collaboration will remain at the margin of the celebration. According to the original idea, this was to take place in the autumn. As I shall be seventy on 5 October and as my brother shall be seventy-two on the 19th of the same month, it might still have passed as a family occasion. But certain last minute hitches have made this impossible.' The Jubilee was attended by the President of the Republic, Albert Lebrun, and seven ministers, twenty-seven ambassadors and forty-seven fellows of the Institut. Auguste Lumière's absence led many people to conclude that he was dead. On being reassured, Gaumont said he'd go to Lyon by car to fetch him. 'Don't,' said Seyewetz, 'He'll throw you out.' It was thought that the brothers had quarrelled. The misunderstanding was the responsibility of the organizers who failed to appreaciate the extent of Auguste's involvement in the invention of the Cinematograph. This letter could be read as an apology, though perhaps not an enthusiastic one, judging by the last lines.

2 Charles Fabry, fellow of the Institut, chairman of the Société Française de Photographie et de Cinématographie. This is an extract from his speech: 'The most striking thing about this work is its homogeneity; the problems solved have been very varied and each time the inventor has drawn on innovative techniques and new faculties of invention; but if he has thus gone round, as it were, all physical chemistry, all his work or most of it centres on that fine thing known as photography, a discipline so complex it is hard to know whether it should be categorized as a science, a technique or an art, in which light itself is asked to print the things it shows,' and further on, the following quotation from Auguste Lumière, 'In the brief intervals afforded us by the management of our industrial concern, we considered this problem [cinema] and I had conceived of a theory, the basic elements of which I no longer remember, when one morning towards the end of 1894, I entered my brother's room. He had been unwell and had taken to his bed. He then told me that, having been unable to sleep, he had enumerated the conditions required to attain our goal and thought up a mechanism capable of fulfilling those conditions. . . This was a revelation and I realized that I must abandon the precarious solution which I had been thinking of. In one night, my brother had invented the Cinematograph!' A sudden revelation that must have been inspired by many hours of considered thought.

3 See Auguste Lumière to the Académie des Sciences, 22 March 1935. Charles Flahaut (1852–1935), botanist, taught at Montpellier from 1883 to 1927, then travelled in Europe and North Africa. He established an Institute of Botany at Montpellier in 1890 and in 1903 the Hort-Dieu botanical garden in the Aigueval Mountains.

Alphonse Seyewetz to G. Méker[1]

24 December 1935

Monsieur Méker
Secretary-General of The French Renaissance
Asnières

Dear Sir,
    Thank you for your letter of the 18th of this month, together with the

texts of speeches given at Monsieur Louis Lumière's Jubilee. I am most grateful to you. I am now returning these texts. I showed them to Monsieur Auguste Lumière, who says that he no longer wishes to discuss cinema. He requests that you do not write to the newspaper in Lyon, a cutting from which I sent to you.

Perfect harmony is now restored between the two brothers and there is no longer any fear of discord. This is all their friends were asking for.

Yours sincerely,

1 This letter relates to the deplorable consequences of the organizers of the Jubilee's tactlessness. The misunderstandings now seem dispelled.

Castanet to [Auguste] Lumière

Pontaillac, 30 December 1935

Maestro,

This year, as every year, it is my pleasure to send you my best wishes.

I read in *L'Illustration* an article that was so well written and so true called 'A Great Scientific Jubilee' which must have touched all your friends. Everyone is indeed surprised to discover that creative genius can also be allied with generosity and greatness, in the close and fond collaboration of two brothers sharing the same ideal. A fine thing. A great thing and a very French thing.

This combination of philanthropy and high scientific thought has inspired me to write. Will it see the day? I do not know, I have sent the foreword in to *L'Illustration* but have not had any reply.

With best wishes, again,

Yours sincerely,

Marius Chapuis[1] to Louis Lumière

Champfromier, December 1935

At a time when the whole world is full of praise for the father of the Cinematograph[2], I cannot resist the temptation of adding the humble expression of thanks of a stranger who, forty years ago, took advantage of the Lumière Brothers' invention to go on a fine journey upon which he would never otherwise have embarked.

I was hired as cameraman-projectionist, among the many you sent all over the world, to show the results of your beautiful work and I was sent to

Russia. The journey lasted eighteen months. A great event which has left me with wonderful memories and also the one great regret of my life: that I was too young (eighteen years old at the time) to make use of the benefits that were offered to me; and so I chose another route which has led me, in old age, to think of my loss.

Forgive me, Maestro, for detaining you with this slight story, but your name is on everyone's lips and it has awakened the thoughts and the memories of one of your humble and respectful servants of forty years ago, who wishes now to tell you of his considerable esteem.

M. Chapuis

1 At the age of seventeen, in 1896–7, Marius Chapuis was sent to Russia to work for the Lumière family as cameraman-projectionist. He lived a surprising and adventurous life, outside normal social conventions. Eventually, he became a cabinet-maker, then Mayor of Champfromier, a village in which he lived. His travels are documented in letters to his family and a notebook he kept throughout his Russian adventures.
2 Louis Lumière's Jubilee has just taken place. A glossy publication of 123 pages was issued for the occasion, on 6 November 1935. Delegates from all over the world expressed their thanks to Louis Lumière at the ceremony. The President of the Republic attended. As we have seen, a misunderstanding led the organizers to claim for Louis Lumière sole paternity of the Cinematograph, as a result of which, Auguste did not attend the ceremony but chose, instead, to write the preface to a book of conjuring tricks.

Louis Lumière to Marius Chapuis

Neuilly-sur-Seine

Many thanks for your kind letter and for the memories which it evokes. I am most grateful.

The Russian programmes which you enclosed were of great interest to me and I shall keep them preciously.

Once again, thank you.

Louis Lumière

Telegram from Nasierowski to Auguste Lumière

11 January 1936

Monsieur Auguste Lumière
45 rue Villon
Lyon
Warszawa 23–55–11
10.15 a.m. by wireless

A thousand apologies that I cannot in person tell a great French scientist how much I admire and respect his measureless works; with all my heart, I join his collaborators in a single act of veneration.

Nasierowski

Auguste Lumière to the Académie des Sciences

Lyon, 15 February 1936

The Perpetual Secretaries of the Académie des Sciences
Palace of the Institut
25 quai de Conti
Paris 6è

Dear Perpetual Secretaries,

In accordance with your request, I sent you yesterday two copies of a note on my research.

Yours sincerely,
Auguste Lumière

Auguste Lumière to the Académie des Sciences

Lyon, 23 February 1936

Please do not include me on the list of candidates for the seat left vacant by the death of my friend, the late lamented Professor Grignard.

Yours sincerely,
Auguste Lumière

Louis Lumière to F. Pellin

Neuilly-sur-Seine, 26 March 1936

Monsieur F. Pellin
Optical and Precision Instruments
59 avenue Jean-Jaurès
Arcueil

My dear Monsieur Pellin,

Thank you for your letter of 24 March and for indicating your price for the supply of a polarized colour meter[1] which I requested.

I note that you call the figure which illustrates it no. 35, whereas in the catalogue you sent me it is numbered no. 30; the one I want is figure 30 in the catalogue.

I also asked you by telephone if I could not, initially, receive the device without the cut quartz[2] if it would shorten the delivery time, because I do not need the quartz until later. You have not answered my question.

In any case, I should be grateful if you would do everything you can so that I may receive this instrument in as short a time as possible.

Yours sincerely,
Louis Lumière

1 Measures the intensity of colour in a liquid. Probably connected with the manufacture of industrial paint.
2 A part of the device, used for its electrical properties.

Group of twelve employees to Auguste Lumière

Lyon, 17 June 1936

Dear Monsieur Auguste,

After the painful events[1] that have just taken place, those of your old employees who cannot forget all the good you do and all that they owe you but who have been forced to take part in action they deplore, wish to take this opportunity of expressing their gratitude and ask you to believe in their long-lasting, affectionate and sincere devotion.

1 Strikes that were particularly bitter that year.

Edmond Haraucourt[1] to Louis Lumière

Paris, 11 February 1937

Dear Sir,

I am proud of and grateful for the congratulations you were kind enough to send me, all the more so because they provide me with an opportunity to tell you how much I admire your work and the respect in which I hold your name. It is one of those names of which France may be proud and it is a pleasure for me to pay tribute to it.

1 Edmond Haraucourt (1857–1941) exercised a variety of professions before publishing in 1882 *La Légende des Sexes*, a collection of licentious verse which caused a scandal. Numerous plays by him were performed between 1887 and 1893. He was friends with

Debussy and Leconte de Lisle; in 1894, he became curator of the Trocadero Museum and in 1903 of the Cluny Museum. He was also a Fellow of the Victor Hugo Foundation. Louis Lumière is probably congratulating him on one of his many plays.

Society of Friends of André-Marie Ampère to Louis Lumière

19 June 1937

Monsieur Louis Lumière
Fellow of the Institut
President of the Society of Friends of André-Marie Ampère
156 boulevard Bineau
Neuilly-sur-Seine

Dear President,

The Members of the Board of the Society for the Friends of André-Marie Ampère, assembled at Poleymieux, were informed of your letter of 9 June addressed to Monsieur Dumont, Delegate General.

They offer you their greatest sympathy and wish you prompt recovery. They hope that your state of health will enable you to maintain the office of President of the Society of Friends of André-Marie Ampère for a long time to come as you have brought to this office much energy and the brilliance of your name.

Yours sincerely,

Ten signatures, including: Hellot, M. Mathieu, J. Berthenod, Grosselin, Ch. Fabry, Jawandowski

Auguste Lumière to A. Sabatier

Lyon, 4 October 1937

Monsieur A. Sabatier
Editions Albin Michel
22 rue Huyghens
Paris 14è

Dear Sir,

I receive letters every day which provide evidence that *Les Horizons de la Médecine*[1] is appreciated.

About fifteen patients have come to the clinic as a result of reading the book and many others have asked me for advice. I am very pleased that some leading personalities to whom I did not send my book and who bought it, spontaneously wrote to me to congratulate me. Today has brought two more such, and not the least: Senator Henri Sellier, former Minister of Health, and Ambassador Rammerer.

Several medical journals have published articles on the book as a result of readers' requests and Doctor Vigne wrote in *L'Avenir Médical* a long article which I shall have sent to you.

I hope that, for your part, you are satisfied with sales.

I wish to congratulate you on the way you have contributed to this success.

A. Lumière

[Handwritten note] Only the major medical papers have not covered the book, but that is hardly surprising and I am used to their ostracism. Mandarins do not admit that one is entitled to innovate if one is outside their purlieu; my research is an obstacle to their self-esteem or their financial interests.

1 *Les Horizons de la Médecine*, by A. Lumière, 252 pages, Albin Michel, Paris, 1937. A work of popular medicine which seems to have had some commercial success.

Auguste Lumière to Henri Lumière

13 August 1938

My dear Henri, my dear Yvette,[1]

I was told last night that my letter might find you at St Tropez and I am keen to give you news. Nothing much, because nothing much is happening at Monplaisir, but that is better than telling you about Hitler's plans or another devaluation.

This country is pretty empty. Fewer patients at the Clinic (seventy to ninety per morning – many people on holiday). This is a good thing because I couldn't manage if we had our usual crowd. Gradon is on holiday, Baullet too; Mademoiselle Simonet[2] is convalescing after an accident to her foot; Bertholon is out of action because of a verruca on each of his thumbs. Daugal, Morel and Profesor Dumas[3] are away on holiday. Mademoiselle Marin[4] is resting, as is Madame Machino. If you take into account that I am without Collet, you will see how much filling in I have to do! Anyway, I have more work than usual. We have Dr Depoorter[5] on an internship at the Clinic with his son, a medical student. He has come especially from Bruges, with a splendid present: a magnificent copy of a famous picture by Memling, the Flemish fifteenth-century master. On his departure, he left a substantial order with Caillat.[6] He was badly injured in the war – one leg amputated at the thigh. He is also very kind and learned. He is Queen Elizabeth's doctor. I think I told you that an Argentinian doctor, Dr Duhan,[7] and his sister had come to us for treatment. They are delighted with the results. Naturally, I don't charge doctors but Dr Duhan, who is now in Paris, has just sent me a cheque for 5000 francs which was nice of him.

I hope you are not having bad weather, but I can't say I am confident because here we've had storms and rain for the last two days. I'd be very sorry if you could not enjoy your holidays.

Marguerite has a new chambermaid I shall call La mère Cotivet[8] to give you an idea.

Give my regards to Léon and hug the children for me.

A. Lumière

I am longing for you to come home.

1 Yvette Piperno had two daughters by her first husband, Monsieur Morsaz: Liliane (born 1925, Maurice Trarieux-Lumière's first wife) and Huguette (born 1929). In 1937, she married Henri Lumière who adopted her daughters.
2 Head of the serology laboratory at Auguste Lumière's clinic of Bon-Abri.
3 Professor Dumas was a heart surgeon; he attended Auguste's clinic once a week with Dr Beaulaton.
4 Head of the haematology laboratory at the clinic.
5 Official doctor to Elizabeth of Bavaria, Queen of Belgium.
6 In 1928, after Marius Sestier's death, Caillat took over sales of Lumière Patents. He had previously been chief accountant for a number of years.
7 Friend of Auguste's.
8 Old mother Cotivet, according to Lyon tradition, was a gossip.

Louis Lumière to Bernard Lefebvre

Bandol, 22 August 1938

REGISTERED
Monsieur B. Lefebvre
Tel: 14
Chairman of the Photo-Club of Rouen
5 rue d'Ernemont
Rouen (S. Inf.)

My dear Chairman,
I am sorry to have taken so long to reply to your letter of 9 August which has been forwarded from Paris.

The Société Lumière has taken note of your wishes and will do what it can to satisfy them. You will shortly be receiving whatever they have managed to gather together. Personally, I have very few documents left here.

Finally, I attach a print of my portrait, complete with dedication, as you requested.

Thank you for your kind thoughts.
Louis Lumière

Louis Lumière to Bernard Lefebvre

Bandol, 10 September 1938

Monsieur Bernard Lefebvre
Chairman of the Photo-Club of Rouen
5 rue d'Ernemont, tél 14
Rouen (Seine Inférieure)

Dear Sir,
Thank you for your letter of 5 September. I can send you examples of my work that you are missing, 4.5 x 6 films shot in 1900,[1] as well as a few images from the stereoscopic film[2] which functions horizontally, but these specimens are still in packing cases and I would ask you to wait a few more days.

Yours sincerely,
Louis Lumière

1) A fragment of a 4.5 x 6 film shot by Monsieur Louis Lumière on the day of the inauguration of the 1900 Exhibition, with the help of a special device

which he has just invented.

2) A few frames of stereoscopic films by the same author.

1 For the Universal Exhibition of 1900, Louis Lumière had Carpentier build a camera using 70mm wide film, because 35mm was not luminous enough, and that is what this letter refers to. The machine was ready in time for the Exhibition but for some reason, the film was never used. The public was shown 35mm film projection in the famous Galerie des Machines, a building 400m long and 114m wide, constructed for the 1889 Exhibition. The original idea had been to hang a screen from the first floor of the Eiffel Tower, but the risk that a sudden gust of wind would tear everything down and injure a crowd of several thousand had meant a change of a plan.

2 Probably Louis Lumière's 1937 three-dimensional film.

Louis Lumière to Gauja

Bandol, 26 June 1939

Monsieur Gauja
Head of the Secretariat of the Académie des Sciences
25 quai Conti
Paris

Dear Sir,

I received yesterday, Sunday, notification of a meeting today, 26 June, which did not leave me enough time to make my apologies for being unable to attend. Please inform the committee of the Chateler Foundation that I shall be unable to be present, and similarly for the meeting on the same day of the applications of science to industry section.

Please note that it would suit me to receive such communications with a little more notice in case I can alter my travel arrangements in order to attend meetings.

Yours sincerely,
Louis Lumière

Gauja to Louis Lumière

30 June 1939

Dear Sir,

I write in reply to your letter of 26 June.

Every week, the perpetual secretaries decide on notifications of meetings to be sent out on a following Monday; following well-established custom, these notifications are drawn up on the Wednesday and sent out, not by me but by the Secretary-General of the Institut, on the Thursday, or sometimes the Friday.

I am sure that this is what happened regarding the notification for 26 June which you received on the Sunday. The ushers cannnot have had time to deal with this matter on the Thursday because of the investiture of Monsieur André Maurois.

In order that this inconvenience does not recur, I shall make a note that when you are to attend a meeting, I shall write to you myself on the Wednesday.

Yours sincerely,

Louis Lumière to Jules Richard[1]

Bandol, 18 July 1939

A thousand thanks, my dear Colleague, for your kind congratulations, for which I am most grateful.

Yours sincerely,
Louis Lumière

1 A doctor and one of the main collaborators of Prince Albert I of Monaco, the occeanographer. He was the first director of the Oceanographic Museum of Monaco (1939).

Louis Lumière [to the Military Authorities]

Bandol, 28 August 1939

I, the undersigned, Louis Lumière, ask the competent authorities for a safe-conduct for my technical assistant, Pierre Cuvier, who is to drive from Bandol to Paris and back again aboard a Peugeot 2799 R.J. 8 in order to deal with technical matters regarding National Defence.

Louis Lumière
Fellow of the Institut
Grand Cross of the Légion d'Honneur
Member of the Research and Physical Experiment Commmittee for War

Auguste Lumière to Louis Lumière

Louis, old man,

And now the fearful storm is unleashed. I trust you will not be affected and that you are safe from this barbarian adventurer's atrocities, the worst criminal the world has ever nurtured.

We, for our part, are far from reassured. We are only an hour and a half away from Hundom by plane and the bandits could easily visit us one day or one night.

For the time being, I am working for Bérard again. He has put me in charge of the anti-cancer Centre, no more than that, and I have just completed the first of my daily rounds.

I get to the Clinic early in the morning, see twenty or thirty patients, then head for the Centre. After that, our dear Albert. See what a life I lead.

But it does help forget one's troubles, and fears.

If only I could lay my mind at rest for Henri, but he won't consider it.

Since the factory has been requisitioned, he could perfectly easily be content to be assigned to the Company, but he will not hear of it.

I think you have had news that everyone is well. I hope you got the cheque that was sent.

love,

Auguste

Laboratory at the Centre for Research, Toulon, to Messieurs Lumière

Toulon, 7 September 1939

Dear Sir,

We have inspected the mirrors[1] which you sent us and submitted them to heat. They are much better than the previous set. We should be grateful if you would send us samples to be tested for corrosion and if you could come yourself so that we might discuss the parameters of our experiments. I am also holding some mirror varnish for you. It must be shaken before use, then applied with a soft brush, first in one direction then in another, as with Dulux. Only one coat.

Perhaps you could arrange to have this paint collected from Toulon.

We have also examined the listening device you were kind enough to leave with me. We intend to try it in our listening stand and it would be good if you were able to come and assess its qualities yourself.

We are very glad of your assistance and certain that it will be of use to us in many other fields.

Yours sincerely,

F. Canac

Scientific Director of the Laboratories at the Centre for Research

1 In 1939, Louis Lumière had worked for the National Defence establishment and had had large parabolic mirrors manufactured at the Arsenal at Toulon for marine projection. This letter refers to these experiments.

A. Lesbros to Auguste Lumière

Lyon, [1930s]

My dear Monsieur Lumière,

I have to leave for Avignon in a slight rush today, because of minor problems with my new job. I had not been planning to leave Lyon until the end of the week and I wanted to call on you before my departure. I apologize for not being able to because I wanted to thank you in person for all your kindness to us. I shall treasure my memories of the time I spent in your laboratory. Over the last four years, you have been the most friendly 'Boss', and the most welcoming, always ready to please. I have learnt and discovered many new things in my time with you and I want to thank you: these four years have contributed to my scientific education and I shall not forget that.

We went to the laboratory to collect our envelope and both my husband and I were most agreeably surprised. My husband is continuing to inject the guinea pigs to obtain repeated shock effects.

I have sent a neat, typewritten copy of my thesis to Monsieur Carrot. I await his response and I shall let you know what it is. I shall come and see you as soon as I return, which will be in late October.

Best wishes for your health, to you and yours. My husband asks me to pass on his regards.

A. Lesbros

An unknown correspondent to Auguste Lumière

St Augustine's Day, 28 August [1930s]

Great scientist, our great scientist friend, Auguste Lumière,

In a little pink notebook I found these white sheets and I thought of your name day! Fine, sunny day and here I am by the water! Yes, near the stairs, between a pink bridge and white bridge, the sun is out and the houses opposite are golden and the trees of green velvet! Dancing frills, nice little trains, little boats and patient fishermen! A swallow flies just by me and the water keeps flowing: that is amazing! A pretty green branch on a staircase! I believe that pure and simple thoughts give off a je-ne-sais-quoi! Delightful days for musing, for talking about good times! Watchful of all that and content, I am meditating! And I say: ah! yes, a Great Scientist is a joy ! And I sing Thank God! The heart is at once serious and joyful! That is why they give so much! Poor world here on earth! A blessing on them and those they hold dear!

You know, my dear, dearest Great Scientist, that you are beloved! Old and young. I see your name everywhere! Yes, I take the liberty of wandering around town and I see the little pink squares dancing for the photography competition at the artistic emporium. How pretty the countryside is today! Ah, for it is your name day!

What a pretty thought, this competition! That is knowing how happiness comes! It is so true when one thinks of it! Let our memories chatter, sing and dream! Photo! Photography everywhere! Everywhere! And having these pious and charming pleasures seems so natural, sometimes! O my Great Scientist, you are so good to have found so many fine and gentle things! Thank you from everyone! Let us look, contemplate! Those who have their precious family album and what art there is in photographs!

How lovely it is! What a wonderful gift! A fine intelligence! Conducted by a sunny heart! Oh! Again and again my Great Scientist, give generously all, all the sun that is in you!

Ah! If you were to write all your thoughts in a big book it would be such a gentle gift to the world, such lovely hours of life for that! Oh yes! Oh yes, yes!

I believe your heart is such a lovely palace full of dreaming fairies and great knights! Where infants sing and kindness watches you contentedly!

Happy name day, O Beloved Scientist, these joyous and sincere litanies will bring you your heart's desires! And I shall tell the Good Lord to love you always, I shall set it down more and more in the little pink notebook! And gently I shall sing this refrain! Many lovely returns, my ever lovely wishes! It is your name day! All the infants are happy thanks to Great Scientists! Oh yes!

Happy name day. I wave my little hand each and every way so that air loves you fast.

Louis Lumière to Alphonse Seyewetz

Bandol, 7 April 1940

My dear Seyewetz,

My brother who has just spent twenty-four hours with me here, has told me that you have been ill for some time and that you have had to have an operation which, I gather, has been successful, and which means that you are expected to be back on your feet shortly.

I wanted to send you my best wishes in the hope that you will recover your old health soon and be able to resume your work, and forget all about this bad patch.

As soon as you can, tell me how you are recovering; I hope you do soon.

Yours ever,

Louis Lumière

Auguste Lumière to Henri Lumière, c/o Monsieur Cazajeux,[1]

Montauban, 20 June 1940

My dear Henri,

We are in anguish! We have no news from you. Our telegram to Le Luc received no reply and since we left Lyon, no letter, not a word – apart from this indirect telegram. It is awful.

We thought we might be able to return to Lyon very quickly, but the city is occupied and hostages have been taken. Bollaert, the Prefect, the deputy Mayor, Cohendy, Cardinal Gerlier,[2] the President of the Chamber of Commerce, Charbin, and the chairman of the veterans' assocation, have all been taken into captivity. I am told that my name might also have been added to this list, but I doubt it because I am too old and also only official figures have been taken.

My feeling is that if we can get home that would be much better than remaining here in precarious circumstances. We have a good bed, we can sleep properly, but the children are on mattresses and there is one toilet without running water for five or six people! We can eat at the Hôtel du

Midi, which serves five or six hundred meals per day. You can imagine what it is like.

And the worst of it as that we have absolutely no news. Nothing, neither from Lyon nor from Bandol nor from you. We are in quarantine. When shall we able to give you a hug?

I am writing to Louis to ask if, in the event that we cannot go to Lyon for the time being, he can take us in and give us a roof: there are seventeen of us. Yvette and her two children, Yvonne and her two,[3] Suzanne and her three,[4] Marguerite and me, plus Jean Couchoud,[5] his son, Billon and Suzanne and Yvonne's two chambermaids!

What do you think is the best course of action? I hope that your military status means you are looked after. But where will they send you? To a demobilization centre, I expect. Where?

And what is going to happen overall? The national economy? The franc? We are heading into the unknown. I hope that it will not mean misery. Above all, let us hope we meet up soon.

A big hug Henri, as big as possible, with all our damaged hearts.

A. Lumière

1 Local representative, for photography, of the Lumière company in Montauban. Auguste Lumière and his family spent two days with him during the so-called 'Exodus' when many French people fled in to the south-west of France, away from the German army.
2 A lawyer who came late in life to the priesthood (ordained at 40), Cardinal Pierre Gerlier, took a close interest in social problems. He was taken hostage by the Germans during the Occupation, with a group of people of whom Auguste Lumière might easily have been one.
3 Henri Lefrancq-Lumière (born 1934) and Max Lefrancq-Lumière (born 1936).
4 Renée Trarieux-Lumière (born 1918), Jacques Trarieux-Lumière (born 1920) and Maurice Trarieux-Lumière (born 1922).
5 Marguerite and Auguste's driver. He and his son accompanied the Lumière family on the 'Exodus'.

Auguste Lumière to Henri Lumière

Montauban, 22 June 1940

My dear Henri,

Being apart was hard enough at first, but now that we can't see when we shall see you again, it is much harder to bear.

We have no idea where you are. Some people are saying that pilots who can go overseas are being sent to Morocco!

If it wasn't for the one benefit, which is that we can communicate with you, I should bitterly regret leaving Lyon because this absolute leisure gets at one.

We are awaiting the results of the plenipotentiary talks with impatience; if there is an armistice – it will come as a great relief but I am afraid that the conditions will be so disastrous that France will refuse and the war will carry on! Then we should certainly be cut off from you!

I am just written to the Prefect of Tarn-et-Garonne to offer my services. It would be a relief if he could use me, this inactivity is atrocious. All one can do is contemplate present misfortune.

I can only think and hope that everything in Lyon is intact and that life goes on – slowly, as before. Perhaps we shall see it all again, everything I have painstakingly built up over sixty years.

I pass over our wanderings, our nights in a car. Yvette will have told you about that.

If we were so unlucky as to see the Huns here, I should not leave because this business of fleeing is a tragedy.

Monsieur Cazajeux has taken us in with incomparable kindness. There are twelve of us in his house. There is nowhere else to go. The devotion of this representative and his wife is extremely moving. At least we have a roof. We live and wait.

I am afraid that Yvette wants to leave at all costs if the war goes on, but where can she go? To leave is to face terrible hardship. No petrol. Travel prohibited. Here, at least we can survive. We should so much like to hear from you.

A big hug, Henri.

A. Lumière

Auguste Lumière to Henri Lumière

Montauban, Monday 24 June 1940

My dear Henri,

Still no news from you. We are worried sick. Where are you?[1] When shall we at last hear word and have a little peace of mind?

Yvette is writing to you with the news of our gypsy trip. We are well looked after at Monsieur Cazajeux'. The Prefect has offered us a comfortable room at the Prefecture. The Minister's room! But I'd just as soon stay here, in this friendly atmosphere; Monsieur and Madame Cazajeux are extremely kind and completely devoted to us. We take our meals at the Hôtel du Midi, where there is enough food and it is not too bad for the moment, and we have decent beds. If you were all right too, we should be happier.

We have had some information on German demands from the Geneva wireless service. Their conditions are harsh. And what will Mussolini want?

I hope the armistice comes quickly! So we can know where you are, what you are up to, if you are in good health! That is our most important wish and hope.

We also trust that an armistice will enable us to go back to Lyon and not stay here too much longer. I have nothing to do and it is harder and harder to be apart.

But I want you to know that we are in good health. Luckily, no trouble on that front.

I saw the Prefect again yesterday; he has been most kind and obliging, but he had no information for me because the military authorities in the headquarters here keep him totally in the dark – they are not in contact with him!

A big hug, Henri, from your mother and me, with all our heart.

A. Lumière

1 Henri is a pilot, always on the move. The armistice is about to be signed. Auguste is in the 'free' zone, Henri in the occupied zone. Communication is, therefore, difficult. The worry expressed in this letter is perfectly justified by events.

Auguste Lumière to Henri Lumière

Lyon, 11 July 1940

My dear Henri,

We had no trouble coming back. There are no obstacles to travel. We reached Vienne by lunchtime and your mother insisted on our having one last lunch chez Point,[1] where nothing has changed. We ate exactly the same meal as before the war! Lots of everything!

Point was amazed by the way the Germans behaved. He said they were polite, tactful and disciplined. They celebrated the armistice in his restaurant, but very discreetly, with no noise or applause, no shouting. They asked the staff to leave them alone while they celebrated quietly so as not to humiliate them or hurt their feelings.

I have started working at the Clinic again. Four new patients this morning. If we are careful, I hope we can survive. The number of patients is increasing daily. Dr Perrer[2] came in today. He has been back two days. I told him I could not use his services and he went home. We shall do the same with the other doctors, except for Mademoiselle Simonet, who kept the clinic open during the last few weeks and I think it might be best to keep Delaigue,[3] who came back today. The others will have to look after their private practices, until our clients come back, if they come back.

I have seen Madame Marcelle and informed her of your wish, and mine, that expenditure should be kept as low as possible.

I was surprised to find this morning that there was a considerable amount of correspondence for the factory.

If sufficient activity returned so that we could give all our faithful servants a living, it would be most satisfactory. I presume to hope that things will work out.

But the main thing is that you must come home! Your return would mean so much to all of us!

And it would fill me with joy! I have the impression people were pleased to see me back, which is nice.

I should like to hear from Huguette. If we don't, I shall telephone Bandol.

Poor Seyewetz is in very bad condition, but not as bad as I had gathered from what Jean[4] and Albert had said. He can go on in that miserable state for weeks!

You can imagine how pleased I was to find everything as it should be at home. I was so scared, for a time, that I should come back to a ruin. I expect I shall get back to work. In fact, I am back at work.

Come home soon! Come home, both of you, with the children! Then we shall be able to start living again.

A big hug, Henri and to Yvette.

A. Lumière

1 Point. A famous restaurateur. He trained numerous chefs. His restaurant, La Pyramide, is still in Vienne, just south of Lyon. Point was a friend of the Lumière family. In order to help his clients' digestion, he prescribed Emgé (M.G.) Lumière, a preparation of magnesium salts invented by Auguste Lumière, recommended for asthma.
2 Dr Perrer was Yvette Piperno's brother-in-law (he was married to her sister) and employed in Auguste Lumière's clinic.
3 Consultant at Auguste Lumière's clinic. He worked with Doctor Lyonnet.
4 Jean Lefrancq (1905–89): Yvonne Lumière's husband.

Louis Lumière to Jean Seyewetz

Bandol, 23 August 1940

Dear Sir,

I was deeply saddened to hear of the death of your father, my old friend Seyewetz, and I want you to know that I share in your loss.

Please give your family my profound condolences.

Louis Lumière

Auguste Lumière to Louis Lumière

Lyon, 24 March 1941

Louis, old boy,

It has been some time since we have had fresh news from you; I hope everything is well – I don't mean food, of which there is a lack everywhere – we have to scrap around here and there.

I am writing to let you know what is happening here.

The clinic is reviving – seventy-two patients this morning. As we are five doctors short, there is plenty of work – indeed, I saw sixty-one patients myself this morning.

Doctor Paul Meyer,[1] formerly a prisoner, has returned without anyone discovering either his former nationality or his religion. I am delighted he is back because he is going to take over management of the experimental research laboratories, somewhat abandoned during the war.

Liliane still has albumen. My cold is almost over.

I am writing several pieces. Yesterday, the newspaper published one, but they changed the title I had given it again. It was 'Drawbacks of Conferences'.[2] As I refer to a group of scientists who gather to study tuberculosis in marriage, the editor altered the title to a more sensationalist, 'Does tuberculosis exist in marriage?'

I enclose the article. The new headline may mean that I am attacked by die-hard conformists.

I have received a number of interesting letters about *Les Fossoyeurs du Progrès*.[3]

You might find the enclosed cutting from a Paris newspaper entertaining. The Germans let it pass. You will see the text reads differently according to how it is folded.

Here is another. Do you know the Italians have just inaugurated a new national dish? They are rationed too. But they are not short of meat, nor fat, so I'm told their new dish is: steak wrapped in fat!

The weather in Bandol must be wonderful, if the sunny temperatures we have been having over the last few days are anything to go by. Enough! A big hug to you Louis, old boy.

Auguste

Let us love and respect	Chancellor Hitler.
England, as always	should be put down.
Let us curse and destroy	the men across the sea.
The Nazis there	alone will survive.
Let us support	German supremacy.
The men of the sea	will not survive.
To them alone	fair punishment.
The crown of victory	is all they deserve[4]

1 Auguste Lumière hired and concealed the identity of this German Jewish doctor before providing him with a senior managerial position at Lumière Americanos in Santiago de Chile, where he remained from 1942 to 1955, manufacturing cyogenin. He shared Auguste's interest in the matter of injecting insoluble substances in order to help scar tissue formation.
2 Scientific meetings, which might today be called seminars. The article was probably polemical since Auguste Lumière's notion that tuberculosis was not contagious was controversial.
3 Auguste Lumière: *Les Fossoyeurs du Progrès: Les Mandarins contre les Pionniers de la Science* [The Gravediggers of Progress: the Establishment against the Pioneers of Science], 322pp, Sézanne, Lyon, 1942. An eminent doctor of Lyon was to declare, 'Sometimes, a light (= Lumière) should be hidden under a bushel' which gives an idea of the ferocity of attacks against Auguste Lumière.
4 This text was designed to fool the Germans. Read across two columns, it appears to support them. Read in single columns, it vilifies them.

Louis Lumière to Cachard

Bandol, 12 July 1941

Monsieur Cachard
Lumière Factory
25 rue du Premier Film
Monplaisir, Lyon

Dear Sir,

Following Monsieur Bizet's request which you have forwarded to me, I enclose a copy of the note which I delivered to the Académie des Sciences on 24 April 1922; I do not know whether Cluny is in the 'free' zone or in the occupied zone, and consequently I am not sending this note directly to the signatory of the letter which I also enclose, in order that you can arrange for him to receive this note.

Yours sincerely,
Louis Lumière

Auguste Lumière to Louis Lumière

Lyon, 14 July 1941

Louis, old boy,

I hope the journey back was not too hot and that there were no mishaps.

We have had our first Council meeting. The Mayor made a formal speech. Nothing else. The Mayor then asked me to drive with him round the War Memorials of the last two wars.

Le Journal published one of my articles this morning. I enclose it.

I should like to do something of this sort, something social. And I should like to rebel against the competitive fury of sport which is destroying the hearts of young people. But there are considerable interests at stake.

None of this will distract me from my medical research, which has pride of place in my activity.

I hope your work is going well. A big hug.

Auguste

Auguste Lumière to Louis Lumière

Lyon, 25 July 1941

Louis, old boy,

We are in much the same position as you, regarding food. We have meat once a week and since our cow was replaced, get no butter. From time to time, some fish appears.

I hear that there will be no meat at all from August onwards. Slaughtering will not be allowed. The tax on vegetables is driving them off the markets. Luckily, Villié-Morgon provides us with food.

Yvette is coming home from Saint-Nectaire tomorrow night. Apparently, Liliane's rest-cure has done her good. You congratulate me on my municipal activity, but I have nothing to do except attend sessions, as an observer, not even as audience because I cannot understand a word they say. The acoustics of the hall are very bad and street noise interferes with the sound, so that the sessions are complete torture as far as I am concerned.

I have written to the Mayor to ask if it would not be better if I resigned, but he is not having any of it. He is deaf too, and after asking me verbally not to resign, he wrote me a note of which you will find a copy enclosed.

A patient has come up from Bandol. I see him every day and I have started treatment. If I fail, he will not survive, but his is similar to a case I have treated successfully in the past. I do not despair.

It is very hot. Thirty-one degrees outside the north door at 7.30 p.m. Marguerite is moaning. Tomorrow we are going to lunch at Saint-Paul – my weekly meal. It is well earned. I hardly have a moment's rest.

Someone told us a nice little story: about a lady selling newspapers in Paris and a German customer who comes every day to fetch his newspaper. If you do not know it, I shall tell it to you. A big hug, Louis old boy.

Yvonne and Jean are staying at Chamonix – you probably know that Yvonne gave us a scare – but she is fine now.

Auguste

Auguste Lumière to Louis Lumière

Lyon, 25 October 1941

Louis, old boy,

Thank you very much for your good wishes. I am most grateful. I am afraid that your prayers regarding my miserable carcass may not be answered, as the warning signs of decay are becoming insistent.

I am getting deafer. I feel constantly dizzy, which is a bother. I sense unease in the heart, due, probably, to deposits of calcium on the aorta. I work less easily. I fall asleep at my desk. I feel continuous pain in my joints and muscles. None of this is particularly alarming, but it is not cheering either.

I am working at my new book all the same; I have written *Les Slogans de la Médecine*[1] and I think it will come out by the end of the year.

I have written to the Mayor to complain about a proposal to spend fifty-five million on new sports facilities for Lyon.

Adolescents are the worst hit by rationing, and they want to encourage them to play football, a violent game with disastrous consequences. That is the opposite of physical education. Adolescents need sofas now, football will kill them. But the policy is a vote winner. It will please the people and there are such vested interests around this evil, spectacular sport!

I have protested to the Mayor, but I have also told him I will not fight the project, because I am no longer in any condition to fight a battle which could be very tough, given the particular interests at play, and I only get involved when I know I can win. Which is not the case.

But I am prattling away about myself and not asking you what is becoming of you. I fervently hope that you are still working and that you will provide our nation with sensational inventions. I hope you do not suffer from rationing much more than we do. The good old meals we used to eat are long gone, but we have enough. There is not much variety; there is almost no meat on the table, it is meagre, but it is enough to live off. And on Saturday, we are going to lunch at Saint-Paul where Charles is better provided.

The Prefect has been to visit the Clinic, after having lunch in the factory restaurant, but the Clinic was completely empty and there was no point.
love
Auguste

I can hardly do any laboratory work: there are no books, no patients, nothing to show!

1 Translator's note: *Slogans of Medical Practice.*

Auguste Lumière to Louis Lumière

Lyon, 11 November 1941

Louis, old boy,

When there is a shortage of food, colds need monitoring. I want to know whether you are better. Marguerite is still suffering from neuralgia between her ribs, but less so: she sleeps better at night, but during the day she is still irritated by the stabbing pains of neuritis. She is doing radiotherapy, but I do not know whether they are going about it properly.

Fabry to Auguste Lumière

Les Lecques, 17 December 1941

Dear colleague and friend,

I have learnt with great pleasure of your elevation to the highest rank of the Légion d'Honneur, which is a well-deserved homage to your incomparable scientific achievements.

I wish to echo all your friends, and all the friends of French Science, in congratulating you most sincerely.

Louis Lumière to Lacroix

26 June 1942

Many congratulations, my dear and eminent friend and colleague, for the Osiris prize which you have just been awarded.

I much regret not coming to Paris from time to time to attend the Académie and see my friends there.

Louis Lumière

Auguste Lumière to Henri Lumière

Lyon, 7 August 1942

My dear Henri, my dear Yvette,

You will have been gone eight days tomorrow and I imagine you will be wanting news of your old folks left behind in Lyon. This is all the easier because none of our news is bad and the most important bit is excellent. I mean food, of which we have had a great deal since your departure, and largely thanks to you.

Your meat gave us an opportunity to invite Vigne to lunch yesterday. Hébrard brought two big baskets full of vegetables, small fish for frying which we shared with Yvonne, and crayfish, which I hadn't so much as seen since before the war! We also got a packet of coffee for you and we have put it aside for your return. There was also a basket of peaches, one third of which were rotten. I enclose the sender's card which you may be able to decipher. We ate the good ones, not the bad ones, not being able to forward peaches to you.

Furthermore, Montagné, one of my patients, who had sent us three food parcels that were stolen, sent us a fourth which got through. Then we had beans from Charles, pears from Mademoiselle Bony, some more pears from Madame Rey,[1] vegetables from one of André Winckler's suppliers.[2] Anyway, it was a blessed week such as we had not seen since before the famine.

Vigne is in Lyon at the moment and very sorry to have missed Henri because he wanted to talk to him about a gypsum business which he thinks is particularly interesting.

I received a letter from Bourjon[3] this morning. I do not suppose Henri wants me to answer it.

The temperature has fallen suddenly (fourteen degrees yesterday morning, fifteen today). I hope this has not affected you and that it will not prevent you from swimming.

Madame Ebenrecht[4] passed on to us yesterday the news you had sent her and told us you had been able to go fishing and caught some fish, which was nice to hear.

As you can see, everything is fine here. Have your holidays and do not worry.

Much love to both of you and Liliane and Huguette.

A. Lumière

I have received the enclosed picture which is of no use to me so I am sending it to Huguette.

1 Chief buyer at the Lumière plant.
2 André Winckler (1909–67) son of France Lumière and Charles Winckler.
3 A doctor from Lyon, Bourjon rented his apartment to Jacques Trarieux-Lumière in 1941–2.
4 Yvette Piperno's mother's maiden name was Ebenrecht.

Auguste Lumière to Louis Lumière

Lyon, 20 August 1942

Louis, old boy,

Last night Jean called as I had asked him to let us know the results of your ophthalmological tests in Toulon. We were reassured to hear the news, but I ought to tell you that we think we have several times observed that eye trouble can be improved by prolonged use of Emgé in pill form.[1]

If the product does not disagree with you, I think you might try taking one pill with every meal, or at least at lunchtime.

I have seen two instances of white-haired patients recovering some colour in their hair after taking steady amounts of Emgé orally.

Emgé seems peculiarly effective against problems associated with ageing, and a cataract is one such.

A big hug.

Auguste

1 Emgé Lumière, a medicine. See note to letter of 11 July 1940. Manufacture of this product lapsed some years ago, though as of 1994 there is apparently interest in both Japan and in the United States in starting to make it again.

Auguste Lumière to Louis Lumière

Lyon, 12 March 1943

Louis, old boy,

I am sending you a Wood filter[1] and Gallois' note.

About your question concerning twenty-five cycle current, you should let Gallois have reference numbers for the lamp and transformer; they are written inside.

If you send them this information, they will let you know straight away if something needs to be done. More and more patients. One hundred and fifteen this morning. I am going to bring back Dr Berger, who was here before the war.

Suzanne arrived yesterday, but I have not seen her yet. She is well.

I work more than ever. The contagious party are launching a new attack and I must act.

I have started on some new articles for the medical journal. [*Here a line is missing*]

Meanwhile, one forgets the worries of the era.

A big hug, old boy.

Auguste

1 Auguste and Louis Lumière appear to have resumed their collaboration. Auguste is hard at work at his clinic, but also finds time to work on X-ray equipment. This Wood filter, addressed to Louis, provides evidence of this.

Louis Lumière to René Monduel

Bandol, 3 August 1943

AUTHORIZATION

I, the undersigned, Louis Lumière, hereby authorize Monsieur René Monduel to direct a script entitled 'And the Illusion Was', which is based on a part of my life, on condition that the text which I have been shown and which consists of forty-eight typewritten pages – of which a copy resides with the Society of Film Authors in Paris – is not altered in any way, unless such alterations have been approved by me. If this condition is not kept, then this authorization may be considered null and void.

Louis Lumière

Signed by Monsieur Louis Lumière,

signature certified by the Mayor of Bandol, 9 December 1943

Louis Lumière to Jean Grémillon[1]

Monsieur Jean Grémillon
Chairman of the Cinémathèque Française
7 avenue de Messine
Paris 8

Dear Sir,

Thank you for your letter of 12 April. I am sorry to have to tell you that it would be difficult for me, especially at present, to assemble the documents you request on behalf of the Cinémathèque.

I will, however, look through fifty-year-old documents and I hope to be able to give you some elements and some information, but part of what may be of interest is now out of my laboratory at Bandol, which I had to evacuate completely last May and I cannot undertake any research until I can get back to the south. I do not know when that will be because my state of health forces me to take refuge here in Lyon, at my brother's, 96 cours Albert Thomas.

I shall certainly be in touch with you as soon as I can let you know what I have found.

Yours sincerely,
Louis Lumière

1 Jean Grémillon directed among others, *Gueule d'Amour* (1937), *Remorques* (1941), *Lumière d'Eté* (1943). He was chairman of the Cinémathèque Française, a semi-private organization set up by, among others, Henri Langlois, to preserve and show prints of films and thus provide something like a living museum of cinema.

Auguste Lumière to Henri Lumière

My dear Henri, my dear Yvette,

What a nice surprise! Your letter dated yesterday took only twenty-four hours to arrive. We have already had news indirectly and we know that you arrived safely. I know Henri does not much like to write and we are very grateful to him for taking the trouble.

As you suggest, we shall try to call you between one and four.

Nothing has happened since your departure. Since the factory has closed it has been even quieter here than before.

We spent Saturday afternoon at Saint-Paul, whence I brought home some frying fish which Madeleine[1] enjoyed, though Marguerite does not like pond fish.

It is very hot – the weather is most unpleasant. Needless to say, Marguerite has been complaining.

Nothing new at the clinic except that a new doctor arrived this morning, Dr Berthezène,[2] who happened to appear at a session with half-a-dozen extraordinary cases, by which I mean unidentified problems for which the patients have consulted, unsuccessfully, several famous doctors before coming to us.

I believe no one sees as many curious and interesting cases as we get at the clinic.

You seem happy with your holiday, which pleases us. Enjoy it as much as you can and we hope that no incidents unsettle your well-earned rest.

A big hug and to Liliane and Huguette too.

A. Lumière

---

1 Madeleine Koehler (1895–1970), daughter of Jeanne Lumière and René Koehler. Her father named a starfish after her: Magdalenaster.
2 A friend of Auguste's. He remained at the clinic until Auguste's death.

Louis Lumière to Perrot

Bandol, 22 September 1945

One can only say that the figure representing the earliest machine in this book (*Histoire du Cinéma* by Coissac[1]) does not depict it at all and represents an experimental machine I built some time later in order to introduce a system of running the film through a multi-angled prism corrector. A second mistake in the illustration concerns *L'Arroseur Arrosé* which is not the version I shot but the version shot with Aimos.[2] Aimos' *Arroseur Arrosé* is a copy of mine, induced by the success of mine.

I never met Aimos and I have never wanted to get him into trouble by denying certain affirmations which he went so far as to sign.

L. Lumière

---

1 Georges-Michel Coissac established, in 1903, the first professional journal of cinema. It was called *Le Fascinateur* and appeared until 1914. After the war, he launched *Le Cinéopse*. His *Histoire du Cinéma*, which appeared in 1925, is essential to an understanding of the early days of cinema.
2 Actor of the 1930s and 1940s actor, playing working-class Parisian types. Aimos claimed to have played the lad in Louis Lumière's famous early film, *The Gardener Takes a Shower*. Actually, he played the part in a Pathé remake.

Louis Lumière to André Berthomieu[1]

Monsieur Berthomieu
Chairman of the Union of Cinematographic Production Technicians
2 rue Wilham
Paris 15

Dear Sir,

Your kind letter has reached me in Lyon and I thank you for it. Allow me to inform you of the following:

As soon as I received a telegram on 26 December, signed 'Cinematographic Industry Technicians', asking me to send advance thanks to the organizers of a ceremony they were arranging on the occasion of the fiftieth anniversary of 28 December 1895, I immediately did so in the belief that what was meant was a commemoration of the opening of the first public Cinematograph Lumière projection theatre and sent a telegram addressed to 'Film Technicians, 92 Champs Elysées'.

I have just learned by press cuttings that have been forwarded to me that a procession, led by you, proceeded to go to the building in the boulevard des Capucines where the Grand Café used to be and had a plaque fixed there the text of which pays tribute to a number of technicians who, while they may be considered 'pioneers' of moving photography, none the less had nothing whatsoever to do with the first public performance of the Lumière Cinematograph, which is the only thing celebrating its fiftieth anniversary on 28 December 1946, whereas for the people in question, the date is no anniversary at all.

Naturally, I am among the first to recognize the merits of the 'pioneers' in question, as I showed when a plaque was inaugurated on the house of my lamented and close friend Marey who, I am certain, if he were still alive, would not have failed to protest because he was a loyal and honest man, as I had occasion to discover. And was I not also Méliès' sponsor when he obtained the Légion d'Honneur?

I should applaud with all my heart the fixing of commemorative plaques on all the places made famous by the 'pioneers' you mention, on the houses they lived in, or honoured by their presence, or their work, but I am deeply shocked that the successor building to the Grand Café should have been chosen as the site of a plaque, the wording of which is unobjectionable, but the siting of which would only seem to me to be justified if it was anywhere else than the place you have chosen.

I know that this misunderstanding is not of your doing, but it nevertheless warrants the complaint I am making, which I trust you will note.

    Yours sincerely,

    Louis Lumière

1 André Berthomieu (1903–59), a prolific, late 1930s director. Some years, he made as many as four or five films. These include *Pas Si Bête* (1928), *Mon Ami Victor* (1931) and *La Mort en Fuite* (1936).

Louis Lumière to the Government Commissioner

Paris, 27 January 1946

The Government Commissioner to the National War Supplies Board
Council of State
Place du Palais-Royal

Dear Sir,

I am pleased to acknowledge receipt of your letter of 7 January with the enclosed description of contracts signed by me with the Ministry of War and the Aeronautical Corps between January 1915 and February 1918.

I must first express my considerable admiration for the scrupulous method of your department which has taken a mere twenty-eight to thirty years to monitor sets of accounts in a manner I certainly cannot fault. In any case, your archives have been carefully preserved and I must congratulate you.

I regret, however, that the same attention has not been devoted to all the documents concerned: if it had you would have been spared the trouble of making quite superfluous demands, of which I should be perfectly within my rights to complain if my eighty-one years of age had not provided me with a sanguine philosophy of life.

I should add that in 1914, at the request of the Aeronautical Corps, I conceived and manufactured a catalytic heater[1] which proved entirely satisfactory. I made a number of these devices and gave them to the State at cost, because I wanted to avoid making a profit at the expense of the National Defence effort.

An increase in the number of orders enabled me subsequently to make these heaters on an industrial scale and therefore at a much lower unit cost. When I came to finalize my accounts, I realized that I had made a profit. I wrote to the Director of Aviation Manufacture and to the Director of War Supplies to ask how and to whom I could reimburse the profit I had made.

As a result, I gave the Financial Receiver for the Department of the Rhône,

on 22 June 1918	50,400.00 F (War Supplies)
on 28 August 1919	33,596.25 F (Aviation Manufacture)
on 16 October 1918	41,996.25 F (Aviation Manufacture)

In other words a total amount of 125,992.50 F
on a turnover of, according to your accounts, 556,758 F.

Perhaps I should add that I received the grateful thanks of both services, which were reflected in the form of a decree offering the Ministry of Armament a credit corresponding to the amount I had repaid, and published in the Official Record.

You will understand, after this simple account of the facts, that I should feel somewhat dismayed at receiving the demand in question from your services which does not even have the justification of memory lapse, since it has gone back thirty years to make the claim.

For your personal interest, I enclose photographs of the various documents which have enabled me to provide you with this account. I am keeping the originals in case my grandchildren receive the same demand in 1975 or 1976.

Yours sincerely,
Louis Lumière
Fellow of the Institut
Grand Cross of the Légion d'Honneur

1 See Louis Lumière to Guignard, 22 May 1918.

Government Commissioner to Louis Lumière

Paris, 5 February 1946

Monsieur Louis Lumière
Villa Lumen
Bandol (Var)

Dear Sir,
Following your remarks on the subject of supplies certified by the state no. 1 of 7 January 1946, I am pleased to inform you that I have decided on

this day to exempt you from any forfeiture or obligation.

Yours faithfully,

The Government Commissioner

Auguste Lumière to Yvette Piperno

Lyon, 9 August 1946

My dear Yvette,

Your nice letter was all the nicer because it brought such good news and that we had none since your departure.

As to us, it is very quiet here. The house has fallen silent.

Since Marguerite has come home, I feel as though I am on holiday myself because I no longer have to do the housework and I have gone back to my ten hours of work a day, my usual work which seems so simple now.

Monsieur and Madame Ebenrecht called on us yesterday, together with their Cairo daughter and son-in-law. They seem very pleasant and we spent an agreeable hour with them.

Nothing special since your leaving, except Monsieur Magnier's death, but I don't think you knew him and consequently this event need not upset your holidays.

Have a good rest. A hug to all three of you.

A. Lumière

Louis Lumière to Georges Sadoul[1]

Bandol, 3 September 1946

Monsieur Georges Sadoul
Paris

Dear Sir,

I have just spent two months in bed, as a result of a serious and painful cardiac and kidney crisis, complicated by breathing problems. Consequently, now that my health has improved, I have only just been able to gather together the comments I wished to make on your book, *The Invention of Cinema*.

This work is now complete and I enclose it. I have to say that I very much regret that a number of statements and facts about me in your book seem pejorative and tendentious. This is no doubt due to the hostility of some of your informants. It looks pretty nasty to me.

Yours sincerely,

Louis Lumière

I am taking the liberty of enclosing with these documents, a number of documents which may be of interest to you.

1 Georges Sadoul published the first volume of his *Histoire Générale du Cinéma* (Denoël, 1947) under the heading *L'Invention du Cinéma*. A new edition appeared in 1948. This had been corrected and revised to take into account of, among other things, Louis Lumière's criticisms. The initial contact between the two men was abrasive. They had opposing political beliefs, and Sadoul had, in perfectly good faith, used mistaken and sometimes malicious sources. But they soon made friends and a real mutual respect grew up which allowed Sadoul to glean invaluable information on the early films, among other things.

Louis Lumière to Georges Sadoul

Telegram: 16 September 1946

Thank you for your letter. Shall be very pleased to see you end of the month. Come to a simple lunch. Must go to Lyon twenty-eighth. Grandson's wedding. Please telegraph whether you can be Bandol twenty-seventh at latest. Letter follows.

Best wishes,

Louis Lumière

Louis Lumière to Georges Sadoul

Bandol, 16 September 1946

Monsieur Sadoul
3 rue de Bretonvilliers
Paris 4

Dear Sir,

I write to confirm the telegram which I thought I ought to send you in case a letter did not reach you on time and to say, once more, how much I should like to see you at Villa Lumen, where I trust you will not refuse to come to lunch, frugally because we are not fortunate with our rations in this lovely part of the country, but we shall then have an opportunity of discussing in detail the various points which have occasioned the correspondence you and I have just exchanged, and I hope to be able to hand over to you a number of documents which you wish for.

They are, of course, incomplete, because it has been so long, and also because I left Lyon more than twenty years ago, after an oppressive number of deaths in the family. I remain merely Technical Consultant at the Société Lumière.

Everything concerning the early days of the Cinematograph has been dispersed (make way for youth!) and our negatives, which repeatedly went from one attic to another, suffered a great deal from all this removal, particularly as our staff was not particularly careful, thinking it was all old junk anyway.

I am sorry to be slightly pushed for time and I should be grateful if your visit could be before 27 September at the latest, because I am leaving on the 28th and I cannot alter this commitment.

Yours sincerely,
Louis Lumière

Louis Lumière to Georges Sadoul

Bandol, 7 October 1946

Monsieur Sadoul
3 rue de Bretonvilliers
Paris

Dear Sir,
Shortly after your departure from the Villa Lumen, returning to my study, I noticed that you had left your Reynolds[1] behind and I immediately sent it registered to your address in Cannes. As I have not heard since, I would be grateful if you would let me know whether it got lost or whether you received the precious little thing.

Thank you in advance.

Yours sincerely,
Louis Lumière

1 A pen, no doubt.

Louis Lumière to Max Lefrancq-Lumière

Bandol, 9 October 1946

My dear Max,

To go with the little engine I am sending Henri, I am sending you a little device you may already know. It's a gyroscope and it can do some very curious things. Ask your father to show you.

It is very fragile, so don't let it fall on the floor or it will go wrong.

I hope you enjoy it and that it gives you some quiet fun.

A big hug, and to your baby sister and to Daddy and Mummy too.

Pépé[1]

I enclose a bit of cotton straw for Florence[2] because I promised her some to thread the pearls on her necklace.

1 Translator's note: common French term for grandad.
2 Florence Lefrancq-Lumière, born in 1942, is the daughter of Yvonne and Jean Lefrancq.

Louis Lumière to Georges Sadoul

Bandol, 14 October 1946

Monsieur Georges Sadoul
3 rue Bretonvilliers
Paris 4

Dear Sir,

Thank you for your kind letter and I enclose a copy of the patent taken out by my brother and me, under the heading, 'Device for direct viewing of cinematographic images, known as kinora.[1] This patent is dated 10 September 1896.

The name Casler was forced upon us by its bearer as a result of a complaint from the Casler French Company for Mutoscope and Biographs,[2] at the time when the device was put on the market by Gaumont, to whom I had applied because it required mechanical elements which we were not equipped to handle.

We gave him the patent and all the cutting and assembly tools which I had developed and used to make the pictures. I don't think the business yielded much and it was abandoned shortly afterwards.

Perhaps you could return the copy of the patent to me when you have

had a chance to look at it.
   Yours sincerely,
   Louis Lumière

P.S. Reading the copy of the patent I am enclosing, I notice that it was drawn up appallingly badly by the patents clerk; the description is ridiculous. I apologize.

1 A kinora is a small device with shows positive frames of films, by means of a key-wound spring system, in quick succession, so as to give the illusion of movement. Some Lumière films were shown in this way, lit by natural light.
2 Herman Casler was a mechanic who had worked for Edison in 1891 on the kinetoscope. With Dickson, who had also taken part in the invention of the kinetoscope, they invented the mutoscope, in 1894 and 1895, and then, in 1896, called it the biograph.

Gabriel Doublier[1] to Louis Lumière

Lyon, 4 November 1946

   Monsieur Louis Lumière
   Villa Lumen
   Bandol (Var)

Dear Sir,
   I am sorry I did not reply immediately to your letter of 25 October requesting the list of cine-negatives, but it has taken me some time to identify the numbers and the All Saints' holiday then intervened.
   Please find enclosed two lists of box numbers. I am sending a copy of the same list to Monsieur Bessy,[2] who had asked for it too.
   I hope you are well.
   Yours sincerely,
   Doublier

1 Gabriel Doublier's father, Edouard Doublier, supplied the Lumière factories with barrels to contain chemical products. He had an accident and died in 1890, so Antoine Lumière hired four of his eight children. Philippine became head of the paper operation, Jenny was cashier, and Francis became a cameraman-projectionist. Gabriel became head of the 'colour department'. When Louis Lumière moved to Paris, they corresponded frequently about the factory archives.
2 Journalist and cinema critic, screenwriter and the editor of many film periodicals (*Cinémonde, Le Film Français*). He wrote a book with Lo Duca called *Louis Lumière, inventeur* (Prisma, 1948).

Louis Lumière to Gabriel Doublier

6 November 1946

Monsieur Gabriel Doublier
Colour Service
Lumière Factory
25 rue du Premier Film
Monplaisir, Lyon

My dear Gabriel,
I received your letter telling me about the lists of negatives which you have been able to identify and box up, and indeed these lists were with your letter.
Thank you very much for all your trouble.
Good health and fond memories.

Georges Sadoul to Louis Lumière

Paris, 5 December 1946

Monsieur Louis Lumière
Villa Lumen
Bandol

Dear Sir,
Forgive this long silence. I am six weeks late in thanking you for the 'kinora' patent you sent me. I shall send it back to you soon but I wonder whether I can keep it for another month, until I have finished revising my next volume, the new edition of which is coming out next month.
If I have been so slow to write to you it is partly because I have had so much on my hands, but partly also because I wanted to be able to tell you something definite regarding the making of prints of films currently stored at your factory at Lyon.
I am enclosing two of the precious documents which you were kind enough to lend me: 1) Your 1897 catalogue,[1] and 2) The list of negatives currently in store at Lyon. With the agreement of the Cinémathèque Française I have chosen some 300 films from this latter list, which adds up to about 6000 metres of film to print up. The Cinémathèque Française will take responsibility for making these prints; its Secretary-General, Henri Langlois, will go to Lyon some time next week to meet Monsieur Doublier. I wonder if I may request that you recommend Henri Langlois to your factories at Lyon and to Monsieur Doublier, and in particular that he may

make a selection from among the cases of negatives. Perhaps you would let me know under what conditions the negatives can be entrusted to the Cinémathèque and whether you can agree to their removal to Paris where the Cinémathèque has, according to Monsieur Langlois, had a special machine made to print shrunken films with only two perforations per frame. As soon as these prints are ready, I shall set to work on the pamphlet I intend to write, which I shall call 'Louis Lumière, film director'.

I have had several opportunities to see the precious copy of the first eight films you made, which you were kind enough to give me. These films have raised general enthusiasm wherever they have been seen. My pupils at l'IDHEC,[2] who had just seen Edison's film strips, broke into spontaneous applause at the marvellous photographic quality of your films, and especially the excellent framing of *Lunch with Baby* and, above all, *Boat Leaving Harbour*.

I hope you are in excellent health and that you are still at work on your invaluable research.

Georges Sadoul

1 During 1897, the Lumière firm published a list of films shot by their cameramen. It contains the first 786 entries of the general catalogue of the firm which came out in 1905 and contains 1425 films in all.
2 Translator's note: IDHEC: until recently the name of the National Film School in Paris, now called FEMIS.

Louis Lumière to Gabriel Doublier

9 December 1946

Monsieur Gabriel Doublier
Lumière Factories
25 rue du Premier Film
Lyon

My dear Gabriel,
The list you drew up for me has turned out very useful, and I want you know to that Monsieur Henri Langlois, Secretary-General of the Cinémathèque Française (an official body) is going to come to Lyon to view a number of these films which he has chosen with Georges Sadoul for reproduction on a machine specially adapted to compensate for the shrinkage of these old films and to give them a standard four perforations per frame.

They intend to reproduce three hundred films in this way and I should be grateful if you would do your best to help him by showing him the films and handing over to him, for the Cinémathèque, any negatives he chooses. I know that what I am asking means a lot of extra work for you, but I think it is essential that we take advantage of the current favour of this group to avoid the first class funeral with which modern style film-makers would bury anything that is not modern.

Thank you in advance. A handshake.

Louis Lumière to Georges Sadoul

Bandol, 9 December 1946

Monsieur Sadoul
3 rue de Bretonvilliers
Paris 4

Dear Sir,

Thank you for your kind letter of 5 December.

I have written to Lyon to prepare them for Monsieur Henri Langlois' visit so that he is given every assistance in his dealings with Monsieur Doublier, in order that he can choose whatever he wants in the boxes containing films, the list of which I sent you.

I see no reason why these films should not be sent to Paris and kept at the Cinémathèque, if it is useful. I only ask for a receipt for the lot.

I am pleased to learn that your screening of my early films was of interest to your pupils at the IDHEC and I thank you.

May I suggest that you send me the text of your new edition of your book, *The Invention of Cinema*, before it is printed, in order to avoid further misunderstandings, or would that be indiscreet?

Once again thank you.

Louis Lumière

P.S. My health is not brilliant at the moment because I am having bad heart trouble which is preventing me from working. One mustn't be too greedy at my age!

Louis Lumière to Jean Lefrancq

9 December 1946

My dear Jean,

I received this morning a most amiable letter from Monsieur Sadoul who asks me to take the necessary steps to ensure that Monsieur Henri Langlois, Secretary-General of the Cinémathèque Française, is well received at the Factory and introduced to Gabriel Doublier so that he can examine and choose from the boxes in which Gabriel has tidied away and classified the old films which were hidden away in some attic.

Sadoul informs me that the Cinémathèque intends to reproduce about 300 of these films, adapting the perforations to modern standards, and that they wish to keep the negatives in Paris. I see no reason not to accept this request and I hope that you will do your best to welcome this Langlois, whom I do not think I know, and that you will give him every facility so he can accomplish his mission.

Sadoul is a new man: all sweetness and light. He is producing a new edition of his history of the 'invention of cinema' in which I believe, from what he has told me, he intends to correct a number of gross errors which appeared in the first edition.

I had thought to explain all this to you by telephone this morning, but you had not warned me that you would be asking for me today. We shall probably be speaking tomorrow or the next day. But it is as well you should be warned of citizen Langlois' arrival and that he should be well received.

I have had a bad few days during which my nervous condition had me crying like a calf; I called Doctors Charmot and Bonnet, who suggested I try a medicine called 'pneumogeine Renard', which is a mixture of theobromide, potassium, iodine and caffeine. It is a strange mixture, but it has done me much good. I feel better, though I have also been taking digitalis. I'd like to get out of this mess, but nothing seems to work and I spend about three-quarters of my time in bed. I am hopeful though.

I hope you will be giving good news tomorrow of Poussy's jaundice and everyone else's health.

A hug, Jean. All my ancient and unchangeable affection.

Louis Lumière

Georges Sadoul to Louis Lumière

Paris, 12 December 1946

Monsieur Louis Lumière
Villa Lumen
Bandol

Dear Sir,

Thank you for your kind letter of 9 December.

Monsieur Henri Langlois intends to travel to Lyon towards the end of next week, about 20 December. I have advised him to contact Monsieur Gabriel Doublier directly in order to arrange the exact timing of his arrival.

Have you received the catalogue and the list which you lent me and which I returned to you with my last letter?

Your state of health sounds worrying. I hope your heart problems do not prevent you from working too long.

As regards the new edition of The Invention of Cinema, I shall not have finished my corrections until the middle of January. The book is due out towards the end of April. I think I shall therefore be able to send you copies of the passages which concern you in early spring.

Yours sincerely,
Georges Sadoul

Louis Lumière to Georges Sadoul

16 December 1946

Monsieur Georges Sadoul
3 rue de Bretonvilliers
Paris 4

Dear Sir,

Thank you for your kind letter of 12 December. I apologize for not letting you know I had received the 1897 catalogue-relic I had lent you, as well as the list of films discovered in the factory attic. I did get them with your letter.

Regarding Monsieur Langlois' visit to Lyon, I should be grateful if you would ask him to go to 25 rue du Premier Film in Lyon and ask for Monsieur Jean Lefrancq, my son-in-law, who manages the plant and who will introduce him to Monsieur Doublier, about whom you know. I have informed my son-in-law that he is to expect this visit.

I should mention that Gabriel Doublier is one of the old guard of cinema.

He was, I think, with us from the start. His brother, Francisque Doublier, helped launch the Cinematograph in New York and settled there. He has been successful there and is now, I think, head of a publishing company which is, I believe, very prosperous.

Gabriel is still with us but in charge of colour photography.

My health, about which you are kind enough to ask, is making my life diffiult at present and is reflecting, as it must, the decrepitude of my cells. I can hardly hope to turn the clock back because I have no relationship with Mephistopheles. Still, things seem to be getting better and I hope to find a bit more energy to continue my studies into diverse problems, which are currently in abeyance.

Thank you for all your kindness. I note that you expect to finish the new edition of your *History of Cinema* in the spring and that you will send me the text regarding my own work.

Yours truly,
Louis Lumière

Georges Sadoul to Louis Lumière

Paris, 20 January 1947

Monsieur Louis Lumière
Villa Lumen
Bandol

Dear Sir,

I am sorry not to have replied sooner to your letter of 16 December, but I have just spent a month in the country to finish the second volume of my *General History of Cinema*[1] and I have not had a minute's break. I have been in Paris for a few days and I have seen Monsieur Grémillon, President of the Cinémathèque Française, and his Secretary-General, Monsieur Henri Langlois. They were back from Lyon and delighted with the welcome which, thanks to you, they had received from Monsieur Lefrancq, Monsieur Henri Lumière and Monsieur Gabriel Doublier.

As you probably know, your precious negatives have been sent to Paris where the Cinémathèque has had a special machine built to make prints. I have asked to be told when the boxes arrive and, if I am in Paris when it happens, I shall attend the opening.

Messieurs Grémillon and Langlois intend to use enlargements from your films and some documents they already possess to organize a Louis

Lumière exhibition in Brussels next June. This exhibition would then transfer to Paris in the autumn. I do not know if they have informed of you this project, nor whether you have given your agreement. If you do not wish to agree to it, perhaps you would let me know.

As soon as the first prints are ready, which will be in February, I expect, I shall start work on the leaflet I told you about, 'Louis Lumière, film director'.

If you do not mind, we should like, Monsieur Grémillon and I, to pay you a visit in Bandol in a month or six weeks or so. Monsieur Grémillon is currently in Italy. I am due to give a series of lectures for the Ministry of Information in Alsace-Lorraine next month. But from 20 February onwards, we should both be at your disposal.

I am glad your health is improving and that you have been able to work.

I am due to give my publisher the text for the new edition of *The Invention of Cinema* in February. I should have the proofs around 15 March. I shall send you the chapters relevant to you, as agreed.

Yours sincerely,
Georges Sadoul

1 *Les Pionniers du Cinéma*, volume two of *Histoire Générale du Cinéma* by Georges Sadoul, Denoël, 1947.

Louis Lumière to Georges Sadoul

27 January

Monsieur Georges Sadoul
3 rue de Bretonvilliers
Paris 4

Dear Sir,
Thank you for your kind letter of 20 January and I am sorry not to have replied sooner but my health obliges to me to spend most of my day in bed and to put off to the morrow what I should be doing on the day.

I willingly authorize you, as well as Messieurs Grémillon and Langlois, to enlarge images from certain of my films for the exhibition in Brussels at the end of June, which you mention.

I should be delighted to receive you with Monsieur Grémillon at the Villa Lumen towards the end of February if such a project comes off.

I shall also be pleased to receive the proofs you are thinking of sending me for the new edition of your book, regarding those passages that concern me.

See you soon, I hope.

Yours sincerely,

Georges Sadoul to Louis Lumière

Paris, 2 March 1947

Dear Sir,

I am sorry to have been so slow to reply to your last letter but I was away from Paris longer than expected and in any case I did not wish to write to you before completing an inventory of the negatives which you have entrusted to the safe-keeping of the Cinémathèque Française.

I hope that your health has improved and that you are now totally recovered. But this hard winter is dragging on and I am afraid that even in Bandol you feel it.

I had told you that towards the beginning of this month of March Monsieur Grémillon, President of the Cinémathèque Française, would come and see you and that I should accompany him, but Monsieur Grémillon is currently away from Paris in pre-production on a film and he will not be able to go to Bandol for many weeks.

Perhaps I could come with Monsieur Langlois, Secretary-General of the Cinémathèque, Saturday or Sunday next, 8 or 9 March? If the date is convenient, could you possibly confirm by telegram?

I come now to the inventory of negatives which I completed the day before yesterday with the help of the Cinémathèque's employees. We have re-classified the films using the numbers on the boxes, and this has enabled us to reconstitute those of your catalogues I do not have in my possession. It also enabled me to identify certain boxes, the labels of which had become illegible and which thus were not recognized by Monsieur Doublier in Lyon.

We should like immediately to make prints of your 'complete works' for a large exhibition of French films which is due to open in Warsaw at the beginning of May. I shall also be taking the liberty of asking you certain questions for which I must first establish the current list of films which you claim are by you. The numbers are the numbers in the catalogue. Unless otherwise stated, the negatives are at the Cinémathèque. (Trarieux) means the film is kept at your Paris subsidiary.

Films by Monsieur Louis Lumière[1]

  1 *Spinning Plates*
  2 *Aquarium* (two negs)
  5 *Arriving by Car* (Trarieux)
  8 *Arrival of a Train at Villefranche*   no
  9 *Boat Leaving Harbour*   missing
 11 *Sea-bathing*   missing
 32 *Leaving by car*
 37 *Disembarkation (Nice)*
 40 *Demolishing a Wall*
 41 *The Cat's Lunch*
 43 *Children with Toys*
 57 *Launching a Ship*
 64 *Weeds* (film by Monsieur Auguste Lumière, Trarieux)
 69 *Fishing for Goldfish* (Trarieux)
 73 *Game of Cards* (Trarieux)
 74 *Tic-tac*   missing
 99 *The Gardener Takes a Shower*   missing
 62 *The Blacksmith*
105 *The Transformable Hat*   missing
107 *Mechanical Pork Butcher's*
109 *Sack race* (two copies)
108 *The Photographer*   missing
128 *Place des Cordeliers, Lyon*
129 *Place Bellecour, Lyon*
653 *Arrival of a Train at La Ciotat*
655 *The Invalid Who Isn't* (two negs)
 91 *Leaving the Factory, rue Saint-Victor, Monplaisir*   no
Uncatalogued:
Disembarkation of the Congress of Photography   missing
Conversation between Messieurs Janssen and Lagrange   missing[2]

Films that could be by Monsieur Louis Lumière:
 27 *A Game of Bowls*
 45 *Children out Shrimping*
 46 *Children and Dogs*
 55 *Bicycle Lesson*
 60 *Washerwomen*
 72 *A Game of Bowls*
 67 *Baby's First Steps (Marcel and Madeleine)*

I apologize profusely for submitting another list after you had so kindly sent me a list of films 'that may be by Monsieur Louis Lumière' and I shall give you the reasons for my attributions.

Children out Shrimping, Children and Dogs, Baby's First Steps, A Dog has Lunch, A Children's Quarrel, Children, Home from a Trip out to Sea, School break at La Martinière: Some of these scenes have Marcelle and Madeleine on the box which seemed to suggest that they were family scenes shot by you. As regards La Martinière, I did not think you would send one of your cameramen to a place where you had been to school. *A Children's Quarrel* seems to me to be the film described by André Gay in *Revue Générale des Sciences* in 1895. *A Barge at La Ciotat*: it seems to me that you wouldn't have had a cameraman down to shoot such a scene in a town you visited regularly.

71–79, four scenes involving firemen: was not *A House on Fire*, shown on 11 July 1897 and reviewed by André Gay a collage of these films? And were they not shot by you?[3] If my hypothesis is correct, then these films would be of considerable historical importance because the fact that these four films were assembled and shown together would make them the first 'montage' and the first dramatic story of cinema. This series of 'firemen' was much imitated in France, America and England over the next ten years. Americans consider that their first dramatic and edited film was Edwin

Porter's *Life of an American Fireman* in 1902 and which is very much plagiarized from this series I am attributing to you.

André Gay also notes that among the films shown in July 1895, there was *Trick-riding* which seems to me to correspond to no. 194 in the catalogue, *Barrack House Joke*, which could be *Jumping the Blanket* (193), whereas *Soldiers at Riding School*, which Monsieur Coissac says was shown at the Grand Café, could be nos. 182–185.

I will have contact prints made of all the films I have taken the liberty of attributing to you and perhaps you could tell me from these images if you recognize them as yours or not.

I have two more worries. *Leaving the Factory* and *A Train Enters the Station.*

Leaving the Factory is described by André Gay[4] after the 11 July 1895 representation thus:

'We saw Messieurs Lumière's workers, men and women, leave their workshops for the midday break, young girls getting out of the way of carriages and bicycles, running alone or in groups.'

For its part, on 30 December 1895, in an article which is often quoted, *Le Radical* wrote 'Also worthy of particular note is [a view of] the entire staff, carriages and so on, leaving the workshops in which the device somewhat off-puttingly baptized the Cinematograph was invented.'

But in the film which is currently shown under the title *Leaving the Factory*, there are no carriages, nor do the factory girls have to make way for bicycles because the two or three bikes in shot are pushed along by hand by their owners.

The negative entitled *Leaving the Factory* (or, more precisely *Leaving the rue Saint-Victor Factory in Monplaisir*), which I have not been able to view fully yet, does have several carriages. This film bears no relation to the film usually shown under the same name, but is it not the one which was shown in 1895?[5]

For my part, I am inclined towards this hypothesis, if you can confirm it, because since our discussion last September, I have looked into the dates carefully. The first Edison kinetoscopes arrived in Paris towards the end of September 1894 (first description in *La Nature*, 20 October 1894) and as far as you are concerned, your research did not begin until after these machines had arrived in France. As the factory girls and workers are wearing summer clothes, the film shown on 22 March does not seem to me to have been the one usually quoted as being your first film. I am inclined, therefore, to think that the first film must be the one with the carriages, which is the one at the Cinémathèque.

Regarding *Arrival of a Train*, a 1903 English, Urban catalogue,[6] being a translation of your catalogue made by your English agents, contains the following two films, either of which could be the right one:

8 *A train Enters the Station at Villefranche*
653 *A train Enters the Station at La Ciotat (France)*

In an article published in *Annales* in 1896, Henri de Parville calls this film *A Train Enters the Station. Five minute halt.* Whereas a letter from a member of the audience at the first performance of the Lumière Cinematograph, published by Monsieur Ramsay, and quoted by me in my *Invention of Cinema*, refers to a film called *Entry and Departure of a Train*.

Arrival of a Train is a very fine film. It is generally regarded as the one shown at the Grand Café. I have found it under the box number 653. It does not figure in the first Lumière catalogue, dated 1897, which you were kind enough to send me. However, a quite different film, discovered in an unnumbered box, may easily be that other *Arrival of a Train* which does appear in the 1897 catalogue and which may comprise an arrival and a departure.

I have thus decided upon two hypotheses and I should be grateful if you would tell me which of the two is closer to the truth.

1) When you published your catalogue in April or May 1897, your firm, which for a year or so had refused to sell its films, now possessed some six or seven hundred negatives and the 358 films listed in the catalogue are an arbitrary selection from among your film strips, the naming of which was only completed after the publication, very shortly thereafter, of a second catalogue. According to this hypothesis, *Arrival at Villefranche* and *Arrival at La Ciotat* are both 1895 films, and only an accident in the selection process differentiates them.

2) On the contrary, your April 1897 catalogue listed all the films available at the time. According to this second hypothesis, *Arrival at La Ciotat* can only have been made by you during 1897, like, for instance, *The Invalid Who Isn't*, no. 665.

For my part, I favour the first hypothesis, since I have always believed that once you had trained your first cameramen – Doublier, Promio, Mesguich,[7] and so on – from early 1896 on, you stopped making films yourself.

The fact that two films made by you are numbered 653 and 665, and that two films currently held at Monsieur Trarieux', *The Sleeping Coachman* and *The Sleeping Watchman*, may be by you, leads me to conclude that a number of your films may have been catalogued under numbers in the 650 to 700 bracket.

I have to point out that none of the films currently held at the Cinémathèque is numbered between 648 and 730. Two crates containing these films must still be in storage in Lyon therefore, and likewise a third crate containing nos. 1300 to 1346.

Aside from these two or three whole crates, quite a few boxes are missing from the inventory. These gaps rarely amount to as much as 10% of a crate. They are unfortunately more prevalent in the first half of the catalogue (up to no. 600) which relates to the oldest and most precious films.

I shall have copies taken of my inventory and I shall send one copy to you and one to Monsieur Doublier. I apologize for the interminable length of this letter, but if I could call on you in about a week's time, I should be very pleased to discuss with you some issues about which I have written at too great a length.

Yours sincerely,
Georges Sadoul

I expect to have proofs of the new edition of my *Invention of Cinema* during the month of April. I intend to start writing my booklet, 'Louis Lumière, film director' as soon as the Cinémathèque has made prints of your complete works.

[Handwritten addition] I am sorry about the typing of this letter. My secretary is ill and I have had to stand in for her.

1 The list of films by Louis Lumière dates back to Sadoul's conversation with Louis Lumière at Bandol on 24 September 1946. On a copy of the Lumière Catalogue, Lumière had put blue ticks next to the films he thought were his. Now Sadoul is requesting a second identification. These will remain 'probably Louis Lumière' films, in *Lumière et Méliès*. Films 76 to 79, 82 & 83, 192, 194 will definitely be attributed to Louis. No. 82 was identified by Louis himself. In both lists, some films lose the attribution: 5, 20, 37, 45, 46, 52, 72, 182 to 184, 191, 665, 666 and 667. In 1974, Vincent Pinel reattributed 5, 37, 20, 52, 72 and 665 to Louis Lumière.
2 Jules Janssen was an astronomer who invented, in 1874, the photographic revolver used in 1874, in Japan, to study the passage of Venus before the sun. He was Chairman of the Congress of the French Societies of Photography in June 1895 at Lyon and as such filmed in conversation with Leo Lagrange, Member of Parliament for the Rhône, by Louis as the congressman disembarked from a river ferry at Neuville-sur-Saône.
3 Alas, we do not have Louis Lumière's reply to this question.
4 Former student of the Ecole Polytechnique, André Gay gave a detailed account of the 11 July 1895 performance of a Lumière Cinematograph in the reception rooms of the *Revue Générale des Sciences* in Paris.
5 The first version of *Leaving the Factory* shows a team of piebald horses facing the camera; according to Pinel, this was shot in mid March 1895 and is the earliest Cinematograph film. This is the version which would have been shown on 22 March at the Society for the

Advancement of Industry, 44 rue de Rennes in Paris. In the second version, the carriage is drawn by only one horse and in the third version, which figures in the 1897 Lumière catalogue as no. 91, there is no horse at all.

6 Louis Lumière had compiled a catalogue for advertising purposes, selecting the films he regarded as best. Some films remained uncatalogued, a real headache for film historians.

7 Felix Mesguich (1871–1949), became a Lumière cameraman-projectionist upon completing his military service. Trained at Lyon by Perrigot. in June 1896 he was sent to the United States, where he achieved considerable public success. He was forced to leave by American protectionist backlash. In 1897, he arranged displays of the Lumière Cinematograph all round Russia, and was deported for filming a dancer known as La Belle Otero, dancing with an officer subsequently driven to suicide. In 1898, he made the first advertising film (for Ripolin, a brand of paint). In 1933, he wrote his memoirs under the title *Tours de Manivelle* (*Cranked up*).

Georges Sadoul to Louis Lumière

Paris, 17 March 1947

Monsieur Louis Lumière
Villa Lumen
Bandol

Dear Sir,

Thank you very much for giving Monsieur Henri Langlois and me such a tremendous welcome. We hope that we did not exhaust you and I am sure that as spring is coming, your health will soon improve.

As I said, I stopped off in Lyon for two days on my way home. I was very well looked after by Monsieur Lefrancq, and Monsieur Doublier went to a great deal of trouble to find what we were looking for. Monsieur Doublier managed to dig out the four crates missing from the first lot sent to Paris. I hope these crates left Lyon today, Monday, and I trust they will reach the Cinémathèque Française by the end of the week.

Monsieur Doublier is also hunting out the list of all the various machines which he sent to you some time ago and the crate numbers for the crates in which they are kept. He will send you these soon.

Monsieur Lefrancq allowed me to enter the library which is in your father's old studio. I was able to work there for many hours and I found some interesting documents.

As soon as an inventory of the new crates is drawn up, the Cinémathèque will embark on its print-making programme.

I enclose a list of negatives currently held by Monsieur Trarieux. I do not think this list is complete, but it is the only one I have got.

I shall return the various catalogues you have lent me once they have been copied or photographed; there are spare copies in the library in Lyon.

I hope your health improves rapidly.

Yours sincerely,

Georges Sadoul

Louis Lumière to Georges Sadoul

Bandol, 25 March 1947

Monsieur Sadoul
3 rue de Bretonvilliers
Paris 4

Dear Sir,

Thank you for your kind letter of 17 March. It was very pleasant to see you in Bandol a few days ago.

Upon examining the list of films which you have found in Monsieur Trarieux's at the Lumière company headquarters, I note that a fair number of them were indeed shot by me but there are some which are not by me. I shall probably be able to be more precise when I have received still frames printed on paper which you have promised to send me. When I have them, I shall do my best to let you know.

This list, in any case, is wanting the list of mauve films[1] which I have given you.

Yours sincerely,

Louis Lumière

---

1 Printed in mauve and white instead of black and white, which tones down the contrast, although the colour does not show through in projection.

Henri Langlois to Louis Lumière

Paris, 28 April 1947

Maestro,[1]

We apologize for being so slow to complete the making of prints, which is due to our workshops being overburdened. We are returning to you, as promised, the mauve prints of the first performance at the Grand Café which you were kind enough to lend us so we could copy the negatives.

Monsieur Grémillon and Monsieur Sadoul and all the members of our Board have asked me to thank you for your generosity to the Cinémathèque Française, and we shall be pleased to count you among our benefactors.

As we discussed when we met, the Cinémathèque Française has been asked to arrange an Exhibition on the birth of cinema, on the occasion of the World Festival of Film and Cinema which is to be held in Brussels in June. We intend to organize loop projections of some of your film strips, to reconstitute the Photorama and to exhibit anything concerning you and your work.

As we are now assured of receiving the financial support required, we should be most grateful if we could receive, as you indicated that we might, a copy of the poster for the Lumière Cinematograph which you promised us for our archives, the photograph of you filming Janssen upon which you were unable to lay your hands that day and a Photorama projector,[2] the original Lumière machine and all the various versions which you may still possess including one or more Kinoras, and any documents which you feel are appropriate to this exhibition.

We should also be most grateful if you could lend us some of the drawings you mentioned.[3]

In order to avoid disturbing you unnecessarily, we have asked Madame Musidora,[4] under Monsieur Sadoul's guidance, to liaise with Monsieur Doublier in Lyon and with yourself in Bandol, as soon as we have received your definite authorization, in order to arrange the logistics.

I remind you that the Brussels exhibition is transferring to Paris in the winter.

I shall send you from Warsaw photographs of the Lumière Room which we are setting up in an Exhibition on the History of French Cinema from the earliest days to the present.

Regarding the original negatives which you have entrusted to us, we are having stills printed up and sent to you. We shall then install a special Laboratory for these negatives at the Cinémathèque. None of the tests we have conducted in commercial laboratories has been satisfactory.

Yours sincerely,
Henri Langlois
Secretary-General

1 The following story is told about Louis Lumière. An admirer wishing to heap him with praise kept on calling him 'maestro', in French, Maître. Lumière eventually said, 'Maître is not enough, old boy, call me Kilomaître.'
2 A device invented by Louis Lumière in 1900 which projects panoramas by means of a central image cylinder around which twelve lenses rotate, and an inverter which fixes the image on the cylinder; the screen was slightly elliptical, 20m wide and 6m high. A complex

set of mirrors and prisms was required to project the image on to the screen. Photorama performances were held until 1903. A catalogue was published. It contains more than 1000 panoramic views.
3 Louis Lumière was the author of dozens of drawings, not all of which have survived.
4 Musidora (1889–1957), a singer at the Folies-Bergère and other music halls. From 1913 on, she was a Gaumont film star. She appeared in tight black satin in Feuillade's *The Vampires* (1915) thus launching the term 'vamp'. She was a friend of the writer, Colette, and later in life became a writer herself. She is the author of numerous memoirs, novels, screenplays, short stories, plays and articles.

Musidora to Albert Trarieux

Paris [1947]

Dear Monsieur Trarieux,

I am sorry to importune Monsieur Lumière's son-in-law – you, the extension of that light.[1] I am sending you a man tormented by a thousand promises of work at the Cinémathèque Française. He is Feuillade's famous cameraman, G. Guerini. He will tell you briefly that he will willingly accept, and above all from you, any work compatible with his capabilities, which are numerous.

Thank you for doing what you can for him. If, in these difficult times, you can do something.

Gratefully,
Musidora

Louis Lumière
Louis [sic] Gaumont[2]
Louis Feuillade
'L's and wings[3] of fame.

and a little drawing to cheer you up
Musidora
thanks the three Louis who made her name . . .

1 Translator's note. Feeble pun on the word *lumière* – light.
2 His first name was Léon.
3 Translator's note: The French for wings is *ailes*, pronounced like the letter L.

Louis Lumière to Henri Langlois

Bandol, 5 May 1947

Dear Sir,

Thank you for your kind letter of 28 April. I shall be delighted to make available to you, as far as I can, the various objects you request for your exhibition in Brussels. My health has got worse since I had the pleasure of seeing you at the Villa Lumen and I cannot go and search my laboratory for the things you want because I can hardly leave my house.

I hope that, as the fine weather returns, I shall recover some of my strength and that I shall thus be able to satisfy you, in part at least, though there is one absolute stumbling block. As I told you when I saw you, to set up a photorama projection room would be a considerable task and would take much longer than you have got: you would need to build a solid walkway twenty metres long, with no pillars for support, a Fresnel lens and pool of the same dimensions, a stone pillar three metres high and very solidly built, an opaque, circular screen, thirty-one square metres in dimension and so on.

The only thing which would be possible would be to show the machines themselves, if, that is, there are some in Lyon (projectors), you can certainly have them if they have not all been dispersed; camera, which you already have; and enlarged prints, even very large, on bromide paper.

As soon as I can, I shall send you what I have got. Thank you in advance for all your trouble in organizing this project.

Please give my regards to Monsieur Sadoul.

Yours sincerely,

Louis Lumière

Louis Lumière to Henri Langlois

Bandol, 31[sic] June 1947

Thank you for your kind letter of 26 June. I am writing to say that I willingly accept your proposal regarding the permission you request for Venice.

Yours sincerely,
Louis Lumière

Louis Lumière to Max Lefrancq-Lumière

Bandol, 6 August 1947

My dear Max,

Thank you for your nice letter, which Florence has given me.

I am glad to hear that you like the fine country you live in now and that you get on with the nice family who have taken you in for the holidays. I hope they like you and that you repay their kindness to you by excellent behaviour.

And you'll come home talking English like Churchill!

I look forward to having you and your brother to stay for a few days.

Keep well.

I have been getting better this week, but I have trouble walking.

It is very hot (thirty degrees in the bedrooms) but getting cooler. At last there is some mistral.[1]

A big hug, Max.

Pépé

I have trouble reading and writing, even more, because my eyesight is failing . . .

1 Translator's note: Mistral: a cold north wind that blows in Provence.

Louis Lumière to Gauja

Bandol, 17 October 1947

Monsieur Gauja
Head of the Secretariat
Académie des Sciences
3 quai Conti
Paris

My dear Monsieur Gauja,

It has been ages since my dreadful state of health has allowed me to leave Bandol and I am very sorry that it has been more than a year since I have been to the Académie, where I used to come to see you and my colleagues with such pleasure.

The object of this letter is to ask you whether Gauthier-Villard could print a hundred or so copies of my note to the Académie dated 8 June 1945, of which I enclose one of the last remaining copies in my possession. I should pay for the printing.

A newspaper in Nice mentioned this note recently and since then I have had a revival of interest; I now get daily requests from people who have had a cataract operation hoping to achieve for themselves what I have managed to do.

Perhaps the block with the illustrations has been kept; if not, could you have another engraved?

Thank you very much in advance. Please give your wife my regards.

Yours sincerely,
Louis Lumière

Note: This work related to a 'new system for recovering normal sight without increasing the size of retinal images through orpasia compensation as a result of a single or double cataract operation' inserted in the account of proceedings, volume 220, 8 January 1945.

Gauja to Louis Lumière

Paris, 22 October 1947

Dear Sir,

I was very pleased to hear from you in your letter of 17 October because, as you say, we had not had the pleasure of seeing you for some time here.

The printer's blocks for your note no longer exist: they were destroyed shortly after publication because we are so short of materials. We shall therefore either have to compose again or photograph the originals.

I am asking Monsieur Lefort, who manages Gauthier-Villard, to look into the matter and he will write to you.

Yours sincerely,

Gauja

Louis Lumière to Henri Langlois

Bandol, 20 December 1947

Monsieur Langlois
Secretary-General
Cinémathèque Française
7 avenue de Messine
Paris 8

Dear Sir,

Thank you for your letter of 28 November. I have been unwell and I was not able to reply sooner, for which I apologize.

You know almost all the documents I possess because you have seen them either in Paris or in Bandol or in Lyon or in Brussels. There have been so many events of this sort that I have not much left.

All I can do is to authorize my son-in-law, Monsieur Trarieux, to give you the autochrome photograph in his possession, in which I appear, apparently, in the midst of my family. As to finding photographs of my cameramen-projectionists, do not even think of it because they rarely did more than pass by the factory on business and I do not have any record of what they looked like. Everything has been dispersed long ago and I am sorry that I cannot do better for you.

I am delighted to learn that you have had almost two hundred 18x24 prints made from my films and these have come out very well. I should be delighted to have copies of whichever you think you may be able to obtain for me.

Monsieur Sadoul is very well informed about all the above-mentioned matters and I am sure that you will find he has more documents than I do because many have never been returned.

I am, unfortunately, in bad health and I cannot attend my laboratory any more. Perhaps, when the fine weather comes, perhaps, with your assistance, I may be able to look for objects of interest for your exibition.

Yours sincerely,

Louis Lumière

Henri Langlois to Louis Lumière

Paris, 26 February 1948

Monsieur Louis Lumière
Villa Lumen
Bandol (Var)
Service: General Secretariat
Reference: AMG/HL

Maestro,

I am glad to inform you that we have just completed a conclusive test: we shall now be able to make prints of your films at Monsieur Mayer's (Monsieur Mayer, SIM, Bd de la Pie, St Maur des Fossés, Seine). We were sent to him by Monsieur Trarieux. I am taking advantage of parallel credits to have three or four hundred metres printed up immediately.

Monsieur Braunberger has, however, approached me to say that he wishes to have prints of a number of films made, and that you have given him permission to do so, on the understanding that the prints in question will remain the property of the Cinémathèque.

But your letter refers to only a few films and Monsieur Braunberger is talking about almost all your films, so that we can later make inter-negatives. Monsieur Sadoul has, like us, seen the press release announcing a montage film composed of your films, in which both of us were attacked, even though we had not even been informed.

I should be most grateful, Maestro, if you could let me know whether you have reached an agreement with Monsieur Braunberger, that he may freely print and obtain inter-negatives of all your films or whether you approve of the precautions which I have taken, namely insisting that the bills be drawn up in our name, so that your rights are unaffected: the rules of the Cinémathèque forbid us from disposing either of prints or of inter-negatives without your approval. No one can use Cinémathèque films without the owner's permission.

Yours sincerely,

Henri Langlois

Pierre Braunberger to Louis Lumière

Paris, 3 March 1948

Monsieur Louis Lumière
Vila Lumen
Bandol (Var)

Dear Sir,

On 7 November last, you were kind enough to write me the following letter:

'I authorize Monsieur Pierre Braunberger to use a few negatives belonging to the collection of "early Lumière films" currently at the Cinémathèque, with a view to making prints for the film he is planning, and with the agreement of the Cinémathèque.'

I am most grateful to you for this letter and take this opportunity of thanking you again.

Because we are about to undertake work of considerable importance on your negatives, and in order that there may be no misunderstanding with the Cinémathèque, I should be grateful if you would stipulate that you authorize me to make prints from all the negatives currently at the Cinémathèque Française, for the purposes of the film which I am now preparing.[1]

Naturally, we shall give you credit for these archives.

I am sorry to disturb you a second time. Thank you again.

Yours sincerely,

Pierre Braunberger

1 Here is testimony to the relations between Pierre Braunberger, producer, and Louis Lumière, inventor. It provides a context for this letter, which relates to a film Braunberger was both producing and directing (with Nicole Védrès): 'In 1894, my father, then a young doctor in a hospital, went to see my great-uncle, Professor Weill, in Lyon. He accompanied him on his consultant's rounds, and examined Louis Lumière who had been in bed for more than two months. An idea for a new course of treatment occurred to my father and he asked his uncle for permission to look after this patient. Within a few days, Louis Lumière had recovered. Lumière was so grateful, he gave my father a trunk full of photographic plates. The day he was due to return to Paris, Lumière said to him, 'I know you love photography, and I've got a surprise for you; I've invented moving photography.' I think my father must have been the first person in the world, apart from the inventor's own family, to witness cinematographic projection, in Lumière's own room. He had occasion to see the Lumière Cinematograph again at the University of Lyon, eight or nine months later, at the first public screening. He also attended the performances at the Grand Café in Paris, where almost none of the films corresponded to the ones he had seen in Lumière's room, except *Lunch for Baby*.

This episode, in which my father looked after Louis Lumière, unconsciously influenced my career but it also had an unexpected epilogue, some fifty years later. I was finishing, in 1946, a film which I had conceived long before the war, called *Paris 1900*. I had included a large quantity of Lumière archive. Just as the film was about to come out, I received a telephone call from Henri Langlois to say that he had just received a registered letter from the Lumière brothers formally prohibiting any commercial use of their work. I tried, unsuccessfully, to get hold of them. Forty-eight hours later, I mentioned this difficulty to my father over lunch. He told me not to worry. He said he would write a letter to Louis Lumière and that I was to deliver it. I took his letter and went round to the Lumière office, in the rue du Quatre Septembre, in Paris. A few minutes after the janitor had given him the letter, Lumière appeared in fits of laughter. 'The answer is yes, of course,' he said. This is what the letter said: 'In 1894, you asked me what you could do for me. I've been thinking. Let my son use your films.' And that is how I was the only person to receive Lumière's permission to use his archives for commercial purposes.' (From *Pierre Braunberger, Producteur*, CNC-Centre Georges Pompidou, Paris 1987.)

Auguste Lumière to Henri Lumière

Bandol, 19 May 1948

My dear Henri,

Everything is fine here. Louis told me a rude story at lunch and went down to his laboratory and stayed there for three hours! His doctor cannot believe it! Nor can we.

He would like to have an ordinary little clock or watch, except that he wants one with twenty-four hours instead of twelve. He says that when he wakes up he does not know whether it is day or night. Could you ask Mademoiselle Bonnard to do this for him, and send me the thing as soon as you can? Please also, when you ask her to do this, thank her for her news and tell her to thank Dr Berthezène for the letter he sent with Mademoiselle Bonnard's.

I am always pleased to hear your news and I should like to know how Yvette is. I hope the journey was not too tiring and that her health is improving.

I have said that everything is fine here in Bandol, but that was not exactly true. There is one thing wrong: the fishing. Fishing in the afternoon is nowhere near as good as fishing in the morning. I've lost about 50% compared to last year. But no matter because I think I am getting better and I shall return in good condition.

Marguerite is not overfond of Bandol, but this time things are better because Madame Brun[1] is here and she is staying as long as we are.

Since yesterday, the weather seems to be getting better.

A big hug, Henri, to Yvette and the children too.

A. Lumière

Tomorrow we shall have been here a week; almost half our stay gone already! Time is flying by – I feel as if I have only just got here!

1 Madame Brun, a friend of Marguerite Lumière's who kept an antique shop in the Brotteaux district of Lyon.

Auguste Lumière to Paul Meyer

Lyon, 29 May 1952

My dear friend,

We were all very upset to hear that you have had several bad weeks of illness and we were awaiting with great impatience news of the results of the operation which you have had to undergo.

Happily, we have heard today that you are recovering quickly and, needless to say, I long to see you cured quickly. We are longing to see you back in Lyon too, in the same good health you always used to have.

Henri is in Morocco, coming home in four or five days' time. I know that he will be pleased to hear that your operation has not caused any complications. In fact, he has not yet heard what a hard time you have been having.

For my part, I have only good news to tell. I seem to be bearing up reasonably well despite my ninety years of age, since I continue to work and spend every morning at the clinic.

But I deeply miss the days when we worked together; it was such a pleasure to be with a uniquely brilliant researcher. I have never come across another researcher as learned, as competent, as able and as conscientious as yourself. I was always sorry you left and now more than ever.

Apart from the staff, I have only good old Perrin as a collaborator, and I hardly use him because I cannot do any pharmaceutical research these days. My research labs are deserted and my own work is still ostracized. They won't forgive me for proving that tuberculosis is not contagious and they stifle anything I do.

The fiftieth anniversary of anaphylaxia has just been celebrated in Paris, with not a word on my work on the subject.[1] They are unaware of the mechanisms of the problem, even though I have analysed it. They prefer to remain ignorant, rather than take account of the two books and thirty papers I have written about this over the last thirty years! It is very sad.

When you come to Monplaisir – soon – I shall show you what I have been publishing, without obtaining any kind of recognition from the establishment.

But none of this matters to you. What matters is that you should recover your old state of health, which is I what I fervently wish for.

Yours ever,

A. Lumière

1 Auguste Lumière was one of the great experts in this field. He published innumerable works on the subject. This refers, perhaps, to a study published in *L'Avenir Médical*, a periodical founded by Auguste Lumière, entitled 'Strict diets cause certain food allergies' (1940), unless to 'The stagnant pond of anaphylaxia.'

Auguste Lumière to Georges Panuel[1]

Bandol, 20 September 1953

Dear Sir,

I am most grateful to you for the loyalty with which you have preserved the memory of our time at La Ciotat, all those years ago. Thank you very much indeed.

You were kind enough to ask me where I thought your project should be realized and I can only congratulate you on the choice which you and the Council have made.

It is a spot from which the whole magnificent bay is visible, and the grandeur of it has, perhaps, not been appreciated sufficiently.

When I had to leave the area, and our house, it was with dread in my soul, a heavy heart and tears in my eyes.

Since I am about to embark upon my ninety-second year, I cannot think that I shall live to see your project achieved, but I thank you and the Council with all my heart for the eternal monument which you propose, so spontaneously, to give us.

Thanks to you, I can depart in the knowledge that something of our work and something of us will survive in one of the most lovely spots of the French coastline.

Yours sincerely,

the Grateful Survivor

A. Lumière

1 Chairman of an association for a monument to the Lumière family, which was inaugurated at La Ciotat on 10 August 1958.

Appendix I
The Cinematograph

We are most grateful to Messieurs Lumière who have been good enough to loan us their device and who have given us every explanation we wanted.

'Let us suppose we have obtained – and we shall see in a moment by what method – a strip of positive film P (fig.1 no. 1) upon which images appear as ordinary photographs, light tones represented by light tones and dark tones by dark tones. This strip is not more than fifteen metres long and is about three centimetres wide. Equally spaced holes are perforated on either side of the strip, corresponding to each image. The images, each one corresponding to a fifteenth of a second, are rigorously identical: in other words, if two such images were to be superimposed, the parts representing fixed objects would coincide exactly, and the distance between the parts representing moving objects would represent the movement accomplished in the interval between the two images being taken. This strip, P, is rolled up and placed in a box which sits on top of the Cinematograph. It is held in place by a metal rod. It emerges through a gap, descends and passes around spool, G, ascends, passes over a rod and wraps its around a third rod, T. The strip is driven by a crank M, which, by a gear system, drives a camshaft. On this camshaft sit: a reverse lever which drives T; a triangular eccentric drive; a drum V (figs. 1 & 2); and a double disc.

Having said all of that, we can watch what happens as the camshaft revolves. The mechanism moves into bottom position and locks; the sprockets dig into two holes in the film situated on the same horizontal; but a rod starts to draw them back towards the drum, P, so that they are completely free when the shutter moves upwards. This upward movement is such that the mechanism moves exactly the same distance as separates two holes, such that when it locks into its upward position, the sprockets are exactly opposite the next two holes. For a moment, the mechanism is immobile as the other rod pushes the sprockets into the holes, in such a way that they drive the film. The drum P gives into the pressure and unravels; the drum P (fig. 2), activated by a rotation of rod T, rolls up and, the next time the mechanism stops, the sprockets disengage from the film again, a new frame will have replaced the old frame in front of the aperture E (fig. 1) which is located in the path of the beam that will project the images on to the screen. All these movements, which take so long to explain, are complete – in the example we have chosen – in one fifteenth of a second. A new turn of the camshaft will bring a new frame and so on, up to nine hundred frames per minute. It is easy to imagine the precision required in making the machine in order that the film remains undamaged by all these movements, despite its frailty and despite repeated usage. For this reason, the sprockets must start moving and stop as gradually as possible. The backward pull or forward push of the sprockets does not begin until the film has come to a complete stop, in order not to damage the holes. In addition, the film passes round another, upper rod, before winding back. The reason for this is that when the film stops, rod T is still turning, tending to force the film and pull it. This motion is proportionally less brutal – so we discovered in our experiments – the more horizontal it is. We so arranged things that the tangent off drum P, emerging at epsilon and giving approximately the direction followed by the film strip, should be horizontal at the end of the roll, which is where the mass, alternately stopped and in motion, is at its greatest. When the film is immobile, a small plaque at E is kept in place by a light spring mechanism (not shown on our drawings) which prevents it being affected by the traction exercised by T (fig.2).

The mechanism is such that the film strip is motionless for two–thirds of the time; the other third moves it downwards. If light hits the screen while the film is immobile, everything is as it should be; but if light hits the screen while the film strip is in motion, the fixed image is affected by the impression of film descending; there would be a drag effect corresponding to the light tones. Consequently, the light must be masked for the last third of the cycle. This is what the machine does. Only successive still images are projected on the screen, at a rate of, say, nine hundred per minute. Because these images persist on the retina, the eye fails to register the black space in between each frame. Also, because the light only shines for two–thirds of the total time, the light required is not particularly powerful. Successive images impressed upon the eye give an astonishing sense of reality where the differences between frames, accountable by the motion of people and objects during exposure, gives a complete illusion of that motion. The same machine serves to make the negative print and to make a positive print from the negative. The apparatus devised by Messieurs Lumière will be of considerable assistance to the photographic study of motion. Not only does it enable us to capture movement in its various stages, but we can recompose it at will, since the crank is hand–operated. Motions can be slow, very slow if we wish, so that no detail escapes our attention; and then, subsequently, we can accelerate it, should we so desire, back to normal speed. We shall then possess absolutely perfect reproduction of real movement.'
Louis Lumière
The Cinematograph
La Nature, 12 October 1895

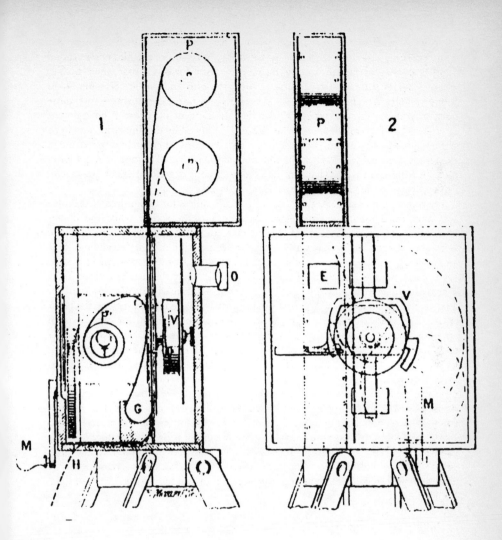

Fig. 1 Lengthways view.
Fig. 2 Sideways (or vertical) view, showing lens.

P shows film unreeling.
T shows the rod around which film spools.
V shows the cylinder.
O shows opening through which light strikes film.
M shows crank.

Appendix 2
The Autochromes

In 1862, Ducos du Hauron sent a memoir entired 'Solution to the colour problem', accompanied by photographs, to a member of the Académie des Sciences. In this memoir, he laid the basis for an 'indirect method' of photographic reproduction of colours, which avoided the principles of synthetic addition and subtraction.

'If the picture which nature provides, which seems to be one, is divided into three distinct pictures, one red, one yellow, one blue, and if from each of these pictures one obtained a separate photographic image, in the specific colour, then the three pictures need only be combined for an exact representation of nature to appear, complete with shading and colours.'

His ideas were met with contempt. At the same time, another researcher, Charles Cros, obtained similar results. He put them forward to the Académie des Sciences and was similarly attacked. Becquerel launched a great diatribe against these ideas. 'Let anyone who feels like it and who has the means put these ideas to the test.' Which is what, a few later, the Lumière brothers were to do. As Charles Cros wrote in verse, some time later,

'I have willed the grace and colour,
of all that lives in a mirror,
the folly of an Opera ball,
and evening reds and shady green,
on inert plates to be seen
I have willed it, it shall befall.'

Ducos du Hauron and Cros were involuntary rivals. They confronted each other with courtesy, in an exchange that did nothing to diminsh their mutual respect. See also Ducos du Hauron's fine letters to Louis Lumière, reproduced here.

It seemed, therefore, as though colour photography might be achievable by the direct method, even though considerable practical obstacles stood in its way: the subject had to pose without moving while three different shots were taken on three different plates, each one of which was sensitive to only one of the three primary colours, because of a complementary filter. Each of the three negatives then had to be printed in monochrome on paper and coloured with one of the colours. Finally, the three monochrome prints had to be assembled exactly together. A highly complex process in which a very large number of parameters all needed strict controlling: sensitivity, colour sensitivity, the precise tints of the filters, varying exposure times for each of the three negatives and the three positives, and so on. Even the experts found it exhausting.

On 12 February 1891, Professor Gabriel Lippmann presented the Académie des

Sciences with a new method, which he called 'direct interferential', for obtaining colour photographs with a single exposure. The principle was much simpler: colours are recorded on a photographic plate, the emulsion of which is in direct contact with a film of mercury which acts as a mirror. 'Once the plate is developed,' Lippmann observed, 'colours appear. The picture obtained is negative, by transparency – in other words each colour is represented by its complement – and positive by reflection: the colours themselves appear.' Colours form in strata, according to two sets of interferential waves. Lippmann's studies were revolutionary. They prefigured holography.

The Lumière brothers were fascinated by Lippmann's discoveries and set about making smooth plates for tests. Lippmann had so far taken only one photograph: a solar spectrum obtained after three hours' exposure. In May 1892, thanks to the Lumière brothers, he was able to show the Académie des Sciences some photographs his associates had taken: stained glass with four colours; a plate of oranges with a red poppy; a parrot; a group of flags. Each photograph was still the outcome of several hours' exposure. One year later, on 11 May 1893, Messieurs Lumière showed the Paris Photo–Club projections of bunches of flowers (the *Le Temps* reporter said they were only missing scent), the park at La Tête d'Or in Lyon, cloth and so on. These photographs required only thirty minutes' exposure. Shortly after, the brothers had got this down to four minutes. Now, portraits were possible, provided the sitters were patient and not too fidgety. At the International Congress in Geneva, August 1893, the Lumière brothers showed a self–portrait with one of their sisters, sleeping with her head on a table laden with fruit. This was a universal success. At the Congress of the Photographic Society in London, where the pictures were introduced by Captain Abney, one of the pioneers of bromide printing, and the projectionist was Warnecke. The pictures then made their way to the United States where they were much admired. On 28 March 1894, the brothers received academic awards; in June the Académie bestowed its grand medal on them. After this success, the brothers took stock of the difficulties which still faced them in their pursuit of colour photography along these lines and which were probably insuperable: the image was shiny, and varied according to the angle from which it was viewed. Above all, it could not be reproduced. It had one final disadvantage which must have been unacceptable to them as scientists: identical procedures, using identical photographic plates, did not lead to identical results.

So the Lumière brothers decided to start again from scratch. Their modesty, in working from a completely different basis, annulled several years' research, publications, lectures and exhibitions. A new patent was taken out on 17 October 1903. The new method is a simple one, well described in Borgé and Chardère (*Les Lumières*, Payot, 1985, pp. 127–8): 'A glass plate is coated with a layer of microscopic, trichrome particles coloured blue, red and green. This layer is then coated with a second layer of black and white, panchromatic, light–sensitive emulsion. Provided the plate is exposed 'the wrong way round', with the trichrome layer nearest the light, a normal developing and fixing process will produce a colour negative image with colours – yellow, blue–green and magenta – complementary to the original colours.' Considerable problems remained. The red, green and blue emulsion layer must somehow be made to adhere to the glass; the colouring of its particles must be rendered stable, so as to avoid blotching. It must be varnished with a varnish whose refractive index is the same as its own.

The ideal components turned out to be specks of potato starch, 15 to 20 thousandths of a millimetre across; divided into three lots, these particles were then dyed red, green and blue with special dyes, then mixed together. This is how Louis Lumière described the principle, in a handwritten text dated 30 May 1904, (Lumière file, Académie des Sciences): 'The method is based on the use of coloured particles forming a single coat on a glass plate, varnished with an appropriate varnish, and then coated with light–sensitive emulsion. This plate is exposed with its back to the light; the resulting image is developed and then reversed, so that the true colours of the subject appear. We have had considerable trouble in our research into this method but the results show that this is not insuperable. The details of the process are as follows: treat potato starch so as to obtain particles 15 or 10 thousandths of a millimetre in diameter; divide these particles into three lots and dye each lot respectively red–orange, green and violet; dry thoroughly and combine the powders obtained in appropriate proportions; using a brush, spread this powder on glass plate which has had some adhesive coating applied to it; with care, it is possible to obtain a perfectly smooth surface with not a single particle protruding; by the same process of scattering, it is then necessary to block any interstices which would allow white light to pass through; this can be done with any fine black powder, powdered charcoal for instance.'

Louis obtained 3000 grains of potato starch per square millimetre, a figure which, by 1907, had reached 9000. It was soon found necessary to compress the grains. Unable to find a machine capable of producing the five tonnes of pressure per centimetre without breaking the glass plate, Louis Lumière built one which, instead of pressing down vertically, pressed in at a tangent with needles 1.5 millimetres in diameter. . . Similarly, Louis had to resolve the difficulty of sorting the particles of starch in such a way that the colours were evenly spread on the glass surface, that they stuck to it, that the colours did not blotch and so on. In order to achieve this, new workshops were established in the Lumière factories, and new machines brought in, to powder, varnish and spread. The results were good but Louis remained concerned. Would the meticulousness of the process put the public off?

It came on the market in 1907. It was so successful that it lasted thirty years and for thirty years innumerable letters and learned articles were written, competitions were set up and so on. Production expanded from 6000 plates per day in 1910 to 70,000 per day in 1914. Albert Kahn sent photographers the world over with these plates and assembled a collection of some 70,000 autochromes. In 1960, a French expedition found plates frozen in Antarctic ice, where they had been abandoned by an Australian expedition in 1910. Despite the cold and the weather, they were still in usable condition, which is an amazing measure of how well they were made.

'Of all the things I have invented,' Louis Lumière said, 'Cinema cost me least and making practical autochromes gave me the greatest pleasure.'

Appendix 3
The Lumière Family Tree

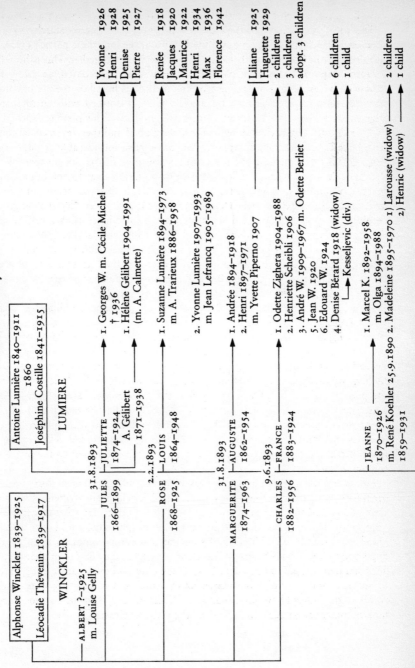

Appendix 4
Chronology

1854 Antoine Lumière, an orphan, learns carpentry at Armand Dovine's shop, with Onésime Gayon, at Marcilly, in the Aube, a department of the Champagne region.

1855 Antoine goes to Paris, and becomes an apprentice sign–painter with Auguste Constantin.

1859 Ducos du Hauron starts researching colour photography.

1860 Antoine designs Nadar's luminous shop sign, boulevard des Capucines in Paris.

1861 Antoine Lumière marries Jeanne–Joséphine Costille.

1862 19 October. Auguste is born in Besançon.

1863 At the School of Industrial Art, Antoine attends Jeanneney's painting and drawing class.

1864 5 October, Louis born in Besançon. Antoine obtains first prize in painting.

Ducos du Hauron describes a process for projecting moving pictures. This device will never be built, but the patent mentions slow motion, speeding up, special effects, animation, tracking shots.

1865 Antoine teaches painting at the School of Industrial Art. Antoine becomes partners with Emile Lebeau and opens two photographic studios, at Montbéliard and at Baume–les–Dames.

1869 Antoine sings in bars at night.

In the USA, J.W. Hyatt manufactures celluloid.

1870 The Lumière family moves to Lyon, rue de la Barre. 2 April, Jeanne is born.

Heyl presents his phasmatrope.

1873 30 September, Mélinie–Juliette is born

1874 Antoine designs and builds a studio so that he can practise photography on metal plates. His camera has twelve lenses.

Janssen studies the passage of Venus before the sun using a photographic revolver.

1878 Antoine's portraits are noticed at the Paris Exhibition.

Edison invents the phonograph. Reynaud starts selling his praxinoscope.

1879 Antoine orders Van der Weyden's electrical system which improves photographic lighting

Reynaud establishes the Praxinoscope Theatre.

1880 Muybridge's zoogyroscope projects images of horses in motion.

1881 Louis devises a formula for photographic emulsion which is faster and smoother than Monkhoven's: dry bromide plates. Soon, they are on sale at Larochet the chemist's, in Lyon. Auguste, a soldier with the 96 regiment at Chambéry, witnesses an epidemic of typhoid.

1882 18 September, France is born.

Reynaud combines his praxinoscope with a projector. Marey invents the fixed plate chronophotograph.

1883 Louis' first patent which, as he is under age, is taken out in his father's name. It refers to metal containers for photographic plates.

1884 18 November, Edouard is born. Louis and Auguste manage to save the factory which has been in financial trouble since the early 1880s. They employ about ten workers. Great commercial success of Blue Label plates which are extra–fast. The family moves to Monplaisir.

1885 Auguste signs an agreement with Balagny for the manufacture of film.
Louis perfects his photogravure process. His first photogravures come out in 1887.

1887 Goodwin invents supple, clear film made from cellulose nitrate. This is what the first films are made of.

1888 Louis Le Prince takes out a patent for a zootropic camera with 16 lenses. Edison and Dickson build an optical phonograph. First chronophotograph images on strips of paper by Marey.

1890 Jeanne marries René Koehler.

Planchon builds an 'autotensile' film factory, destined to replace photographic plates. The Lumière company buys it from him.

1891 Auguste and Louis manage to take colour photographs by the Lippmann method. The Lumière firm manufactures colour plates for the Lippmann method.

Edison's kinetoscope is perfected. Lippmann presents the interferential method of colour photography to the Académie des Sciences.

1892 The Société Anonyme Antoine Lumière, a family company, is set up. Auguste is the chairman. Production of photosensitive silver citrate and bromide paper begins.

Demenÿ invents the phonoscope, which reconstitutes motion. Reynaud displays three tapes of luminous pantomimes at the Musée Grévin. The Edison Kinetoscope Company is founded to manufacture the kinetoscope.

1893 Mélinie–Juliette marries Jules Winckler and Auguste, Marguerite Winckler. Lippmann method colour photo products are put on the market.

Edison's kinetoscope comes on the market.

1894 Antoine is given the Légion d'Honneur. Louis and Auguste are given academic awards for their work on colour photography. The factory runs into financial trouble. Vermorel gives his support. The first prototype for a moving picture machine, developed by Auguste and Charles Moisson, does not work. Louis takes over.

1895 13 February. The brothers obtain a patent for a machine which takes and views chronophotographic images. 22 March, they show the Society for the Advancement of National Industry, their chronophotographic pictures and colour photographs which obtain a resounding success. 10, 11 and 12 June, at the Congress of the French Photographic Societies in Lyon, they show eight films. Carpentier works on industrial production of the Cinematograph after receiving an order from the Lumière Company. 28 December, first public performance of the Cinematograph at the Salon Indien of the Grand Café, boulevard des Capucines in Paris.

Skladanowski's bioskope performs at the Winter Garden, Berlin.

1896 Antoine purchases a house in Evian–les–Bains, now the town hall. Auguste embarks on physiological and pharmacodynamic experiments with Auguste Billiard (who will change his name to Alexis Carrel), in an old hotel which he turns into a laboratory.

Louis Lumière makes several films with Fregoli, the illusionist, at Lyon. Méliès uses a bioscope to make his first films, inspired by Lumière's.

1897 First Lumière film catalogue published.

1898 Louis enters the Astronomical Society of France. Birth and death of Jean, Louis and Rose Winckler's son. Auguste establishes his own pharmaceutical laboratory; sales are managed by Marius Sestier, a former chemist, and also a cameraman.

Gaumont puts Demenÿ's chronophotograph on the market. Pascal, once a teacher of the Lumière brothers at La Martinière, takes out a patent for a colour chronophotograph.

1899 The Lumière Company manufactures photographic plates for the army. No proft is taken on the transaction. This is the first military contract.

Méliès shoots a fiction film, *The Dreyfus Affair*.

1900 Louis invents the photorama, which projects, by means of 12 lenses, images on to an elliptical screen 20m long and 6m high. Apotheosis of the Lumière Cinematograph: at the Universal Exhibition of 1900 in Paris, a giant screen 25m high by 15m wide enables films to be seen by 25,000 people at one sitting.
   Auguste works on telephotography.

Grimoin–Sanson's cineorama balloon, or cosmorama, allows the photograph and projection of panoramic moving pictures in colour. Launched during the 1900 Universal Exhibition of 1900 in Paris, at the foot of the Eiffel Tower.

1901 The 'Château' is built at Monplaisir. The Lumière North American Company Ltd is established in Burlington.

1902 Merger between the Planchon Film Co. and the Lumière Co. Louis opens a photorama theatre which lasts for two years.

1903 A Lumière autochrome patent is taken out. A new factory is built, under Planchon's management, at Feyzin, near Lyon. France Lumière marries Charles Winckler.

Edwin S. Porter makes *The Great Train Robbery* and *The Life of an American Fireman*.

1904 Auguste founds *L'Avenir*

Médical, a periodical. LNACL
sells its first extra–fast plates in
the USA.

1905 First Lumière diaries put on sale.
A complete photographer's guide,
with information on all Lumière
products, including Auguste's
medicines.

1907 Autochromes on the market.

1908 Auguste given the Légion
d'Honneur by Edouard Herriot
and Jules Courmont. Antoine is
forced to retire. He gives the
company to his children in
exchange for a comfortable
income.

Emile Cohl starts making
cartoons and animated films.

1909 The manufacture of acetate in
sheets by Rhône Poulenc enables
the Lumière company to put non–
flammable film on the market.

1910 Auguste establishes a dispensary,
run by Gélibert.

1911 11 April. Death of Antoine
Lumière, from a brain
haemorrhage, at Château
Lumière, Monplaisir.
Establishment of Union
Photographique et Industrielle
Lumière et Jougla Réunis, a new
company structure.

1914 Auguste takes over the X–ray
department at the Hôtel–Dieu
hospital in Lyon. He works with
his daughter, Andrée, and doctors
Bérard, Gélibert and Koehler.
Louis sets up and pays for a 100–
bed hospital.

1915 20 December, death of Jeanne–
Josephine. Failure of LNACL.

1917 17 February, death of Edouard in
      the war.

1918 Andrée dies of Spanish flu, two   Charles Pathé buys a factory, Rue
      weeks after the armistice is   des Vignerons in Vincennes,
      signed.   outside Paris.

1919 Auguste becomes a correspondent
      member of the Académie de
      Médecine and Louis a fellow of
      the Académie des Sciences.

1920 Auguste and Louis leave
      management of the factory to
      Albert Trarieux and Henri
      Lumière. Louis invents
      photostereosynthesis.

1923 Death of Rose, Louis' wife. He
      goes to live in Paris.

1924 5 January, death of Mélinie–
      Juliette. 4 March, death of
      France.

1926 26 November, death of Jeanne.
                                            1927 *The Jazz Singer* launches the
1928 Commemorative plaque on the   talkies.
      Grand Café. Lumière factory built
      at Chotska, near Kiev. Jougla
      leaves the firm which retrieves its
      old name: Lumière.

1931 Death of René Koehler.

1932 First Lumière films produced at
      Chotska factory. Henri is given
      the Légion d'Honneur.

1935 Louis remakes *Arrival of a Train
      at La Ciotat* in three dimensions.
      Louis Lumière Jubilee at the
      Sorbonne. Auguste writes the
      preface to *A Practical Guide to
      Illusion and Conjuring* by Rémi
      Cellier.

1936 Commemorative plaque placed on the house the Lumière brothers were born in, in Besançon, a few yards from the house Victor Hugo was born in. Auguste enters the Académie de Lyon, as does Louis as correspondent member.

1938 23 December, Dr Gélibert dies.

1948 6 June. Louis dies, at the age of 84, in his villa at Bandol.

1954 10 April. Auguste dies, aged 92, in his villa at Monplaisir.

Index

AL refers to Auguste Lumière; LL refers to Louis Lumière.